Nuclear Weapons and European Security

ADELPHI LIBRARY 13

Edited by
ROBERT NURICK
Assistant Director, IISS

Published for
THE INTERNATIONAL INSTITUTE
FOR STRATEGIC STUDIES
by
Gower

Published by

Gower Publishing Company Limited
Gower House
Croft Road
Aldershot
Hampshire GU11 3HR
England

British Library Cataloguing in Publication Data

Nuclear weapons and European security–(The
    Adelphi Library: 13)
    1. Atomic weapons   2. Europe–Strategic aspects
    I. Nurick, Robert   II. Series
    358'39'094   UF767

    ISBN 0-566-00678-2

Printed in Great Britain by
Biddles Ltd, Guildford, Surrey.

0 566 00678 2

NUCLEAR WEAPONS AND EUROPEAN SECURITY

The Adelphi Library

Contents

Introduction

Would the United States risk Chicago for the sake of Hamburg? In that crude question is contained the enduring dilemma of 'extended deterrence' — the credibility of the US threat to employ her nuclear weapons in defence of Europe, in the full knowledge that her own territory would thereby be vulnerable to devastation. For some observers, this threat — which is central to NATO's doctrine of 'flexible response' — may have been credible at a time when the US enjoyed superiority at the strategic nuclear level, but is no longer so in an era of parity. For others, it is the 'first use' element in NATO doctrine that is especially problematical; in this view, the threat of nuclear retaliation can deter nuclear attacks, but it is both implausible and dangerous to rely upon using nuclear weapons to deter or to defeat conventional attacks as well. And cutting across these and similar lines of criticism is the belief that, while NATO's nuclear posture and doctrine may still be adequate to deter the Soviet Union, they no longer reassure Western publics, nor command sufficient public support to ensure their credibility over the longer run.

As the essays in this volume make clear, these are hardly new issues. Indeed, a good deal of the debate about nuclear policy in the United States for the past 20 years has turned, at least implicitly, on the question of what makes the US nuclear guarantee to Europe credible (or what undermines that credibility). Similarly, much of NATO's own history might be written as the search for a doctrine for nuclear weapons which is adequate to deter, and yet sufficiently general to accommodate both the understandable tendency in Europe, as the potential battlefield, to emphasize the threat of escalation to central strategic war as the best deterrent to any aggression in Europe, and the equally understandable American desire that making good on its nuclear guarantee should not *automatically* entail her own devastation. Given this underlying difference in perspective and interest, it should hardly be surprising that the role of nuclear weapons in European security has been a contentious issue in intra-Alliance politics.

Nor has it been an issue for United States nuclear forces alone. As Peter Nailor and Jonathan Alford point out in Adelphi Paper No. 156, the debate in the UK about the future of Britain's nuclear deterrent has never taken place in isolation from the larger context of Western security; in their view, a UK decision either to maintain or to discontinue her independent nuclear deterrent can be seen as 'not a British decision at all but a European one'. In part, this is because of the increased political weight the UK deterrent is thought to confer, both vis-a-vis the US and within NATO councils as a whole. In part, however, it is also because the British force has been justified as a means of adding to Soviet uncertainty about how the West might respond to aggression (the unspoken assumption being that, if a decision to respond with nuclear weapons were the province of the US alone, then Soviet uncertainty would be decreased), and as a hedge against a 'radical change in the diplomatic alignments between East and West in Europe'.

Barring such diplomatic realignments, however, the debate will probably continue to revolve around the contribution of US nuclear forces to deterrence and defence in Europe. In Adelphi Paper No. 175, Anthony Cordesman identifies four criteria essential to making 'extended deterrence' credible: the risk of escalation must be limited enough to avoid unacceptable damage to the US; the US must have sufficient survivable strategic forces so that even relatively large exchanges in defence of NATO will not leave too few warheads to deter a Soviet strike against US territory; the forces must be flexible enough to control collateral damage and make limited options possible; and the US must be *seen* as determined to extended deterrence to the territory of NATO Europe. Cordesman reviews the evolution of US nuclear force structure and doctrine (with particular emphasis on the initiatives of former Secretary of Defense James Schlesinger), traces their implications for extended deterrence, and comes to the conclusion that extended deterrence remains credible now, and is likely to be reinforced as the US continues to improve its capabilities and plans. What both Europeans and Americans must accept, however, is 'the fact that extended deterrence can never again be tied to US strategic superiority'.

What, then, is the role that US nuclear forces in Europe should play? Is NATO's doctrine of 'flexible response' still credible? Francois de Rose is not at all sure that it is. In the Survival article reprinted below, de Rose argues that 'flexible response' derives from, and is tied to, the bygone age when NATO enjoyed superiority in theatre nuclear forces (TNF). Now, in the light of Soviet conventional superiority and its continuing TNF buildup, 'it is the West which whould run the greatest risk if it took the nuclear initiative as called for by current doctrine'. De Rose thus recommends that the doctrine be modified: among other things, NATO should adopt

the principle that, whatever the level of a Soviet nuclear attack against Europe, the response would immediately involve a nuclear strike against military targets on Soviet territory. Many Western defence analysts would share de Rose's worries about NATO's present military posture but his suggestion that the Alliance move towards a doctrine of 'inflexible response' raises the old dilemmas: would the United States be willing to adopt a policy of automatic escalation tq the homeland of the Soviet Union? And would the threat be credible?

The inevitable tensions between European and American perspectives, and the inevitable uncertainties surrounding the US nuclear guarantee to Europe, are central themes in both Gregory Treverton's Adelphi Paper and Christopher Makins' *Survival* article. Terverton argues, for example, that the recent US debate about the survivability of its land-based ballistic missile force is 'essentially a problem for deterrence in Europe'. In his view, US strategic nuclear forces retain their extended deterrent effect, but parity at the central strategic level and the increase in Soviet theatre nuclear capabilities will make it even more difficult for any US President to make 'the agonizing decision of nuclear release in a European conflict'. Treverton devotes considerable attention to the need for NATO to fashion a more realistic doctrine, and has a number of sensible suggestions to make: NATO's nuclear arsenal should be re-assessed, to reduce Soviet temptations to pre-empt and to shift the emphasis toward longer-range systems; strategies of 'nuclear defence' should be laid to rest; and conventional forces should receive greater weight (and, very possibly, more resources) in NATO's deterrent strategy as a whole. In the end, however, the problem of nuclear weapons in European defence is a political problem which cannot be solved once and for all; dealing with the problem, concludes

Treverton, means 'making it politically manageable'.

Makins, too, cautions against the belief that there may be some magical solution to these issues. Like Treverton, he sees no wholly satisfactory means of using nuclear weapons to compensate for inadequate conventional forces; indeed, he is sceptical that even a 'measurable US advantage in long-range homeland-based nuclear forces would change the fundamental dilemma' for the Alliance. But the West *can* influence Soviet calculations — especially, in Makins' view, by increasing the survivability of its own forces so as to deny targetting options to the USSR, and by developing new mid-range systems which can strike mobile targets deep in Warsaw Pact territory. The point, as Makins emphasizes, is that the uncertainties surrounding the use of nuclear weapons work both ways; if the West cannot hope to eliminate its own, it can at least make sure that Soviet uncertainties persist as well.

Robert Nurick
Assistant Director, IISS

1 The Future of Britain's Deterrent Force

PETER NAILOR AND JONATHAN ALFORD

Introduction

If the British independent nuclear deterrent force is to be replaced, the decision must shortly be made as to the kind of system that should be procured. Another way of looking at the same problem is to declare that deferring the decision too long will amount to deciding not to renew the deterrent force for there will be no time to design and build a force to succeed the four *Polaris* nuclear ballistic-missile submarines (each carrying 16 A3 missiles) by the time they become obsolete. The timing is generally acknowledged to be a very important factor in the debate. Yet there appears to be no consensus either as to how long *Polaris* will last or as to what a successor system should look like, if there is to be one. This confusion arises partly because few can predict the operating life of the four *Polaris* submarines to within five years, and partly because it will be the nature of the system chosen to succeed *Polaris* that will dictate the lead time – and so the decision point. Until the nature of the new system is determined, it is hard to know when its construction must begin. Technical factors are not the sole arbiter of timing; political factors and the impact of the chosen system on the British defence budget will also play decisive roles.

The debate now beginning on the successor system to *Polaris* will have to take into account many complex arguments, and inevitably one whole aspect of it will be heard *in camera*, since it will deal with matters which are likely to remain sensitive. The authors of this Paper know that, because a number of important facts remain obscure, they cannot be comprehensive, but they present the arguments on the basis of what is ascertainable. They reach what may at first sight appear to be somewhat tame and conventional conclusions. People generally do not want to hear that what they have now is good enough and will remain so for as far ahead as one can see with any clarity – but that is the thrust of the argument presented here.

The debate is of course not solely, or even mainly an internal British one. It cannot be isolated from either the larger context of Western security, or from the dynamics of arms control and perceptions of the shifting balance of nuclear power. It is not enough to say that what Britain can contribute is certain to be militarily insignificant when compared with the nuclear inventories of the super-powers. The decision to maintain or discontinue an independent strategic nuclear deterrent will have a political significance out of all proportion to the relative military power involved; it will be interpreted as a clear indication of resolve or lack of it. It may also be interpreted as not a British decision at all but a European one, implying much about Europe's willingness to take the necessary steps to defend herself against a growing threat to European security.

Jonathan Alford

1

The Strategic Context

Jane Austen begins her analysis of *Pride and Prejudice* with a rather cynical generalization, and it is not entirely inappropriate to adapt her words to explain why a discussion of British strategic nuclear weapons policy seems appropriate now: it is a truth universally acknowledged that a medium power in possession of a deterrent must be in want of a decision about its replacement. Clearly there is a limit to how far one can push a fanciful literary allusion, but in something of the same way that poor Mr. Bingley became an object of interest as soon as he arrived at Netherfield, the question of what might supersede the *Polaris* weapon system as the basis of the British strategic capability became a matter for speculation soon after the submarines, in which it is mounted, were deployed. Concern was based upon an appreciation of the political and strategic changes of the 1970s and assumptions about the changing military and technological factors that might alter previous calculations about the utility and effectiveness of the force. The fundamental question was whether nuclear weapons could or should have a place in the spectrum of British power. All these questions concerned not only the *Polaris* system itself, but also a continuing debate, sometimes active, sometimes dormant, about why and how Britain should maintain a strategic nuclear weapon capability. 'Why' is not confined to ethics, it is also about purpose; and 'how' is not confined to engineering capability, it is also about costs and politics.

More recently, the debate has quickened. It was set in train by the report of a Parliamentary committee in 1973, and has been taken up in various ways. The Royal Institute of International Affairs produced a substantial contribution in 1977 in a programme of studies about British foreign policy, and a number of Adelphi Papers, books, articles and pamphlets have carried the matter forward.[1] The timing of this activity can be

explained largely by the practical issue; if the existing force is to be replaced, then decisions ought to be taken in time to allow any successor force to be deployed without any hiatus. And before decisions can be taken, there will have to be discussions about what the decisions should be. Over and above the continuous question of whether there should be a replacement on ethical grounds, one reason why such discussions should be both extensive, and as public as such things can be, is said to be the need to debate whether Britain's place in the international system of the 1980s and beyond will require the continuation of a policy which for the last 30 years or more has attributed significance to a British strategic nuclear capability. In short, the question is *cui bono*?

The Historical Arguments

Although the debate about British policy towards strategic nuclear deterrence has been more or less continuous since about 1954, it has been rather unsatisfactory. Critics who have sought to alter Britain's policy, and specifically those who have wished to dispose of her strategic capability, have always been in the position of *demandeurs*. It is they who have had to make the case for change, and to explain why they think the policy should be altered: and, particularly in the British political system, where the government has more effective power to determine the limits of policy debates than in some other parliamentary systems, this requires both a wide range of support and a convincing set of reasons. The reasons adduced do not hang together well, in so far as there have been at least three major lines of argument, which overlap but do not easily integrate. The first is that the possession of nuclear weapons is not only ethically wrong but it also makes Britain even more vulnerable to attack than she would be if she did not possess them. The second argument is

2

that the time is past when Britain's power and interests required a strategic nuclear capability in support, or as a manifestation of the role that she should seek to play in the Atlantic Alliance. The third argument concentrates upon the utilitarian perception that, given her restricted resources, Britain would do better to employ the skills and monies she has to enhance her conventional forces, rather than to divert them to maintain a marginal increment to the nuclear strength of the United States. There have been other arguments, including that of technical and military inadequacy, but these three lines represent what has been the basis of the case throughout the period.[2]

These criticisms have been directed at a continuing policy maintained by her successive governments, which, although defended with varying degrees of vigour over the years, has not essentially changed.

Some trimming has been done, at the level of declaratory policy, but the *status quo* has been maintained. It is not that the criticisms have fallen upon deaf ears, but that they lack either substance or weight enough to force a discontinuity. Successive governments seem to have been sufficiently sure that their adopted (or inherited) policies are correct and effective enough to warrant continuation, and do not arouse major public concern. The evidence to support this is largely circumstantial. Governments normally confine their explanations about strategic nuclear weapons policy to short descriptions of current functions of the nuclear forces, and the annual British Defence White Papers, the defence debates in Parliament, and the foreign-policy debates that touch on this aspect of British security concerns, yield relatively little about strategic purposes or security doctrine. Certainly by comparison with the United States and French official explanations and legislative discussions, the material about the objectives of the policy, rather than the capability to execute it, is thin. In the early Sixties nuclear technology and delivery system technologies were changing as rapidly as the pattern of foreign affairs was shifting. The level of public debate in Britain was rather tentative and assertive and similar debates being carried on elsewhere were no more positive. Everyone was struggling with the implications of this awesome new type of power.

However, there are a number of features about British exploration of the changing environment that are worth noting. First, Britain was very early in the field; both her scientific and her political experience with nuclear weapons dated back to wartime. Her drive to reap the benefits of this experience was developed against a background of a hostile post-war world in which a relationship with a powerful ally was the major defence factor. In so far as nuclear weapons were concerned, self-help was the only way to overcome the largely instinctive reluctance of the US Congress to sanction scientific and technical co-operation, even after the American nuclear monopoly had been broken by the Soviet Union. Secondly, the scale of the projected British programme up to the transition to thermo-nuclear weapons, relative to the projected US programme, was of a size and type, that directly derived from the familiar pattern of wartime burden-sharing that conditioned so much post-war security planning. The British programme would, when complete, be relatively small but still a significant component in the joint armoury. It would both contribute to matters of joint concern and cover some matters that were of special interest to Britain. (The standard example quoted was the targeting of Soviet submarine bases). It would embody a specific military utility and a wider political utility, both within the alliance and *vis-à-vis* the major adversary. It looked as if, in technical and financial terms, this could all be done without detriment to other defence objectives. However, the interpolation of the production order for the V-bombers into the Korean War re-armament programme made this aspiration less than fully realistic.

Lastly, although the transition to thermo-nuclear weapons and missile delivery systems came about very quickly, challenging earlier expectations about the military, political and financial consequences of nuclear weapons programmes, the shape of the British programme did not materially change. Instead, there was what might be perceived as a cautious reassessment. One of its principal elements was unwillingness to discard nuclear weapons when they were obviously becoming much more powerful and significant to the super powers: giving up the race at what was virtually the first awkward hurdle did not seem to be very sensible, since the length and difficulty of the course was unknown to all the competitors. Second, there was an acknowledgement of the need to limit both the testing and the spread of nuclear weapons – on general and international as much as on national grounds. The danger and the importance of nuclear weapons were substantially enhanced by the significantly more powerful thermo-nuclear weapons. A third conclusion seems to have been that the cost of maintaining a strategic nuclear capability must be kept within reasonable limits, in scientific and production terms, as well as in money costs. Reopening a line of technical co-operation with the United States offered a chance to share some of the new delivery system technologies without wildly upsetting the balance of the defence programme generally. As a result, the sort of nuclear deterrent that Britain could afford, or chose to afford, was still a credible military instrument, in terms of the calculations which were then becoming familiar about deterrent values and goals. Thermo-nuclear weapons made small deterrent forces inherently more capable of dealing a politically significant blow to an adversary.

In short, Britain's capability stayed pretty much at the sort of level originally conceived, in terms of weapon numbers, even though the two super-powers were beginning to develop large and increasingly diversified nuclear armouries. Later, the French nuclear forces, though they became more diversified than the British, followed a 'British pattern' of assessment in assuming that a relatively small nuclear armoury was sufficient to achieve national objectives.

One deduction that can be drawn from these levels of force is that Britain and France have concluded that the capability needed to maintain a policy of mutual deterrence that is credible to an adversary is relatively small. Both states have been able to take into account the parallel threat that the United States must always pose to the Soviet Union: but both states have never set themselves the objective of crippling the Soviet Union's industrial-military power, which has been the US aim in planning its forces. They seem to have a more conservative analysis of their requirement; but to the extent that they have had more pressing economic and technical constraints to meet, it seems their judgments of what is an adequate level of deterrence are not seriously at odds with those pressures. What they can afford will do – though the costs of affording it have had quite different political and economic consequences for their separate security postures. In the early 1960s both states might have explained their separate national objectives, in this sort of syllogism: 'If you should ever attack us, we have the capacity to punish you, even after the event, by destroying this many of your cities, and consequently part of your industry and population. This would not only be a grievous blow in itself, but would materially weaken your capacity to withstand successfully an attack from the United States which, for the purposes of this argument, you will have to assume would be a separate actor'.

This explanation, directed towards the adversary, is only concerned with the effects upon him of what is explicitly a nuclear exchange. Neither the antecedent crisis nor the effect of the precipitating attack upon the home state's own territory are explored. It is not an explanation to the state's people of the issues or interests at stake. It merely assumes the resolution of the government will be supported by the people in the same way that it presumes the adversary involved is also an adversary of the United States. In the mid-1960s French explanations of policy moved away from these limitations, and placed more emphasis upon the circumstances in which French nuclear forces would be used – in particular they stressed the requirements to protect the French homeland from any attack by any enemy.

The British programme has been developed and sustained against a political background of ambiguity. Parliamentary criticism of the policy has never been absent, and support for the policy, particularly among Labour Party supporters, has often been sufficiently equivocal, either to create doubts about government intentions when the Labour Party is in office or to cause government to adopt what is usually called a 'low profile'. The debate about nuclear weapons seems to be intrinsically about a wider issue: Britain's role in international affairs. If this is a reasonable picture of some of the most important political divergencies about the deterrent, it might go some way towards explaining the relative lack of authoritative exegesis over doctrine.

Medium-Power Nuclear Doctrine
Doctrine about nuclear weapons is difficult to determine precisely. Neither academic analysts nor governments are really sure about the risks. There are very substantial differences of opinion

about whether the possession of nuclear weapons can be turned to advantage without running the serious risk that they may need to be used, or whether such risks are so transcendentally unacceptable that possession should be renounced; whether nuclear weapons can be regarded as rather special and terrible weapons of war, or whether they are so dangerous for the future of mankind that mankind will have to take the virtually unprecedented step of relinquishing the consequences of acquired knowledge.

Attempts to analyse and identify the implications of nuclear weapons for the nature of war, and for relations between states, began almost as soon as their existence became known, and it was probably inevitable that most of the analyses were importantly constrained by the political circumstances of the time. It is not therefore surprising that the nature of what we might call the orthodox perspectives, or conventional wisdom, about nuclear weapons owes a great deal to United States concerns, since it was in the United States that public discussion of the nature of deterrence in the nuclear age began.

The resulting tendency for American perspectives to shape orthodox thinking on the subject of nuclear weapons has been supported by American policy. US dominance in NATO has meant that shifts and innovations in alliance strategy have been primarily set in motion by an American initiative, followed by a debate in which the allies have modified or acquiesced in a framework of which the limits have already been determined. The tendency has been supported, understandably, by the perception that what might emerge from a conflict between the superpowers would have global significance.

There is often in the debate an uncertain and loosely-drawn distinction between description and prescription, between analysis and advocacy; at one level, this means that the correspondence between the declaratory aims of policy and action is almost totally untested. Since there has been no use of nuclear weapons since 1945, theories and propositions are untested – and many of them are unverifiable in the normal scientific sense. It is therefore difficult to determine whether propositions about how deterrence can be maintained have the same value as descriptions of what deterrence is.

This concern has particular point for us, for the second limitation that arises from American dominance of the Western 'conventional wisdom' is a preoccupation with an archetypal bipolar environment based upon military power. In recent years some play has been made with multipolar models, most of which have also made distinctions between military and non-military types of power. It is not yet certain, in spite of the emergence of China on the world stage, whether the bipolar description of a world of two superpowers with preponderant military strengths has lost its dominance – especially for European and Middle Eastern states. Bipolarity has assumed some of the attributes of a new balance-of-power theory, and has been used not only as an analytical device, but as an explanation and justification of policy, particularly in regard to the forms and practices of the alliance *blocs*. (From this point of view, some of the intellectual *rationale* behind the French doctrine of *'défense à tous azimuts'* involves a denial of the pretensions to which bipolarity had been pressed, and a reassertion of multilateral, and multi-layered, principles of international power. In this sense, possession of nuclear weapons could be seen as a practical manifestation of a claim to be heard in major international affairs – or to 'have a seat at the top table').

Nonetheless, bipolarity is sufficiently ingrained to be a standard and convenient way of explaining nuclear concerns, even though it is unsatisfactory as an explanation or as a controlling device at other levels of international concern. It is still useful in reflecting a view of the nuclear balance which, for members of NATO and the Warsaw Pact, has some correspondence with reality. It is also a simple concept, enabling arguments to be structured with some clarity. A bipolar world is relatively easy to describe and account for; a three-pole or five-pole structure is inherently unstable, with more parties to account for and manage. This may explain the unpopularity in the United States of France's attempts to provide an alternative doctrinal base for her own policies. It may, perhaps, also explain why British explanations of a distinctive doctrine, incorporated in an unintegrated mixture of official and non-official expositions, have been cast in muted vein.

The French writings tend to postulate a much less stable international environment, implying that alliances will be temporary or fragile, and that the prime responsibility of a state is to maintain its own interests. One of the most

5

interesting aspects is that French expositions have tried to confront the problems that arise not only from co-operation between a super-power and lesser states, but also that arise from the links that have been established over the years between geographically disparate groups of states: in North America and various regions in Europe. The burden of the argument is that France, as a unit of power in the international system, has to provide against a future in which this framework no longer applies – either because super-power dominance is unwelcome or because the links break down. The antithesis is with the assumption that NATO is a core value in British policy and is – by implication, at least – a permanent alliance.

This is a novel concept historically, though it does reflect the current movement towards transcending the limits of state power which the EEC exemplifies. Nonetheless it is a difficult concept to accept readily in the geo-political area where the state first emerged in its current form. It can be argued that French attempts to retain greater freedom of action by suggesting that the Western security structure may change, are self-fulfilling. Similarly it might be argued that British attempts to play down such possibilities by implying that they will not happen might – if changes do occur – require a sharper and more radical response. In reply, one might comment that maintenance of the British deterrent has been seen as an instrument for guarding against some of these possibilities; this is the implication of the 'independent deterrent' aspect of the British nuclear programme which has been emphasized from time to time. The style of the policy has, however, generally been to give both a low prominence and a relatively low priority to the issue. In 1959 Denis Healey explained it thus:

> There is little doubt that the main aim of the British thermo-nuclear striking force is to provide passive deterrence for Britain in case America drops her present policy of active deterrence for NATO as a whole. Though some Englishmen [sic] believe that the political likelihood of Russia presenting Britain with the sort of threat to which passive deterrence would be relevant is too small to be worth preparing against, the majority, including the leaders of both the political parties, feel that the additional expenditure required to mount a passive deterrent on the basis of Britain's existing atomic resources and delivery system

is small enough to be worth making. This majority might dwindle dramatically if its assumptions about the low cost of a passive deterrent prove to be mistaken.[3]

Although the super-power stereotype contained within the nuclear orthodoxies led to a relatively high level of articulation of doctrine in the United States, for a state whose concerns are more limited, the requirement to be precise is also more limited.[4] It may indeed be satisfied simply by a concept of deterrence that emphasizes the inherent power of a deployed capability. The additional argument required to enhance deterrence by relating it to a range of war-fighting options may, for a state like Britain, be sufficiently fulfilled by an implicit dependence upon retributive force. This creates a wider range of uncertainty, which assists deterrence *vis-à-vis* the adversary, though maybe at the price of enhanced uncertainty within the state which adopts such a doctrine. The purposes for which a deterrent is maintained are thus left relatively unspecified. Although traditionally, defence forces have not been required to fit precisely into mission, role and task pigeon-holes, this imprecision goes against modern analysis and specification. However, specific articulation may be one of the privileges of dominance that has been enhanced by the recent technological bias of American doctrines. Particular levels of 'assured destruction' are plainly not so important to a nuclear power that has accepted a retributive posture and a limited purpose. (Also, it may be that the explicitness with which doctrine *needs* to be articulated has something to do with the political system of individual states.)

From French pronouncements an adversary can gain a relatively clear impression of French intentions, even though it is no more certain what the French government would actually *do* in a specific situation than it is certain what the Soviet or United States governments would do. But where Britain is concerned, even the impression of *intent* is unclear. France chose to neglect specific obligations inherent in the North Atlantic Alliance and based her posture upon national and state priorities. Yet she remains a member of the Alliance, and it is entirely possible, even probable, that in an important crisis her decisions would be compatible with those of NATO. The area of uncertainty is, so to speak, positively defined. Britain contracted in: her forces are pledged to NATO, and their involvement in the Alliance is heavily stressed. Their residual independence is a footnote to render their external obligations acceptable in domestic political terms and is, by comparison with the French approach, negatively defined. This has led to a greater sense of uncertainty in the domestic political environment, even to the point where the stress laid upon loyalty to the Alliance minimizes both the contribution to the Allied cause that the British nuclear forces represent, and their residual utility for discrete (but unspecified) national purposes.

There is another type of argument that has been advanced to explain the role that Britain might play as a 'medium nuclear power'. This is that the increment which British possession of nuclear weapons contributes to the Alliance creates an opportunity to exert additional influence on Alliance policy and behaviour. (This is the obverse of the argument about 'additional centres of decision', developed most notably by French analysts, which suggests that a composite and nationally differentiated deterrent posture is additionally inhibiting to an adversary.) The argument put to allies might run thus: 'Because we have assumed part of the burden which you bear in possessing these terrible weapons of mass destruction, and because we stand with you in our determination to deter aggression, we seek to ensure that the responsibility of deciding when and whether this ultimate expression of force shall be used, will also be shared. We have the right, by virtue of this burden, to be heard in your counsels. And you should not forget that these weapons also give us a better ability than some of your other friends to stand aside from your decision, if we do not agree with your proposition.'

Such arguments may have had greater effect when super-power armouries were small and assymetric, and before the advent of missiles foreshortened the time in which consultation and disavowals might need to take place. However, this does not entirely negate the political utility of this argument, the principal weakness of which is that it can neither be proved nor disproved. Many essentially political propositions are assertions of this declaratory type. It certainly emphasizes a determination to take decisions nationally at one level, but only so that similar sorts of decisions will be internationalized at another level. In this connection Britain has made some play with the idea of an 'independent deterrent', and President Giscard d'Estaing has made some distinctions about the different roles of France as an autonomous power and a military power, and stressed her special position 'at the head of the group of powers just behind the super-powers' which may have been intended in part to address this sort of issue.

It is difficult, therefore, to avoid concluding that, fundamentally, both Britain and France developed nuclear forces:

(i) because of a determination, in the earliest post-war periods, not to acquiesce in the abandonment of a capability they had helped to pioneer;

(ii) as a precaution against radical change in the diplomatic alignments between East and West in Europe; and

(iii) to cement their distinctive attributes as major powers, at a time when other attributes, like colonial possessions, were being cut away.

As a *rationale* for acquiring a nuclear capability, these arguments are by no means negligible. Though it is not clear whether they can be applied to maintaining such a capability through generational changes, they do highlight the fact that specific and positive reasons will have to be advanced in order to justify discarding it.

Perhaps the key to this is that the proposition about influencing allies is not an analytical or general proposition but a political device, specifically constructed with the United States in mind. This brings into focus another problem: that the 'medium power' may need to consider whether its doctrine is sufficient to cope with a changing international environment which may bring the need for change to the current orthodoxies. If the number of nuclear weapons states increases, the expository value of doctrine may be enhanced: more fundamentally, the scope of doctrine may have to be reassessed. If there are major technical changes in nuclear weapon or delivery system engineering the 'medium power' may come to feel that it should explain why it does (or does not) follow the new fashion. For the last fifteen years Britain has been able to share in and benefit from the technical plateaux on which significant elements in the conventional wisdoms are based. Nuclear-powered submarines, ballistic missiles and other advanced systems are fitted into a posture which generally conforms to concepts like 'invulnerable second-strike' which are part of the collective wisdom. 'Assured destruction' in this respect is as important to 'medium powers' as to the super-powers. If technical changes were to come in the 1980s as fast as they came in the 1950s, new doctrine might become increasingly important, whether to explain non-conformity or to justify the cost of imitation.

The Question of Status

In connection with doctrine, nuclear capability seems hitherto to have been seen as a significant attribute of statehood, implying a claim to some sort of international or technological status. The fact that it might also indicate a sense of insecurity attracts less attention. In that context, the stake that 'mankind' has in preventing nuclear war implies that some way must be found to bridge the incompatibility that may exist between the particular state's concern and some agreed conception of the general good. It is a difficult question to deal with in an international community which has rapidly become more diverse. It is also a question that has a parallel at a lower level which is perhaps more immediately important for Britain: the question of 'if' and 'when' nuclear weapons should be used in support of alliances. The imbalance between state ownership of nuclear weapons and alliance agreement about their use has never been fully resolved, though an acceptable method of limiting the problem has been found for most NATO members in the Nuclear Defence Affairs Committee (NDAC) and in the Nuclear Planning Group (NPG). These groups discuss and formulate doctrine which will determine the nature of alliance policies and the framework within which national decisions might be arrived at in times of crisis.[5]

Nuclear weapons have a distinct significance that derives in part from their nature, but it also has to do with their restricted range of ownership. It is not clear whether the significance assigned to the United States in the specific NATO case, or the analogous case of the Soviet Union in the Warsaw Pact, can be read across to Britain or France. Other attributes of power and the sheer size of nuclear armoury are lacking here, and we may need to make distinctions about *significance* as we have tried to do about policies and purposes. Are 'medium nuclear powers' more significant to some states than to others? And are they more significant because they have nuclear weapons? It seems as if they may be – though how this significance can be measured is difficult

to determine and is open as much to assertion as to analysis. Perhaps, the 'medium nuclear states' do not gain much by having nuclear weapons; they have resources that enable them to pursue their interests without their nuclear status making much difference – except in the crucial matter of making, or not making, nuclear war. Following this argument we are led to conclude either that what they gain is not worth the price of the investment, or else that what is involved in coming to terms with weapons of mass destruction is so distasteful that it would be best left unexplored. Both conclusions, imply that, by comparison with the policies and interests of the super powers, the 'medium nuclear powers' are out-gunned. Further, on a second level of inference, we must acknowledge that super-power dominance is a stable and basically benign regime in which to be out-gunned is sufficient reason to accept that a nuclear capability has lost any significance related to purely national interests.

The alternative line of argument followed by successive British and French governments, is that super-power dominance cannot be relied upon to be either stable or benign, and that in an international system that is consistently moving away from what 'medium powers' might regard as familiar limits; they cannot afford to neglect any attributes of power that may slow down the rate of change. They are drawn towards policies and practices that legitimize what they perceive as an appropriate standing; and to develop nuclear weapons is no less unsurprising a choice of policy than the maintenance of the system of permanent memberships in the Security Council. An orderliness and a stability has been imposed upon British and French policy, for the purposes of synthesis, that neglects the doubts, the crosscurrents and the inconsistencies that have appeared from time to time over the years. It also implies that these states have adopted a simple 'billiard ball' model of international politics by which to assess their objectives. It does not tell one much about the chances of being able to maintain such a balancing activity in the future.

Perhaps a negative proof is possible; perhaps such states would be less significant if they discarded nuclear weapons? The very act of renunciation may be of prime significance: for a state to give up anything offers an opportunity for its neighbours to reassess their attributions of power, and nuclear weapons may be similiar, in this respect, to colonies, aircraft carriers, industrial production, claims to territory or anything else. There is one possible difference, however: the possession of nuclear weapons may be of particular importance relative to the perceptions of the super-powers. Both the United States and the Soviet Union self-evidently place great emphasis on nuclear weapons. For a nuclear weapon state to renounce possession might affect super-power perspectives more sharply than those of the rest of the world community. The conclusions they drew might be different, as between prospective guardian and prospective adversary, but it is by no means unlikely that any state contemplating a change of status – renunciation or acquisition – would have this particular and important audience in mind.

The Challenge
The international environment in which super-power perceptions are important is the same environment into which Britain has boxed herself by her successful policy of maintaining a strategic nuclear capability. She has done this by keeping down the costs of her deterrent forces. It is delivery-system technology, rather than weapons technology, that has become most costly, and Britain has been able to save both time and money through her co-operative links with the United States. However, the consequence is that any determination to maintain a militarily credible delivery capability in the future is more complex than it would be for France, for example. It inevitably becomes as much an international as a domestic concern, especially if minimum cost is a prime objective. To maintain the American connection is to save the cost of re-creating a specialized industry to produce particular types of rocket motors and ancillary equipment, and that of establishing test ranges.

At the political level, it also demonstrates that there is a connection that can be maintained. Paradoxically, if for some reason the British government came to believe that nuclear weapons had assumed a new level of significance, sufficient to justify a separate national investment, it would be difficult to relinquish the American connection without implying that some fundamental reassessment of the British-American relationship had taken place. And, to displace the connection by preferring to co-operate with another collaborator would be very pointed indeed. But to seek to maintain it is to concede to the United States Government an initiative in evaluating whether the connection still has value. However sure any British government might be about the practical importance of its political co-operation to any American administration, it would nevertheless want to pick its moment for conceding that sort of initiative. Neither Britain nor the US could limit the evaluation to purely bilateral considerations. They must take into account how the world in which nuclear weapons seem to have relevance has changed. For Britain, in particular, the evaluation has to be set in a context quite different from that in which the last decisions of this sort were taken.

Nuclear weapons are militarily significant because of their destructive power; but they have a more general importance for other than specifically military reasons. They give rise to awe and fear, not only because of the damage they could do, but because of the ways in which this damage would be done: the effects could be passed on, in space and in time, in a way that no other weapon has so far had the power to do. It is therefore difficult to discuss them simply as military weapons; their utility is not confined to their destructive role in any particular military conflict. Indeed, any utility that they have which is calculable *before* any conflict may rest principally in the ability they give to their possessor to threaten to use them, rather than in showing an ability to put the threat into effect. This rather indeterminate value arises partly from their relative novelty and the international community's limited experience in dealing with them, and partly from the sense that, if they are used in any extensive way, the act of use will be an irremediable portent of general destruction. The sense of risk which therefore accompanies their very existence gives them a special sort of political significance in addition to their military capability.

This sense of special danger has been an important element in the development of mutual nuclear deterrence, which emerged after the short period during which the United States alone had the weapons and delivery systems that could reach the homelands of her principal adversaries. Mutual nuclear deterrence is both a situation and a policy. As a situation, it describes a current political environment in which none of the principal parties enjoys a significant military advantage at the nuclear level, and so all are constrained not to push their objectives beyond the shadowy limits at which their adversaries would become desperate enough to threaten to use, or actually use nuclear weapons. As a policy, mutual nuclear deterrence describes the determination of states or alliances to maintain this type of political environment by initiatives or responses that will ensure that they are not put at a nuclear disadvantage. It is this distinction which explains both the SALT process and the determination of the US and USSR to remain, qualitatively, at the forefront of the technology available to them.

Nuclear Arms Control

Nuclear arms limitation, like *detente*, has a patchy record; but agreed regulatory mechanisms have allayed some of the previous worst apprehensions. The steps developed in international agreements of the 1960s and 1970s, have all been directed towards limiting the development and deployment of nuclear weapons. Britain has worked within the negotiations and the agreements; she has claimed that it is the possession of nuclear weapons which allows this role to be usefully performed. Her ability to continue to perform this function in multilateral negotiations depends heavily upon the relevance and quality of her policy contribution. In relative terms, of course, her forces are now smaller than they were even a few years ago, but it is all too easy to underplay what they still represent in absolute terms. Their capability is significantly more powerful than any other form of defence power which Britain controls; the ability to lay waste a range of major industrial and urban concentrations is not a negligible attribute. Even so, it may be the relative rather than the absolute comparison that makes the quality of any British diplomatic input to an international forum important. Whether it is rational or not, nuclear weapons, like earlier dominant weapons, seem to be prone to the quantification syndrome. When adding up numbers, it is easiest to assume that a ratio of 5:1 makes something five times as valuable, and less easy to accept the possibility that one side has been quintessentially extravagant.[6] Any effect of the SALT relationship between the super-powers upon Britain's influence to affect outcomes at that particular level of bilateral negotiation is probably not specific to Britain; it is much more likely to be determined by the intensity and the importance of the negotiating relationship, which is always likely to condition consultation with third parties.

The movement of international opinion which led to the Nuclear Non-Proliferation Treaty has been successful in that it established orthodox values about the undesirability of what is now called 'horizontal' proliferation. In other words, it has stopped – or at least slowed down – the acquisition of nuclear weapons by states other than the existing five owners. However, it has done relatively little to stop the qualitative developments that are now called 'vertical' proliferation. Arms-control dialogues and agreements since 1967 have limited quantities and time scales rather than the scope of competition. The one major exception, which is of considerable significance to the smaller as well as to the greater nuclear powers, is the ABM Treaty of 1972, which limits deployment of anti-ballistic missile defensive systems in the United States and the Soviet Union. For Britain, and indeed for France, this treaty ensured that no major recalculations about the size of the nuclear inventories they needed would be required, at least for the time being. It may not be necessary for Britain to update its inventory as regularly as the United States, but there is a very important relationship between the size of weapon inventory and the tolerance which is built into expectations about its performance characteristics. If a state wishes to maintain the smallest credible force, its capacity to stretch the minimum assessment of credible deterrence will be more sensitive to performance degradation. The ABM Treaty removed one of the most obvious ways in which the penetrative capability of a small force could be affected.

'Vertical' proliferation creates other hazards, however. It can be powerfully argued that limitations on super-power armouries and support of the existing non-proliferation regime are to Britain's advantage, because the costs and difficulties that would follow on from a breakdown in the current environment would create greater uncertainty internationally as well as nationally. If there were a breakdown, in the sense that super-power competition became more intense, the other nuclear powers might jointly be drawn towards an emulative response (though, they might also be as anxious as the rest of the international community to defuse the increased level of hostility that would be implied); conversely, if the super-powers sought to limit qualitative improvements – particularly if the limitation took the form of a positive restriction upon technology transfers – the political effect would be of a different order of importance to the technical consequences. The assumption of a restrictive form of distinctiveness by the two super-powers would be a prime concern, reflecting the difficulty that the United States in particular has in co-operating with her principal adversary without down-grading links with her principal allies.

Specifically, if 'vertical' proliferation is not controlled, Britain might face a special difficulty. The technical co-operation with the United States on nuclear delivery systems has brought considerable advantages over the last twenty years. Any loss of independence that might accrue from such an arrangement is much less critical for nuclear systems than it can be for conventional weapons systems, which need spares and replacements for losses in action, and has been far outweighed by the technical and investment advantages. It is not even clear whether at the political level, there is any loss at all that needs to be outweighed. However, it is possible to foresee that the United States hardware might be too advanced, and too expensive, for Britain to maintain a simple continuation of her current policies. This, of course, leaves on one side whether the two governments would be equally content to continue the transactions, or whether the Soviet Union would perceive such a development as an impediment to further stages of SALT.

It seems likely that the technological development of medium nuclear powers like Britain will continue to be defined largely by what the United States and the Soviet Union do. Hitherto the orthodoxy has assumed that nuclear weapons are useful primarily against threats from other nuclear states, and the smaller nuclear powers have been seen as in an inferior position, with a restricted range of possible responses. If horizontal proliferation occurs, the technical aspect of this position will change, but its policy aspect may not change. The supposed utility of nuclear weapons is likely to continue to be based upon the relative technical excellence of weapon inventories simply because the notion of utility will continue to be based upon the need to influence super-power attitudes. A nuclear capability will continue to be primarily important to a medium nuclear power insofar as it creates a state of deterrence vis-à-vis a super-power. Here a special problem arises from the nature of existing British policy. If Britain wants to rejuvenate and re-commit her existing strategic capability in something like the way she has done it before, this implies an international agreement with the United States. Such an agreement, although provided for in the Nuclear Non-Proliferation Treaty, would be the first reached since the Treaty came into force and would undoubtedly stimulate all sorts of criticism, from the genuinely pacifist to the transparently propagandist. Britain's ability to play an active role in the maintenance of the non-proliferation regime might take a knock, and for the British Government to decide to ride out this sort of criticism would be, in effect, a positive and significant affirmation of the importance of nuclear weapons to British interests. Some criticism would be based upon fear that a bad British example on proliferation would encourage states on the edge of a nuclear capability to believe they were justified in their policies. Whether an opposite British example – that of renouncing a strategic capability – would have a similarly definitive effect is not argued so confidently.

Regarding the pace of technological change, the perspective of a medium nuclear power may be different from that of a super-power. The latter, by definition, has the resources and the direct competitive impulse to innovate. It is possible to observe habits of super-power behaviour over the last twenty years that sustain that part of the arms race concept which emphasizes the internal imperative of competition, as well as the external one: the need to sustain the State's and the Service's own views of their requirements, rather than the need to meet the enemy's achievements. A state's armed forces expect to be provided not only with 'good' weapon systems, but also the most sophisticated ones that their government can be persuaded to provide. However, the rate at which the technical proficiency of a particular weapon system becomes degraded is much more difficult to determine in the case of nuclear weapons than in that of conventional weapons. There may be particular and finite dates that can be pinpointed – such as the hull life of the submarine or the safety limits of the aircraft which is the prime delivery system – but the loss of a nuclear weapon system's technical ability to penetrate to target and the point at which its inherent operational reliability becomes positively unacceptable are very much more difficult to quantify precisely. One consequence of this might be that the regular updating of weapons may be less important for a smaller nuclear power, with limited interests and perspectives, than for a super-power. But once again this highlights the relationship between the size of the armoury and the ability to stretch the minimum assessment of credible deterrence, which in the case of a medium nuclear power may depend more upon the relative survivability of the launch vehicle, than upon the proven ability of the system to penetrate effectively to its target. If this is the case, then it remains important for a medium nuclear power to have delivery systems that are, by general repute, up to date.

The crux of the matter, however, is that in the field of international strategic politics Britain has contrived to place herself in a difficult and unique position. Although maintaining a nuclear capability that entitles her to assert that she has had a reasonably consistent view about the importance of nuclear weapons, she has also taken a prominent role in the international movement towards the limitation and reduction of nuclear weapon armouries – thereby distancing herself from France and China, perhaps even to the extent of creating expectations that her future policy will conform more closely to the highest aspirations of that movement than the policies of the super-powers, which are moving at a snail's pace towards their obligations under the Nuclear Non-Proliferation Treaty. To the extent that Britain has snuggled closer to the super-powers than France or China, should she not take this chance to set them a good example?[7]

The opportunity to do this without fundamentally reassessing her security needs is, however, limited by the inflexibly small size of her nuclear armoury. This means that the cut must be all or nothing. A 20% cut in strategic capability would be pointless, since what was left would represent less than the credible level of deterrence. But as Ian Smart and others have pointed out, to forswear a strategic capability is not a wholly convincing solution in any case.[8] It would neither fully satisfy the nuclear disarmers nor totally persuade the sceptics, who might include the

Soviet Union. Britain has a residual nuclear capability, based upon air-delivered and short-range weapon systems, in addition to the *Polaris* boats, and she also has a range of experience and knowledge that would be retained, if even these secondary forces were disbanded. Nuclear disarmament – as distinct from relinquishing a long-range strike capability – is likely to involve a much wider and more extensive set of decisions. As a unilateral act of policy, it would have to be unusually specific and observable, in order to achieve the international effects of exemplary encouragement. It would have to set a new standard of frankness and intrusion into domestic technical processes by national as well as international norms, and it is, as a matter of practical politics, as unlikely to occur as it would be disconcerting if it did.

The Case for a Successor System

International politics has to be carried on at a number of levels. While we have long-term goals that embody expectations of a better and more peaceful state of affairs, we also have to deal with a current environment that falls short of the ideals to which these goals relate. We must not let our goals and our policies become dissonant, but neither must we let the desire to shape the future override our responsibility to cope with the present. If we cannot manage the short-term problems satisfactorily, our ability to move towards longer-term possibilities may become further impaired.

The attributes and the tools of policy that Britain has at her disposal have been changing rapidly. Although in absolute terms she is still a powerful and prosperous nation, with a good deal to offer the international community and a great deal to preserve in the present balance, in relative terms, she, like the other states of Western Europe, is no longer so distinctive as she was, say, twenty years ago; the international community has grown in size and is more disparate in outlook. Despite good relations with many of the new states, and distinctive relations with many important states in NATO, the EEC and the Commonwealth, she feels a sense of insecurity, which, although recently sharpened by an economic slide, stems from the fundamental threat which the Soviet Union poses, militarily and ideologically. If the Soviet Union were prepared to abandon the ideological pretensions that impel

12

a rhetoric, if not a policy, that predicts the domination of other social systems by their beliefs, the tension could be reduced. But the Soviet Union's size and military power, and experience of her policies all continue to make Britain fearful of taking any risks, or accepting any proposals that could be misinterpreted as weakness or irresolution.

If Britain's general security is to be enhanced, she should not be expected to take any new risks, nor to make any expansive military gestures. However, the future is no less dangerous or uncertain, than it was when she originally acquired a nuclear capability, and having shown persistence in maintaining it, there are no major political reasons for her to renounce it. The arguments about providing a bad example, in the context of the non-proliferation regime, miss the point; irresponsibility in that field would more evidently lie in trying to pretend that nuclear weapons are no longer important enough to take seriously. Having been one of the first-generation nuclear states, Britain knows that they are important enough to warrant multilateral regulation; consequently, international co-operation is implicit.

Domestic Support

The way in which budgetary requirements shape views about what are the most desirable ends of policy is perhaps a separate issue.[9] Governments do not always pursue policy objectives knowing precisely what will be the attributable value gained, nor is there always a straightforward relationship between what things cost and what they are worth. Obviously finding the money is a problem, but to want to find the money is at least as important. In that context, maintaining a strategic deterrent capability is not a special sort of problem. True, it is much more common in defence than in other areas to measure input-output relationships, at a crude budgetary level at least, and it is now a standard norm that, for political as well as for industrial reasons, we specify quantities and purposes to the greatest possible extent. But with some sorts of objectives it is not quite so easy to predetermine precisely what the exact outcome will be, or quite what it would be worth to achieve it. We determine that the policy is desirable, that it is worth doing because it fulfils a need that seems right, or good, or proper to meet. It may even be justifiable on

the grounds of expediency, but the point is that it is politically valuable.

To think of the strategic deterrent as if it were only 'another defence programme' is by this reasoning, too limited. The issue of the deterrent cannot be judged as if one were talking about a new class of warship, or a new tank. The deterrent is a political phenomenon, as deterrence is a political value, and to that extent it must be judged by political criteria as much as by cost, or opportunity cost. 'Is it worth having?' is a question that has to be dealt with at the political level – the inductive, subjective level of judgement – rather than solely in terms of deductive assessments of cost.

We cannot ignore costs, however. If the price of re-providing a deterrent capability was so enormous that it would swamp the rest of British defence programmes, then we should have to re-think our priorities very radically. The French example demonstrates what happens if nuclear weapons programmes are given so high a priority that the conventional military forces have to make do for long periods on very low training and equipment budgets. It should be feasible, if we are sure about the general political worth of the objective, to find a balance that will enable us to continue to provide both a nuclear and a conventional contribution to the security of the Alliance, as in the past.

The preceding explanations have in essence amounted to a case that Britain can and should, continue to provide a long-range nuclear weapon delivery capability as a part of her defence contribution to the Western security matrix. The question of cost is primarily of domestic significance. The question of purpose extends beyond domestic political considerations. Nonetheless, its roots clearly lie in the British political conception of what Britain's role in the Western security matrix is. In a democratic state, no international role is long sustained that does not have domestic concurrence.

Defence and foreign policy are two areas in which British governments have, traditionally, been able to exercise their powers in a relatively free manner, so far as any constraints imposed by parliamentary control or the force of public opinion are concerned. These have been seen as areas of special complexity and importance where government is expected to act, and where its stewardship only becomes a matter of domestic political significance in unusual circumstances. However, it is now much more difficult to identify the limits of these fields of policy. The British membership of collectivities like NATO and the EEC blurs previously identifiable limits, sometimes making any distinctive national element hard to dramatize and Britain's particular worth and her government's particular responsibility more difficult to see. What is easier to see is the comparative relationship between Britain and the other partners: the parts, rather than the whole. As a result, the special tolerance extended to defence and foreign policy issues is being more restrictively redrawn. Furthermore, issues of defence and foreign policy are simply not seen as so important as they once were. This has nothing to do with concern over particular issues, but with a general sense that what Britain can do about any particular issue is much less than it used to be. It is an attitude derived from a loss of confidence just as much as from any estimate of a loss of power. How far the attitude penetrates general as well as elite attitudes is a political issue of general significance. It is of special significance for this enquiry to determine whether it is any longer possible for government to presume that any special effort required to maintain the role in the Western security pattern which the British deterrent force has epitomized will receive support. The determinedly 'low profile' support of the exisiting British policy in recent years has in effect conceded an initiative – a tactical advantage, at least – to its opponents. It is beginning to seem that the normal public expectation about Britain's ability to maintain a strategic nuclear capability has already started to shift.[10]

The Support of Allies

Possession of marginally useful increments of nuclear force might in future not be seen to contribute as much or as directly to the defence of the West as Britain (and France too) originally thought it would. Or perhaps it is still seen as important enough to warrant encouragement, rather than seeing Britain divert her resources into some other defence contribution.

It may be that the significance generally attributed to nuclear weapons makes it difficult for other states – nuclear or non-nuclear – to exert such pressure. One factor here may be that the forces of the two European nuclear states in effect cancel each other out: Britain is a loyal collaborator inside the military organization of NATO; France is a partial collaborator on the fringes. For either substantially to change her posture would be to upset an arrangement with which the Western Allies have come to terms in the last twelve years or so, and which does not materially affect NATO's position *vis-à-vis* the Warsaw Pact.

The United States, for example, no longer makes as much as she once did of the necessity for NATO nuclear forces to be centrally directed. There is no longer a need for comprehensive central direction in view of the growth of a direct and extensive relationship between the United States and the Soviet Union and the qualitative and quantitative changes in the American nuclear posture. Nevertheless, the existence of the British and French nuclear forces continues to be a military bonus, and also a source of some political difficulty. This last is probably not very significant at the moment; but if serious discussions about 'forward based systems' were to take place in SALT III, it seems likely that the USSR would want to see that British and French capabilities be taken into account. And it might not be easy to exclude them from SALT III if the European partners wanted 'Eurostrategic' problems to be raised, even though Britain and France are as adamant as ever that their national forces should not be implicated in the super-powers' bilateral negotiations. Yet it is not easy to see how Britain or France could allow the United States to dispose of their interests unilaterally, and the United States has no interest in undercutting the power or prestige of two of the more important Western European states. A basic premise of American foreign policy over the last generation has been the emergence of a stronger and more unified Western Europe and as things now are, it is entirely conceivable that the United States is already reconciled to the emergence in the longer term of a Western European political entity that will have, as one of its attributes, a nuclear capability.

Meanwhile, the United States nevertheless has to juggle her own relationship with the Soviet Union. For the SALT process to be pushed much further it is likely that some division of interest between inter-continental and regional systems must emerge. The likelihood that the United States would see the British and French nuclear forces as a 'forward based system' in a SALT

14

context (i.e., of secondary importance) would cause concern to West Germany as well as to Britain and France. Much of the concern that has recently been voiced about 'the grey areas' and 'Eurostrategic problems' has come from German sources, and it is clear that West German policy, as well as informed West German opinion, is showing signs of concern about the increased vulnerability of Western Europe.

The Alliance in general views with real concern the improved Soviet military potential that has become apparent in the last two years: the recent agreement to increase national defence budgets is one of the most salient illustrations. However, what attracts less attention is a feeling that the categories, distinctions, policies and attitudes of the last decade are changing so profoundly that new responses and new attitudes must be determined.

One contingency that has to be taken into account is that Western Europe may once again become a distinctive strategic area. This runs together a range of possibilities. Western Europe may evolve as the *glacis* between the super-powers; or it may become a distinct military, political or economic bloc. The key factor at the moment seems to be a perception that Western Europe is more vulnerable to Soviet military power than in the recent past because of the qualitative improvements embodied in the SS-20 mobile missile and the *Backfire* bombers, and because this range of forces is not covered either by SALT or MBFR. In some ways the concern is overstated. Europe has been vulnerable to the SS-4 and SS-5 for twenty years, though perhaps rather less so since the Schlesinger selective targeting doctrine was embodied into United States policy. In a political environment that is heavy with a sense of insecurity and hungry for new methods of emphasizing a collective alliance response, West Germany is unlikely to press Britain to forswear her nuclear forces, even for a larger conventional contribution.

A British observer might be forgiven for assuming that it would be easier in these circumstances for Germany and Britain to find common perspectives than for Britain and France to do so. Anglo-French relations have exhibited as many of the characteristics appropriate to natural competitors as to natural collaborators. But Anglo-German relations have not been all that cordial either and in some ways British policy

towards Germany is one of the most neglected aspects of British foreign affairs.

It might be more difficult for Britain than for France to accept any proposition suggesting that there is a distinct Eurostrategic security sphere. This would alter traditional British policy of stressing the Atlantic 'dimension' in the Western Alliance structure and would simultaneously reduce the vital importance of the British role as one of NATO's principal guardians of the Western Flank. But, intriguingly, it might also serve to emphasize the distinctiveness of the nuclear contribution that Britain could make to such a separate environment. But the way in which the concept is formulated is crucial for its acceptance; West Germany, like all her neighbours, would not want to precipitate the sort of decoupling by the United States that would leave Western Europe as a war-fighting zone instead of a security zone protected by deterrence. But the concept could have its attractions, since it could prospectively be aligned to the ultimate emergence of a European political collectivity; and it could be a positive approach to the concern that France should not be the only nuclear weapon state in Western Europe. This is a concern that seldom finds its way into print.

However unreliable and presumptive these suspicions may be, they combine with the other factors to re-emphasize that nuclear weapons are still thought to be important. What they represent is a military potential that, however distasteful and however uncertain in its utility, is distinctive as well as dangerous. The second point that emerges is that against an uncertain future, nuclear weapons are an attribute which, if already available, should not be lightly discarded. This sort of consideration is older and more primitive than analytical theory, and symbolizes the apprehension which characterizes an international community conceived in terms of states. It is perhaps particularly characteristic of that part of the community that has seen its dominance, many of its values, and the sense of orderliness that supported these values, slip away at an alarming rate.

Time to Act

There are a number of issues which, although they are primarily of a technical nature, have important political consequences. Some affect the style and timing of any policy development, but some contribute more fundamentally to the nature of policy.

One very important technical issue is the length of time needed to procure and deploy any successor system; the converse of this is what should be done about the existing capability if it is decided not to go for any successor system, either at all or not in the lifetime of the present government.

It seems to be a matter of some debate how long the existing *Polaris* submarines can continue to operate effectively.[11] The normal operational life of a submarine is usually 20–25 years, though it is possible to extend this by paying special attention to hull structures and ship sub-systems during refits, and 30 years is not out of the question. The matter assumes significance on a number of counts. If it is decided not to go ahead with a successor system, it would then be necessary to determine the scope of *Polaris* deployment. An extra five years or so of hull-life might conceivably be a useful attribute, provided that the weapon system will remain militarily credible for the longer period. But assuming that a successor system will be introduced, prolonging the life of the existing carrier vehicle could affect policy in a number of ways. If we presuppose that any successor system would take 8–10 years to become operational, and that the earliest of the *Polaris* boats would (on a 25 year life) be retired in 1992, then the time available for a decision about what to do only goes up to 1982. That is before we shall know, empirically, whether cruise missiles now being tested in the United States will perform up to specification, or whether the *Trident* 2 system mounted in the *Ohio*-class submarines may prove so much better and more reliable in service than the *Trident* 1 system, that the present *Trident* 1 and *Poseidon* systems will be phased out of the US inventory earlier than current plans now provide. It is also probably well before we can glimpse the final shape of any SALT III agreement, or any definitive agreement on Mutual Force Reductions.

To be able to buy time for such uncertainties to be clarified, even a little, might be considered politically valuable, but the time involved would have to be considerable in order to justify the extra ship refit costs. And these costs might in themselves be an issue of concern, if the time needed for the extra work were to affect the standard operating cycle of the four submarines

to such an extent that the constant patrol availability of at least one, but more normally two, submarines was in question.

The other reason for buying time by extending the life of the present deterrent force would be if the estimated capital cost of a successor system impinged unacceptably on other defence equipment programmes. This is not merely a question of finance, although it has been a constant endeavour of defence managers to avoid peaks and troughs in defence expenditure as far as ever possible. The constraints imposed by the availability of manpower (in industry as well as in the services) and technical capacity are at least as important, partly because they effectively limit any government's ability to foreshorten the time taken to introduce a new system by mounting a crash programme. If we assume another submarine-borne deterrent system, it might be necessary to consider whether a second submarine construction stream should be set up, either to get the new force to sea as quickly as possible, or to minimize the effects upon other submarine construction programmes, notably the nuclear fleet submarines (SSN). More generally, how would a major new capital programme, which so far has not been projected in long-range costings, affect expenditure on other major programmes, such as new battle tanks or new aircraft? The late 1980s are potentially full of such hazards. Although one cannot determine with any precision what a successor system would cost or how those costs would fall, in programme terms, we can draw two conclusions. First the *Polaris* Sales Agreement was an uncommonly good bargain that is unlikely to be repeated. Second, the cost of an appropriately powerful successor force is likely to be sufficiently high for the political debate about its acquisition to be focused upon the economic and financial questions alone, if that is how those in the forefront of the debate decide to play it.

On the time that a new system would take to deploy, the assumption of 8–10 years is a mean, conventional assessment. A strictly national programme would take longer to organize and complete than a collaborative programme with the United States (on the assumption that what Britain was obtaining had already been proved as an effective weapon system). A collaborative programme with any other state, France for example, would probably take as long as a national programme, if not longer; the political as well as the technical parameters of collaboration would have to gestate, even if the conception was straightforward. The full range of possibilities extends from about 6½ years to about 12 years, but a general expectation of 8–10 years provides a 'feel' which is adequate for most political purposes. It covers for example, the contingency that a decision might be sought sufficiently early in the life of a government – or, in the case of a collaborative programme, in the life of an American or French presidency – to preclude any easy option of cancellation by a successor government which favoured a different policy.

The technical credibility of any collaborative programme is another issue of some importance. The great virtue of the Nassau Agreement was that it locked the British into a weapon system that already had effective credentials: though *Polaris* A3 was not yet fully tested, the A2 was fully operational. To the extent that Britain wants to continue to save time and/or money by collaborating with another state, it would always be in her interests to reduce as far as possible the uncertainties that inevitably exist during the research and development stages of any high-technology innovation. These uncertainties would be one of the additional hazards of a strictly national programme, as well as of a collaborative venture into unproven technology. To opt for a proved system might have an added point in an environment constrained by a comprehensive test ban treaty. It is likely that any such treaty will provide for a small allowance of explosive tests to enable stockpile safety standards to be maintained, but, even so, a state with only a relatively small armoury would want the option of assuring itself that the design parameters of its deployed re-entry systems and warheads were not validated only by laboratory simulations and configuration control paperwork.

The choice of any successor system will obviously be a major political decision; but there are subsidiary considerations which ought to be noted. Taking up my earlier reference to the potential significance of domestic and international attitudes to British policy in this field, it may well be more important to choose an appropriate and favourable *political* occasion to make the decision (or at least to announce it) than

to choose some technically desirable time scale. The *Skybolt* and *Polaris* decisions, both taken under duress, were brought about principally by external factors. It looks as if a less constrained environment might be possible, both for discussion of and eventual decision on any future British deterrent system. An interesting point will be the extent to which a national decision on this occasion will be 'externalized' – for just as the NATO allies all have an interest in what happens to the SALT II Treaty and the Soviet-American relationship which it epitomizes, Britain's friends and allies could claim to be concerned about her intentions and decisions over nuclear weapons. The United States or France might have a direct degree of involvement in any collaborative arrangement, but the other European allies will be at least interested to see what sort of European or Eurostrategic gloss is put upon the domestic British discussion and might try to influence the outcome.

The nature of any decision to procure a successor system could also have consequences for the organization of the defence forces. The obvious variation would be if the preferred solution was a force of air-launched cruise missiles, or a mixed force of air- and sea-launched cruise missiles. Not only would there be a need to review command and control arrangements – with both organization and equipment costs to be taken into account – but there might be a need to reallocate responsibilities (as between the Royal Navy and the Royal Air Force). Less fundamentally, even a successor force of submarines, if its mission were more directly related to a 'Eurostrategic' role, might require review of its authority and command links.

In conclusion, there is one further point worth making which, though technical, is fundamental The rate at which technical change takes place is neither stable nor predictable. It is conceivable that a rapid period of change might occur in the 1980s, as it did in the 1950s, when novel technologies up-ended many earlier calculations. For Britain the possibility of getting stuck with another *Blue Streak* or thrown into confusion by another *Skybolt* cancellation must always cause apprehension, which not even close collaboration with the United States can eliminate with complete certainty.

The Range of Choice

JONATHAN ALFORD

Strategic Factors

Rather than give a comprehensive survey of all technological developments in the strategic field, this section will concentrate on those developments that seem likely to affect Britain's choice of successor systems to *Polaris*. The direction which the super-powers choose to follow will be determined largely by what they perceive as the offensive and defensive improvements in the other's arsenal and by their own doctrinal preferences. However, their choices will have the side effect of severely restricting the range of choice for smaller nuclear powers. The three areas of technological development most likely to affect this range of choice are cruise missiles (and defence against them), anti-ballistic missile defence and anti-submarine warfare. Following the technical review, there is a section on the arms control implications. Having set the context, the British deterrent requirements are discussed and the range of possible choices is examined together with their implications – including the option of renunciation.

Some Factors Affecting the Cruise Missile

It seems fairly certain that the United States will shortly begin to invest quite massively in air-launched cruise missiles (ALCM) in order to sustain the 'air-breathing leg' of their strategic triad. Initially at least, these will be carried by B-52 strategic bombers, and it is assumed that 120 aircraft will be modified to carry about 20 ALCM each (giving a total of 2,400 warheads), although it may be necessary to sacrifice part of this potential payload in order to carry short-range attack missiles (SRAM) for defence suppression. This configuration assumes largely the successful outcome of SALT II. It must also be said that ALCM are not yet operational in the United States, although some facts are beginning to emerge from which inferences can be drawn.

ALCM will consist of a light airframe with a small radar cross-section, a very efficient turbojet power plant, fuel tanks, a guidance system and a warhead. Most interest will centre on the guidance system, since the rest of the technology is relatively easy to reproduce. To guide the missile to its target, assuming that the first part of the journey is over the sea, there has to be an inertial system which is accurate to within tens of miles over about 500 miles; greater accuracy is probably impossible, with a relatively slow vehicle affected by surface winds and flying inertially. Subsequently it might prove possible to use the projected American satellite navigation system (GPS *Navstar*), which is expected to give a 30 ft fix in three dimensions, but this may be subject to ECM (electronic counter-measures) and will in any case require a relatively bulky receiver and computer. However, provided that the missile can fly inertially to an area about 50 miles square, the grid system of TERCOM (terrain contour matching) can take over. This system consists of comparing terrain information, obtained by satellite and stored in a computer on board the missile, with the terrain detected by sensors on the missile. Probably the most important – and the most vulnerable – of these sensors is a radar altimeter which allows the missile to fly low but at a predetermined height above the ground. This will probably be vulnerable to degradation from ECM though it is not known what measures have been adopted to overcome this.

Once the missile has located itself on the first grid, it receives instructions from its own computer to fly inertially to the next, more specific, grid until, presumably depending on the size and distance of the target, it can be brought to an accuracy of less that 100 feet.

We have been discussing the two ALCM under test in the United States – the Boeing ALCM 86B and the General Dynamics *Tomahawk* – being flown in competition in 1979/80 to decide which system should be procured. It is reasonable to presume that America will move rapidly from these first-generation missles to second, and even third-generation types. The development is likely to be in the direction of higher speeds (perhaps to give a supersonic dash capability while penetrating Soviet air defences), a still greater 'ground-hugging' capability and terminal guidance to give, effectively, one hundred per cent accuracy. The last function will have to rely upon some kind of photographic correlation. It is also likely that the missiles of the future will be given some ECM capability of their own so as to protect their own radar altimeters.

What can be said with some confidence is that the costs of first-generation missiles will rise sharply for subsequent generations. Also, there are some inherent difficulties in making the system more capable. The first of these is that supersonic flight at very low levels will use much more fuel (how much more depends upon how long the low-level dash must be sustained in order to penetrate Soviet defences and how low the flight). This will mean that either a greater proportion of the total payload must be devoted to fuel or else missiles must get bigger so as to avoid a range penalty: neither is an attractive trade-off. Much the same applies to ECM, electronic counter-counter-measures (ECCM) and terminal guidance.[12] All devices will use up available space and payload – and this will affect fuel carriage or warhead size and weight or both.

By way of conclusion to this brief technical introduction on cruise missiles it is worth making three points. Firstly, assuming that some defence is possible against cruise missiles, the costs of overcoming that defence will either push up the cost and complexity of the missile or else demand that a higher number be flown to compensate for losses. Secondly, the system will produce a high degree of accuracy when compared to ballistic systems, an accuracy which is unnecesary given a nuclear warhead in the 100 KT range. (Only in attacking super-hardened targets would it be necessary to place a 100 KT warhead within 100 ft of a target.) Thirdly, one must remember that the American rationale for procurement of cruise missiles is not likely to be transferable to the strategic needs of other countries.

Faced with the major decision of how to modernize the 'air-breathing leg of the strategic triad,' the United States decided against building the new B-1 penetrating bomber to carry new weapon systems to a launching position and in favour of reworking the ageing B-52 fleet. When considering system costs, it must be borne in mind that, weighed against the cost of a new and very expensive B-1 aircraft fleet, the cost of ALCM, in combination with other strategic systems, makes strategic sense in American terms. It strengthens US second-strike capability, complicates things for the Soviet Union and, for certain important hard targets (i.e. command centres or missile control posts), gives that combination of yield and accuracy that the US requires.

So far the discussion has revolved around ALCM, but there are no fundamental differences between air-launched versions and sea- or ground-launched versions. The launching platform is almost irrelevant except in the case of submarine-launched cruise-missiles (SLCM). In this case the missile must be prepared for underwater launch from a standard torpedo tube. It must therefore be waterproofed, able to be ejected clear of the water before the engine ignites, and must have folding wings and tail in order to fit into a standard canister. Once the SLCM begins to fly, there are no differences of principle except that, in the anti-shipping role, terminal guidance by radar or by command is essential, since the water surface is not differentiated in a way which allows correlation with data carried in the missile's computer; some kind of homing warhead is therefore necessary. On the other hand it seems very probable that the various versions of the missile will not be truly multi-role, in the sense that they could not be easily switched from one type of carrier to another. The differences in launch mechanism are significant, and one would expect that a degree of role specialization will almost inevitably occur over time, although a family resemblance will remain.

Defence Against Cruise-missiles

It is reasonable to assume that the Soviet Union will be forced to invest heavily in an air defence system in an attempt to protect herself from cruise missile attack from the United States. The only sensible deployment for the Soviet Union would be perimeter defence based upon elevated radars and a combination of interceptor aircraft with a 'look down/shoot down' capability and surface-to-air missiles (SAM) with very high rates

19

of initial acceleration. What is known of the Soviet SA-10 SAM leads one to believe that it might prove suitable for this task.

It also makes sense for the Soviet Union to extend her fighter-interception zones outwards over the sea by means of aerial in-flight fuelling – both because it will probably be easier to separate cruise missile radar echoes from ground-clutter over water than over land and because it would be much more economical to strike the ALCM launching aircraft than at the missiles once launched. In the next decade heavy deployment of such very sophisticated air defences should be technically attainable, although at great cost. Dr William Perry, Under Secretary of Defense for Research and Engineering at the US Department of Defense, has put the total cost to the Soviet Union at $50 billion and stresses that the very small radar cross-section of the ALCM will make acquisition and tracking very difficult.[13]

It may be worth reflecting briefly on the British defences against the German V-1 attacks in 1944. Cruise missiles will fly a lot lower than the V-1 and perhaps a little faster (at least in the first generation), and they will be very much more accurate (partly because target acquisition and means of direction have greatly improved in the intervening years). Nevertheless it may not be inappropriate to draw conclusions from the earlier instance.

The defence of London was made very much more effective when anti-aircraft guns were moved forward from London itself to the south coast of England. German V-1 losses by mid-July 1944 (before the move) were attributed as follows: 924 to fighters, 261 to AA fire, 55 to balloons. After the move, the weekly ratio of AA 'kills' to fighter 'kills' changed from 50:180 to 170:120.[14] This seems to argue strongly in favour of forward, rather than terminal, defence. Secondly, however competent the defences, some missiles will get through; this did not greatly matter with HE warheads but would be very significant with nuclear warheads. Professor Jones, in *Most Secret War,* quotes V-1 figures for 28 August 1944:[15]

Total flown	97
Destroyed by fighters over the sea	13
Destroyed by AA fire	65
Destroyed by fighters over land	10
Destroyed by ballons	2
Total detonating on or close to London	7

With the possibility of a British cruise missile force in mind, it would be true to say that Soviet defences erected against the expectation of a massive American attack of some thousands of missiles could effect a much higher rate of attrition against a smaller force. The third conclusion, again quoting Professor Jones, is that 'an analysis of the economics of the campaign showed a large balance in the German favour; the cost of our counter-measures, especially in bombing the sites, exceeded the estimated cost of the campaign to the Germans'.[16] In other words, there are grounds for believing that the absolute cost to the Soviet Union of defending against a cruise missile threat will be greater than the cost to the United States of sustaining that threat. First estimates indicate that a total of 3,000 ALCM, together with the necessary B-52 modifications, will cost one-fifth ($10 bn) of the amount needed for air defences against them.

It follows however that the United States (or any country interested in air- or sea-launched cruise-missiles for strategic second strike) could be forced to invest heavily in a self-defence capability for the cruise missile carriers and in considerable defence suppression if the attrition rate on cruise missiles is not to rise to unacceptable levels. ECM will figure in both, as will some form of SRAM – probably with a nuclear warhead – to destroy enemy radar installations, control sites, defensive missiles and fighter airfields. The idea would be to create holes in the perimeter defences through which subsequent waves of cruise missiles could fly unmolested. Given that long-range fighter cover for the cruise missile carriers will prove uneconomic, they will need some form of self-defence air-to-air missile (AAM), especially since they are likely to have to pull up to a relatively high altitude to launch, where they will be much more vulnerable to interception than during low-level transit. Also, unless the carriers can approach the enemy coast, the relatively limited range of the cruise missile will be further eroded by a long initial oversea flight. There are two important conclusions to this line of argument. First, a substantial part of the carrier's available payload will consist of SRAM, AAM and ECM equipment, leaving much less than might have been expected for cruise missiles. Second, the attempts at defence will lead to the need for some form of ECM on the cruise missile itself (at the expense of fuel, and therefore range), and the need for the missile to fly faster while attempting to penetrate the defence zone and adopt evasive routing (again affecting fuel consumption, and hence usable range). There is as yet no accurate means of costing the second generation of cruise missiles which seems certain to follow hard on the heels of the first, but it does seem likely that the cost of maintaining a sufficient degree of ascendancy over the defence will lead to at least a doubling of costs in real terms in each generation.

It is also likely that point defence against cruise missiles will be feasible somewhere about 1990–2010, even if only towards the end of that period. Indeed defence against cruise missile attack at sea is already close to deployment but there are likely to be considerably greater difficulties with land defences, since terrain masking will reduce the response time of any defending weapon system. Nevertheless, high-energy lasers and radar-controlled guns with extremely high rates of fire and rapid response could, if deployed in sufficient numbers, give a measure of terminal protection against cruise missile attack. Small targets are much easier to protect than large ones, particularly with regard to omni-directional attack.

It is hard to believe that the Soviet Union could or would divert sufficient resources to give defensive cover for all possible targets, civilian as well as military: not only would budgetary costs be high, but the manpower requirements could prove prohibitively expensive. Nevertheless, she would be likely to provide some measure of defence against cruise missile attack for high-value targets such as airfields, dockyards, command-and-control centres and storage facilities. Given that the flight-time of the subsonic cruise missile will be measured in hours, rather than minutes, there would seem little advantage in providing defence for missile silos – they would probably be empty (unless they were being used for reloads).

In sum, American ALCM (and possible SLCM), when fully operational, will cause the Soviet Union to build a dense and moderately effective perimeter defence that might destroy as much as 50% of incoming missiles – either while still on their carriers or in flight. They will also try to provide some terminal protection against cruise missile attack for important military targets, especially since such point defences will also serve against attack by manned aircraft. These two measures will limit damage but will not totally

protect the Soviet Union, because the US can build more missiles for less cost than the USSR can build defences. However, although the United States may not have a great deal to fear from Soviet defences, their effect on a smaller force of cruise missiles could seriously degrade their performance. Quoting Professor Jones' conclusions on the V-1 experience, 'The reduction in the rate of bombardment worked more in our favour than the launching figures suggest by themselves, *because our defences were then less saturated and thus able to achieve a higher rate of success.'*[17] (Emphasis added).

Cruise missile launcher/carriers have some persistent vulnerabilities. In the case of aircraft, there is an important relationship between the degree of assured warning of attack that can be expected and the time taken to get the aircraft into the air. The United States can expect some twenty minutes warning of ballistic missile attack (or some hours in the case of aircraft attack), provided the attack is launched from the Soviet Union or adjacent waters. This warning of launch is more or less assured by satellites and by radar detection. However, the scenario becomes much more alarming if the threat of depressed-trajectory submarine-launched ballistic missiles (SLBM) becomes a reality, because these could be fired by Soviet submarines on station close to the US shores. In this case there might be only some five or six minutes warning of attack – which is close to the time it takes an aircraft standing ready to get into the air (even the B-52 with a rapid start-up capability). By virtue of her proximity to the Soviet Union, Britain can expect only six to eight minutes warning of ballistic missile attack from the Soviet Union and, given the lack of all-round early-warning radar coverage, virtually no warning of attack by depressed-trajectory SLBM fired from the Atlantic.

If the ALCM option appears to have severe drawbacks, some of these can be obviated by taking the cruise missile to sea – either in surface or sub-surface vessels. Surface carriers could either be relatively conventional warships, such as frigates or fast patrol boats or surface skimmers, such as hydrofoils or hovercraft. To some extent each type would, by sheer proliferation of numbers, create difficult tactical problems for the Soviet Union, whose fleet would have to shadow and then destroy a large number of naval units before they could launch their missiles. This

21

would tie down many Soviet surface vessels or submarines – although a prolonged period of conventional hostilities before nuclear release might cause considerable pre-release attrition of the deterrent. The question of whether to have vessels dedicated to the deterrent mission or to put some SLCM on a variety of general-purpose naval units is finely balanced and is argued later for the British case. The cost of dedicated vessels would have to be apportioned entirely to the deterrent; in the case of wider deployment, only the missiles and any additional command and control arrangements relating to the deterrent would need to be so apportioned. It is worth considering small, cheap cruise missile platforms for the dedicated nuclear mission, with survivability as their most valuable and important characteristic.

Defence Against Ballistic Missiles

It is not so much a question of what each super-power *could* do as what each *will* do, for there is not only a treaty constraining ballistic missile defences numerically (the ABM Treaty of 1972) but also a strong mutual interest in not engaging in unrestrained competition. However, there is little doubt that technology has now reached a stage (mainly as a result of rapid advances in computers and micro-circuitry) where an effective close-in defence against ballistic missiles could be deployed by about 1990, if not before. Defence of missile silos is therefore a possible answer to the emerging problem of land-based missile vulnerability, and many will argue that silo defences would not be destabilizing in the way that city defences would be. On the whole though, it seems highly improbable that either side would wish to abrogate what is perhaps the one enduring monument to an earlier phase of detente, but the possibility must be acknowledged – at least to the extent of renegotiating the maximum number of systems allowed under the ABM Treaty for silo defence. If, rather than defending one site with 100 missiles as permitted under the Treaty, the United States was able to defend 200 ICBM, this could in theory protect the bulk of the MX missiles which seem likely to form the core of American land-based deterrent forces. Nevertheless there seems little likelihood that either super-power could or would be able to extend effective ABM cover to all its high-value targets. It follows that any smaller nuclear power

that relies for its deterrent effect on threatening targets of value, rather than the opponent's missiles, will continue to get what has been described as 'a free ride' on the back of super-power ABM restraint.

Much more serious for smaller powers and super-powers is the emerging possibility that other forms of defence against ballistic missile attack could be deployed by the end of this century. There has been a great deal of speculation in the technical press about ground- or space-based defensive systems relying on lasers or charged-particle beams. Both super-powers are spending large sums on investigating these 'exotic' technologies, but there is no certainty that they will turn out to be capable of providing an impenetrable barrier to incoming missiles, and there is considerable debate in the scientific and intelligence community as to the practicability of either lasers or particle beams for ballistic missile defence. The power requirements of charged-particle beams are very high and they are subject to deflection by the earth's magnetic field, although it is theoretically possible to concentrate sufficient energy at the target to disable it. The beam does not have to hit a ballistic missile to destroy it – a near miss could cause extensive damage to the electronic components of the guidance system. Laser beams, on the other hand, must hit the target to cause damage, and they are attenuated by distance, dust or moisture.

Although there is therefore a remote possibility that these technologies might be diverted from their primary thrust (controlled nuclear fusion), it appears unlikely that either side will be in a position to deploy an effective and comprehensive ballistic missile defence based on these principles, at least in this century. A large space-based particle beam generator would be very vulnerable to attack, and it would not be difficult to fool the system with decoys of various kinds. Furthermore, only a platform in geostationary orbit could provide continuous cover, and it is highly unlikely that the weapon could be sufficiently discriminating to be aimed at individual missiles at distances of 36,000 kilometres. Land-based generators are more feasible, but magnetic deflection would create almost insuperable aiming problems for particle beams, and lasers will not penetrate very far in the atmosphere except under conditions of exceptional visibility. At most it might be expected that both super-powers will be close to deploying some form of terminal defence against aircraft or cruise-missiles based on a high-powered laser by the end of the 1980s.

Whether or not these technologies prove attractive, there are grounds for believing that there will be some mutual restraint codified by treaty. If the logic of the ABM Treaty holds good, its language could be clarified to make it explicit that the treaty refers to ballistic missile defence in all its forms, and not just to anti-ballistic missile missiles. Alternatively a new treaty could be worked out to prohibit the use of space for both offensive and defensive systems – either as part of the SALT process or as a result of separate discussions on the limitation of anti-satellite warfare such as those currently proceeding.

Other types of defence against incoming ballistic missiles are hardening, dispersal, concealment and mobility. In the case of ballistic missile silos, the limits to hardening are those associated with the compressive strength of concrete. Most now agree that the accuracies of incoming warheads are likely to produce over-pressures at the target in excess of the compressive strength of concrete, so that hardening is no longer capable of providing security for any fixed land-based ballistic missile. Dispersal of assets – and their multiplication and concealment – are inhibited by the verification requirements of SALT II and by the numerical restrictions of that Treaty. The preferred option for enhancing ballistic missile invulnerability appears to be mobility between fixed firing positions. There is also a 'do nothing' school in the United States which argues that the existence of silo-based ICBMs will complicate the Soviet Union's targeting problems and force her to allocate so many of her available warheads to neutralizing the American land-based deterrent forces that it is not necessary to spend large sums on enhancing invulnerability. The dangers to the Soviet Union of an American launch on confirmed warning of attack are, it is argued, such as to make a first strike against American land-based missiles a very risky option. But it is the reality of large numbers of other secure second-strike systems in the United States arsenal that makes it not unreasonable to argue in this way. The vulnerability of the land-based ballistic missile in fixed sites is such that they can no longer *by themselves* provide a secure second-strike capability. It would be unwise for any nation now to rely exclusively on fixed assets for nuclear deterrence.

Future of Submarine Systems
In considering the vulnerability of submarines both technical and operational predictions have to be made. The technical questions concern detection and means of destruction; operational uncertainties relate to the investment that the Soviet Union will make in anti-submarine warfare (ASW) forces in the future and how she will use them.

Whereas the balance of advantage has rested with the submarine until now, it seems likely that there will be a slow, though possibly marginal, shift in favour of ASW forces. Such a conclusion is extremely tentative, for ballistic missile nuclear submarines (SSBN) will become quieter with improvements in propulsion machinery and they will take advantage of anechoic coating of the hull to reduce the risk of detection by active sonar. The use of decoys by SSBN and the use of the noise of escorting surface vessels or other submarines as cover will make the task of a trailing enemy submarine very difficult, and there is the probablility that de-gaussing equipment in the submarine will make magnetic anomaly detection (detecting the very slight variations in the earth's magnetic field caused by the submarine hull) from aircraft much harder. Offsetting these defensive improvements are satellite detection systems using infra-red (to measure the small temperature differences between the SSBN, its wake and its surroundings) and improved sonar (active and passive), both of which will make it more difficult for a submarine to hide. Once a submarine has been detected, homing torpedoes of many different types will pose the main threat, but the use of nuclear depth charges is clearly feasible. It would also be unwise to discount the possibility that Soviet land- or submarine-based ballistic missiles might be used to spread a pattern of nuclear warheads to straddle the known operating area of the SSBN. To a large extent the effectiveness of ASW techniques will depend upon the sophistication of command-and-control techniques. Provided that satellite detection is possible, that information has to be transmitted virtually instantaneously to a controlling headquarters, which must then either direct ASW forces to the last known position of the SSBN or target nuclear missiles. If, as appears probable, the most effective counter to the SSBN is a hunter-killer nuclear submarine (SSN), there remain considerable difficulties in communicating with a submerged vessel. All that one can usefully conclude is that the extensive use of satellites by both sides for detection and communication will make the SSBN more vulnerable than before, and clearly they will be most vulnerable to detection and trailing when leaving port or when passing through constricted waters. On the other side of the equation, the much greater ranges attainable with modern SLBMs have increased dramatically the sea areas in which SSBN can operate.

However, there remains the important question of numbers – especially SSN numbers in relation to SSBN numbers. Prudently assuming that the Soviet Union would wish to allocate at least two SSN to every deployed Western SSBN, the rate of building becomes very significant. At present the Soviet Union has approximately 40 SSN and 45 cruise missile nuclear submarines (SSCN). Assuming that the latter's prime role is destruction of surface shipping, and particularly the American carrier task groups, it is not expected that many could be allocated to the anti-SSBN role, even if their missiles can be given an ASW capability (technically quite feasible). As there are now 41 US SSBN, together with four British and four (eventually six) French, there is a definite shortage of SSN on the Soviet side. However the Soviet Union is now close to the number of SSBN permitted under the SALT ceilings, so a number of authorities are postulating that in future many more of the Soviet nuclear submarine slipways will be building SSN up to a theoretical annual maximum of six per year. The next decade could therefore see a much more alarming SSN/SSBN ratio, with two on one becoming a reality. Despite manning problems in her navy, the Soviet Union has always accorded a high priority to matching western SSBN which, for her, are in many ways the most threatening of all western nuclear deterrent forces. As noted, the greatly increased ranges of new American SLBM (the C-4 missile is likely to have a range of 4,500 nautical miles and is now being retrofitted into *Poseidon*-armed SSBN) will further complicate Soviet ASW problems. But that is not in itself any reason to make one believe that the Soviet Union will give up her attempts to neutralize the SSBN; it is more likely to cause her to invest even more in ASW forces. The use of SSCN in the strategic role would find them no less vulnerable than SSBN with the added drawback that, because they can only fire a few missiles at a time, they will have to reload between salvoes, creating a somewhat greater chance of their being detected than when they launch their first cruise missiles. The somewhat shorter range of SLCM would also mean that these submarines must close the Soviet coast before firing; this would make them substantially more vulnerable to Soviet ASW forces.

Implications of US-Soviet Arms Control

It is becoming clear that there has been a shift of emphasis in SALT from an attempt to constrain overall numbers to a more realistic – and much more difficult – effort to place restraints on qualitative improvement. This is not to say that numbers will not remain an important element in SALT with, it is to be hoped, a slow and steady downward trend in the numbers of deployed systems, together with ceilings and sub-ceilings on such things as systems equipped with multiple, independently-targetable re-entry vehicles (MIRV), heavy missiles, cruise missiles per launch vehicle and re-entry vehicles per missile. However, for the purposes of this discussion, the shape of SALT II gives rise to some special problems: first, the whole question of the transfer of technology to third parties; secondly, the understanding in SALT II that SALT III should extend the coverage downwards and outwards to bring a number of the super-powers' (and possibly their allies') theatre nuclear systems into the SALT framework; and, finally, the controversial issue of 600-km range limitations on ground- and sea-launched cruise-missiles (GLCM and SLCM) in the Protocol.

It is uncertain at this stage whether the US Senate will recommend ratification of the text agreed between the SALT negotiators. The largest question mark of all, for Britain, concerns the Protocol and whether its provisions will be carried over into a SALT III (the paragraphs which affect America's allies directly are in the Protocol rather than in the Treaty). The Soviet interest is now – and will continue to be – to ensure that the United States cannot circumvent the agreement by transferring either complete systems or the relevant technology to third parties, and the Soviet Union has placed great store by range limitations on GLCM and SLCM, although conceding that ALCM will not be range-limited.

If one takes the worst case, the non-circumvention clause might be repeated in SALT

III (and interpreted rigourously by the Soviet Union) and cruise missile range limitations might also continue to apply; this combination would be severely limiting for Britain's choice in the future. The position of the American Administration at the present moment was spelled out by the Secretary of State on 10 July 1979, during the SALT II hearings:

Our allies had specific interests and concerns in connection with SALT II ... To make clear that nothing in the treaty would prevent continued cooperation in weapons technology and systems, we stated in detail [to the North Atlantic Council on 29 June 1979] our views on the effect of the treaty on alliance cooperation and modernization. We stressed that in the treaty we have undertaken no obligation on noncircumvention beyond the basic tenets of international law and that the treaty will not affect existing patterns of collaboration and cooperation with our allies. Nor will it preclude cooperation on modernization.

We also recall that in SALT II negotiations we rejected a provision on nontransfer of weapons and technology, and we defined in detail our policy on such transfers.[18]

Nevertheless, there is at least a *prima facie* conflict between what the United States appears to be agreeing to in SALT and the Anglo-US Agreement covering the Exchange of Technical Information. It is impossible to judge the extent of the conflict, but it might be assumed that the United States would be at liberty to assist with maintaining or even modernizing existing systems, even if inhibited by SALT from transferring new ones to allies. It is worth noting that the Nuclear Non-Proliferation Bill passed by the US Senate in February 1978 places a significant number of curbs on the transfer of nuclear technology to other states. The former British Secretary of State for Defence, Mr Mulley, however, made clear in testimony to the House of Commons Expenditure Committee that 'We have no reason to doubt the United States' undertaking to support the [*Polaris*] programme for as long as necessary.'[19] This puts the continuation of *Polaris* A3 missiles in a different category from cruise missiles or *Trident*. Furthermore it is reasonable to suppose that, as a result of the Nassau Agreement of 1962, the United States is committed to the maintenance of that system for as long

as it remains in service. Given that large quantities of *Polaris* missiles and spares will become available when the United States phases out the A3 missile in 1985 (on current planning), it seems most unlikely that there would be any constraints on the ability of the US to sell whatever stocks are considered necessary, and they could continue to build rocket motors (specifically second-stage rocket motors) for the A3 if their shelf-life is in doubt. What may cause more concern in the long term is that the data base for missile reliability will be sharply reduced when the A3 missile goes out of service and American experience can no longer be drawn upon.

On the question of SALT III, it seems certain that there will be considerable Soviet pressures for British nuclear forces to be included in one way or another, if not in reductions then at least in a *de facto* limit for strategic systems.[20] Yet it is not clear at this stage whether these pressures will be decisive. France has already made clear that she will not agree to any restrictions on her nuclear forces in the forseeable future and Britain has followed suit: the Soviet arsenal of medium-range nuclear delivery systems is already so large that this would argue against a reduction of the very small British nuclear forces, even on an equal percentage basis with the Soviet reductions; and the concerns of both super-powers in SALT III are not likely to focus primarily on regional nuclear systems in Europe but on maintaining their strategic stability in the 1980s against the impacts of technology and of China's potential emergence as a major nuclear power. For all these reasons it seems unlikely that the next round of Soviet-American arms control negotiations will impose severe limitations on Britain's choice for her deterrent forces in the near future, but uncertainty remains.

One additional point that needs to be considered is that, if there were to be restrictions on the number of test firings that either side is permitted in a given period under a future SALT agreement the United States might be very reluctant to relinquish a share of those firings to an ally. Nevertheless, although *Polaris* test firings take place at Cape Canaveral, the test range makes use of down-range telemetry based on British dependencies. Whereas it would be expensive for Britain to build her own test range, she will retain some leverage over the United States in seeking use of the Canaveral range. This also clearly implies that any *new* British ballistic missile system might yet be an embarrassment to the United States, making US assistance in testing British missiles extremely difficult to come by.

Taking SALT as a whole, there seems little reason to doubt that the current Administration believes itself to be free to do all the things necessary for the modernization of the British deterrent – even to the extent of transferring *Trident* missiles (at a price) – but the doubts remain. In the event that the Soviet Union decided to make an issue of the sale of *Trident* missiles on the grounds that it was inconsistent with the non-circumvention provisions of SALT, the United States might in fact decide not to sell *Trident*. The same could be true for the sale of cruise missiles to allies, at least if they were no longer under US sole control.

Test Ban Treaty

Any *new* warhead for a British missile will run into difficulties with a Comprehensive Test Ban Treaty (CTBT) – even one of limited duration. It is unimaginable that any nation would be prepared to deploy a new nuclear warhead that had not been tested explosively on a number of occasions. Although the exact provisions of a future treaty are very unclear, both in respect of testing for confidence and of whether or not there will be a yield threshold below which testing will be permitted, it can be stated with some confidence that the effect of Britain's adherence to a treaty banning or limiting nuclear testing will seriously curtail future options especially if the CTBT were to last more than three years or be renewed. The super-powers appear to share an interest in stopping nuclear proliferation, and both therefore seem likely to join in putting pressure on as many states as possible to sign a verifiable agreement either to preclude or severely to limit explosive testing. As all British explosive testing takes place in any case in American facilities, Britain will not be a free agent, and significant warhead improvement may be difficult. If the US is herself restricted to a limited number of underground tests for confidence each year, she might be rather reluctant to allocate a proportion of those to any ally, however loyal. Britain might be able to argue for her own (small) number of annual test firings,

but that would almost certainly preclude any major new programme.

Agreements Limiting Space Warfare

Although unrestrained military competition in space would be very destabilizing, there are relatively few implications for Britain. However, if one postulates that satellite systems might be lost in war, it is worth setting out the effects on the Alliance as a whole. There would be some difficulty in communication and therefore the passage of warning information would be slower and the re-targeting 'of nuclear systems more difficult; some of the warning indicators would be unobtainable if reconnaissance satellites were destroyed; current meteorological information would be unobtainable; and, perhaps most importantly, there would be no means of assessing damage. The last point would tend to make selective targeting more difficult.

The question of possible deployment of ballistic missile defences in space has already been touched on, and it is a reasonable assumption that banning them under the ABM Treaty would effectively remove the possibility of using either lasers or charged-particle beams as mechanisms for attacking satellites – at least those in low orbits. There remains the question of attack by sacrificial satellites. There may be some optimism that arrangements can be negotiated to ban all means of satellite attack, but no official communiqués have been issued. Since a comprehensive and simultaneous anti-satellite attack would be virtually impossible to carry through, and since the Soviet Union is at least as vulnerable to anti-satellite operations as the United States, there is hope that this whole area of competition can be closed off before either can deploy a functioning anti-satellite system. There is no doubt, however, that in case of a nuclear war, the temptation on both sides to destroy the early-warning and communications satellites of the other would be considerable.

Summing-up

Clearly, these external developments carry important implications for Britain's decision on the future size and shape of her deterrent forces. To a considerable extent her range of choice will be narrowed and some avenues will be closed altogether. This section describes the limits for the future. The implications for Britain are:

The accuracy and number of Soviet intermediate-range ballistic missiles (IRBM) and aircraft of Soviet frontal aviation will make unprofitable any discussions of European fixed-base missiles. In addition, all British aircraft will be threatened on the ground.

Britain's nuclear forces *acting alone* could inflict very little overall damage to the Soviet nuclear forces. This is partly a function of numbers and partly because Soviet theatre nuclear forces are becoming invulnerable through greater mobility.

Penetration to industrial or civilian targets will continue to be assured if ballistic missiles are used.

Cruise-missile attack strategy must calculate that a very dense air defence network will be set up by the Soviet Union to contain American cruise missile attack; British weapons *acting alone* would suffer very heavily at the hands of this defence.

SALT may reduce the likelihood of American assistance being forthcoming in future, and that assistance may be altogether precluded in all aspects of long-range cruise-missile technology transfer. Britain would be unwise to count on unlimited US assistance in developing long-range cruise-missiles for independent use, and development costings must take this into account.

Submarine missile carriers will become more vulnerable than hitherto, and, although it may be a highly unlikely situation, the Soviet Union could well have the resources to seek out and destroy the relatively few British SSBN or SSCN *acting alone.*

The future progress of SALT will probably include some discussion of the British nuclear forces and, once included, there will be strong constraints against increases in numbers. This, in particular, will make the cruise-missile option unattractive. Assurance of penetration is very much lower for cruise missiles than for ballistic missiles, so that greater numbers of them would be needed.

The Theatre Balance will go on causing West European concern. Britain would therefore find herself under considerable pressure to retain her theatre nuclear forces, however relatively insignificant they may be. This is a difficult period politically in which to signal the intention to quit this area of competition.

The United States has recently agreed to provide new theatre systems for NATO, which opens a new option for Britain: to buy into an Alliance nuclear force, even if that means accepting the reality of an American veto.

Test Ban Treaty progress would seriously inhibit any new warhead development.

Requirements of Deterrence

It is hard to view as realistic any requirement to use the British nuclear forces, except against the Soviet Union.

Although it is not easy to find explicit statements articulating the rationale for the British nuclear deterrent, and targeting information is highly classified, it must be presumed that there are two tasks that the British deterrent force is now required to do. These must be to provide NATO with a certain number of nuclear systems of intermediate range that can be contributed to SACEUR's Strike Plan and assigned targets through the NATO Joint Targeting Machinery in Omaha, and to ward-off any direct nuclear threat to Britain by the Soviet Union. If this formulation is correct, then Britain's present nuclear force (four SSBN, each carrying 16 *Polaris* A3 missiles currently fitted with triple multiple re-entry vehicles), together with her *Vulcan* bomber force and *Buccaneer* strike aircraft, must be capable of different jobs which are to some extent in conflict.

This force must, in theory, help the Alliance to deter the Soviet Union from raising the level of violence from the conventional or tactical nuclear level to the theatre nuclear level by threatening to attack targets in the Soviet Union with a ferocity at least as great in degree, if not in quantity, as that which the Soviet Union might inflict on Western Europe. Because the Soviet Union has the means for selective theatre nuclear attack, weapons which can only threaten a rather generalized counter-value response are becoming less useful in the design of deterrent forces. Subsequently, if intra-war deterrence failed and, for whatever reason, the nuclear threshold was crossed, the British missiles might presumably be used to strike targets that suit their particular characteristics of range, yield and accuracy. Clearly, the *Polaris* system is by no means ideal for theatre strikes: it is rather inflexible and unresponsive (communication with submerged submarines remains difficult), and too inaccurate for most military targeting. It remains a good second-strike system to be withheld as a reserve, although SACEUR's Strike Plan may include some missiles for early firing against large *military* targets, such as Soviet dockyards or distant airfields. However, the main reason why the British deterrent forces are difficult to integrate into a programme of gradual escalation and intra-war deterrence is their small size. What credibility they have depends on their use as a last resort; limited strategic options are therefore not a realistic objective. This does not, however, reduce their relevance for the Alliance, particularly given the renewed Soviet emphasis on medium-ranged nuclear systems such as the SS-20. Though not covered by the SALT definition of strategic weapons, these are considered strategic weapons by all European countries; Britain is as much covered by the SS-20 range as any other West European country. Thus the use of Britain's strategic forces will have to be considered in response to (or to deter) not only a Soviet ICBM/SLBM strike, but also an IRBM/MRBM strike. Consequently they contribute to offsetting the Soviet SS-20 programme, and this gives them – and their modernization – added weight in the eyes of the European members of the Alliance.

Yet it would be wrong to deduce from this that British strategic weapons should be used only in response to a direct nuclear threat to British territory. Britain is a member of the Western Alliance not because she has signed a treaty but because her security is inextricably tied to that of Western Europe by the conviction that Soviet control over the European continent would imply Soviet control over Britain. Her deterrent forces must therefore be seen in the context of those of the Alliance as a whole. In the wake of SALT II and the current modernization of Soviet medium-range systems, there is growing emphasis on the need to modernize longer-range nuclear delivery systems on European territory or in Europe's sea and air space. While this does not by itself argue for a significant change in the configuration of Britain's deterrent forces, it does indicate the growing importance the West European allies are likely to attach to the continuance of a British deterrent and that the political consequences for Britain's relations within the Alliance of a decision to opt out of a nuclear strategic role would be rather far-reaching. Obviously this is a view not universally held, but it appears to be a majority view as the following (admittedly selective) quotations show:

> The possession by the United Kingdom of strategic nuclear weapons is considered to be an advantage by most, if not all, non-nuclear weapons countries of NATO, as it provides for a 'European voice' in the nuclear affairs of the Alliance and prevents a (politically unwelcome) state of US-monopoly. This British contribution is therefore of primary importance.[21]

> The United Kingdom deterrent force ... guarantees the security of the United Kingdom and strengthens its international role, it reinforces the unity and deterrent influence of the Alliance through the sharing of nuclear responsibilities and lastly, bolsters the intention and capacity of Europe to undertake its own defence.[22]

A dissenting view comes from two Dutch parliamentarians:

> The UK's nuclear forces as currently structured would contribute little to the credibility of a European defence.[23]

The Choice for Britain

There are three main choices open, all except the last containing a number of sub-options. These can be set out as follows:

A. To continue with a ballistic system much as presently configured *or* improved:
   1 With continuing US assistance
   2. Independently *or* in conjunction with France

B. To turn to a cruise missile (sea-, land- or air-launched):
   1. By buying into a European nuclear force based on US equipment
   2. Independently *or* with European collaboration

C. To leave the nuclear arena completely.

Ballistic systems

The thrust of the arguments so far in this Paper is that Britain should not necessarily adopt a system solely on the grounds that it is the best for minimum deterrence in a one-to-one confrontation with the USSR: Alliance considerations must affect the decision. But, if ability to act alone *were* considered over-riding, the present *Polaris* system has many merits and, were

28

renewal not necessary because of age, it should continue to be viable as a minimum deterrent as long as Soviet ASW forces do not have the capability seriously to challenge the SSBN's invulnerability or ABM defences to destroy the warheads. But even if Soviet open-ocean ASW forces did threaten the survival of the SSBN, Britain could opt for an inshore submersible which, operating within British coastal waters, would greatly complicate the Soviet ASW problem. The US *Polaris* system, based on ocean-going SSBN, was procured because the relatively short range of the original *Polaris* A-1 missiles meant that the carrier had to approach the Soviet Union in order to bring them within range. Britain copied the American system somewhat slavishly in opting for ocean-going SSBN, when she might equally well have adopted a much less expensive carrier which could operate from inshore waters yet still reach the Soviet Union, even if the target coverage from Britain was somewhat limited. The greater range of the A-3 missile currently deployed makes it perfectly suitable for local (i.e., inshore) deployment. One should also note that a similar argument against procurement of the very expensive *Ohio*-class SSBN is beginning to develop in the United States. This points out that the range of the new *Trident* C-4 (and D-5) SLBM will permit the US to cover most targets in the Soviet Union without going into contested waters, and a much less costly submersible, protected by US ASW forces and coastal barriers, would appear to have the invulnerability necessary for a second-strike system. While this is an alternative worthy of more detailed examination, in practice it may be unrealistic to expect a major departure from the existing pattern of British deterrent forces, if only because the infrastructure is in place and the advantage of close technological exchange with the United States would be forgone if Britain opted for a system radically different from that deployed by the United States.

Turning from submarines to the missiles themselves, the first question is whether the present missile design could adequately perform its current deterrent role into the next century. There seems little reason to doubt that it should. If that is the case, the next question is whether the present stock of missiles can be kept serviceable over a prolonged period. This is a difficult question to answer with confidence. The greatest difficulty seems likely to arise over the shelf-life of

the rocket motors; Britain does not have the capacity to cast solid-fuel propellants of the size required. It is here that the attitude of the United States would appear to be most important. Assuming that she can be held to the Nassau Agreement (it is of indefinite duration) and that Britain is prepared to pay to keep the production line open it should be possible to assure the supply of replacement rocket motors. The alternative, perhaps less attractive to the United States in view of the technology transfer involved, is for Britain to purchase the capacity to cast large rocket motors from the present contractors. In both cases the cost would be small compared with the cost of taking an independent route to an entirely new weapon system.

Should American unwillingness to maintain the nuclear relationship on its present footing close off both these options there are two further possibilities. The first is to turn to France which has progressed further than Britain in missile design and production. By the mid-1990s, France might be in a position to sell Britain tested missiles without warheads; and it is difficult to see why purely commercial considerations would not prompt her to meet a request for 120 M-4 SLBM, to which Britain would add guidance systems and warheads.[24] The cost would certainly be much higher than that of *Polaris*, even allowing for inflation, but British competence being in guidance and warhead design, not rocket propulsion, there is a degree of complementarity between the two nations. More extensive collaboration should be possible with the British having much to offer the French, but this runs hard against American attitudes. It is very difficult to imagine that the United States would magnanimously accept sharing with France what was, at least originally, largely their technology. Any such initiative is quite likely to place at risk the whole transatlantic relationship. The Anglo-American Bilateral Exchange of Information Agreement of 1958 has been renewed for five years from 31 December 1979. And France's adamant insistence on maintaining her nuclear independence is likely to operate against any nuclear interdependence with Britain. At best therefore Britain might enter the market at cost to by SLBM which could be adapted to carry British war heads. However, if Britain faced having to develop her own SLBM and found it difficult, costly and uncertain, it would be worth testing

French reactions to an offer to purchase, before abandoning the ballistic missile option altogether.

The last possibility concerns further development of the warhead by converting it to a MIRV system. The accuracy of such a system would give additional benefits to NATO, as it would fit the deterrent posture of the Alliance rather better than the somewhat inaccurate and hence relatively indiscriminate multiple re-entry vehicle (MRV) warheads now deployed. But there are a number of drawbacks. First, it would be very costly for Britain to develop a MIRV capability independently of the United States and it is rather unlikely that they would transfer complete warheads. Second, the acquisition of a MIRV capability in the 1990's would look remarkably like vertical proliferation and that may not be politically desirable either in arms control terms or in the eyes of the public. Whereas it is possible to argue that a 3 (or even a 6) MRV warhead counts as one, because it can only effectively attack one area target about 10 miles in diameter, a move to MIRV would multiply the number of targets that could be threatened by a factor depending on the degree to which the warhead is fractionated. Next it is quite possible that Britain might run short of fissile material even with recycling. Finally, the United States might be reluctant to provide flight-testing facilities and Britain might find herself bound by the Test Ban Treaty not to test explosively. Both these latter suppositions make it very uncertain whether Britain could have any confidence in her product. Nevertheless, having said all that it remains a matter for concern that ballistic missile defences might, over the next twenty or so years, be able to cause some attrition of incoming warheads. It will therefore be important to retain an option to move rather rapidly to MIRV so as to maintain retaliatory effectiveness against a ballistic missile defence.

To summarize, the present *Polaris* A-3 missile with three or six MRV warheads will remain adequate for British deterrent purposes but, unless US co-operation can be obtained for the maintenance of the rocket motors, it will before long become a doubtful asset. Failing such assurances, the British could turn to the French for a missile which could be topped with a British MRV warhead. If neither route is possible, the British could attempt a copy of the A-3, but the cost would be high and flight-testing difficult. Finally there does not appear to be any need to

build such costly and capable carriers for the missile as the present *Polaris* boats, assuming that the range of current or future SLBM is not less than about 2,800 miles.

Cruise Missiles

Whatever the virtues of cruise missiles for the Western Alliance, the first question to be asked is how well they will serve the needs of an independent deterrent force in comparison with other systems.

Taking their advantages first, they are very adaptable and extremely accurate. They may also be fairly cheap, though this will depend crucially upon the basing mode adopted, its degree of sophistication and the help Britain might expect from the United States. What complicates the assessment of costs is that the cruise missile is a system liable both to pre-launch attrition of the launcher (whether surface, sub-surface or surface-effect vessel, aircraft or transporter) and to attrition by Soviet defences before reaching its target. The first assumption to make is that the independent deterrent requirements will continue to be served by the ability to attack twelve separate cities. Working back from that figure and assuming a rather high attrition (three out of every four missiles could be shot down in an unsupported attack), it is possible to arrive at certain conclusions as to the numbers of cruise missiles that would be required for five different basing modes. These are:

Nuclear Submarines

Vehicles

Fast patrol boats or hovercraft.

Non-dedicated major surface combatants, such as destroyers or frigates.

Strike aircraft.

Clearly there are a number of other possible basing modes with any weapon system which is as flexible as the cruise missile (for example, helicopters, wide-bodied jets or non-dedicated fleet submarines), but they all fall somewhere in the same spectrum of numbers and cost and have not been considered separately.

The other major variable in the costings is the question of whether to buy or whether to make – with the alternative of license production lying somewhere in between. A British sole venture would probably cost some four times as much as buying from the United States.[25] This is mainly because the high research and development costs

30

will be spread among a relatively few weapons. At a conservative estimate, the United States will buy over 3,000 ALCM and the figure for all types of cruise missile may be as high as 10,000. In no case would the British requirement be more than 400, and in some of the options the requirement is considerably lower (GLCM: 150: SLCM on fast craft: 228). Obviously, the fewer missiles required, the greater the need to buy from the United States, for the research and development overhead becomes more penal.

Some of the disadvantages of cruise missiles are matters of fact: there would again be a heavy demand for fissile material for new warheads; cruise missiles would rely upon targeting information supplied by the United States (or else British satellites would have to be built to acquire the mapping data); retargeting would not be as easy as with a ballistic system; and flight patterns would introduce potentially embarrassing tensions within the Alliance for, (unless launched from north of Norway) the missiles might have to overfly the territories of allies at low level. Also, as has already been assumed in the calculations of attrition, British missiles flying in small numbers *on their own* would attract the full weight of Soviet defences designed to cope with much larger numbers of US or Alliance cruise missiles.

The question of fissile material is not one that can be adequately covered here, for there is no way of knowing to what extent the fissile material from *Polaris* warheads can be re-cycled, nor whether the British stockpile of fissile material is sufficient to manufacture the large number of warheads a cruise missile system would need, nor the costs of warhead production, assuming Britain had to reopen nuclear facilities. The costs of the cruise missile option must include an element to cover warhead procurement, but it is not possible to assess what they would be. It is significant in this respect that Britain has decided to build a new enrichment plant, though it is not clear if it will produce weapons-grade uranium.[26]

As noted earlier, targeting information is no longer a simple question of knowing where the target is. There has to be very accurate mapping of the route to the target to provide the necessary correlation. If there were no doubt that the United States would guarantee always to provide that data from her own satellites, Britain could discount the problem; it must be said however, that there would always be an unwelcome degree of dependence that would not ride easily with an assumption of ultimate independence. Setting aside any problems that might arise as a result of agreements that might come into force between the Soviet Union and the United States, the fact remains that, if she wished, the United States might obstruct the use of the British Deterrent by denying targeting data. (In saying this, we discount the possibility that cruise missiles could use inertial guidance to reach and attack distant targets with sufficient accuracy. It is very unlikely that uncorrected inertial guidance alone could be sufficiently sensitive to allow for surface winds during a relatively slow flight of some thousands of kilometres.) It may prove possible to navigate using the US GPS *Navstar* system or other radio navigational update (such as LORAN or *Transit*) for inertial guidance, but that is speculative for the time being, and Britain would still depend on the US for the coded version of GPS *Navstar*.

The use of terrain correlation for flight control would appear to make retargeting harder since, assuming that the on-board computer can hold only a limited number of sets of terrain grid data, reprogramming would be necessary if targets were changed. This is likely to matter less with a dedicated system than with a widely dispersed contingent deployment involving a few cruise missiles being carried on, for example, most fleet submarines. In a dedicated system with relatively high pre-launch survivability it would be a simple matter to have four or more missiles targeted for the same area, to account for attrition *en route*. But with a non-dedicated system there will be problems in assessing what missiles have survived a period of conventional warfare during which a substantial number of carriers may have been put out of action, and it is only after such an assessment that the surviving missiles can be allocated to targets and fed with the necessary data. It would clearly be possible to devise a command-and-control system to take account of last minute targeting, but it would involve both substantial expenditure on data links and also a very real vulnerability in terms of communications, since any breakdown as a result of ECM or enemy strikes against communication networks could paralyze the deterrent.

A disquieting number of uncertainties would also affect cruise missiles as a result of present and future arms control negotiations.

31

The two linked provisions of SALT II that have caused concern for Britain, (and other European countries) are the range limitations on ground- and sea-launched cruise missiles and the non-circumvention provisions. In the worst case, range limitations might be carried over from the SALT II Protocol into a SALT III agreement during the 1980s, although the decision taken to deploy ground-launched cruise missiles in Europe, can be taken as a clear indication that the United States does not intend to carry forward cruise-missile limitations into a SALT III.

But even if one takes the view that the restrictions are only temporary, the effect is to postpone the time when Britain can make a decision in the light of all the facts. If a decision as to the future size and shape of the British deterrent force is to be made by 1980 at the latest (and this must depend critically upon assumptions made about the life of the *Polaris* force) it may not be prudent to make that decision in favour of buying cruise missiles, given the rather large number of present uncertainties that surround them.

Of course this would not necessarily close-off the cruise missile option if Britain decided to make the weapons herself or in collaboration with one or more European partners. Whether that option still looks attractive depends on the British attitude to SALT and what the government of the day will decide to do in relation to SALT III. It may not prove easy to resist Soviet pressure for British nuclear systems to be counted against Western totals of intermediate range systems. If the British system had to be counted at all on the basis of deliverable warheads or of launch vehicles, this would operate strongly against cruise missiles, since many more launchers and missiles would be needed to produce a capability equivalent to the *Polaris* system, and any numerical limitations would operate to the disadvantage of any system subject to high attrition.

How the cruise missile should be carried is secondary to the question of whether or not it can support the burden of independent deterrence. If its attractions – mainly the lower cost compared to other systems – are felt to outweigh the many disadvantages listed here, the missile must still be married to a launch vehicle, and the range of possibilities is very wide. All the costs which follow are for the purchase of US first-generation missiles with British warheads added. Five diffe-

rent modes of deployment are considered.[27] Far the cheapest in capital costs would be ground-launched cruise missiles mounted on trucks (£172m at 1977 prices), though with any land-based system there are bound to be difficulties arising from the relative scarcity of suitable deployment areas. It is possible, however, to imagine a fleet of GLCM vehicles held in secure areas in peacetime and dispersed to under-populated areas at a time of tension. This would be identical to current concepts for US GLCM deployment in NATO nuclear modernization. There would be some vulnerabilty to a pre-emptive Soviet attack, but this danger could be prudently discounted provided that the government was prepared to disperse its nuclear assets at the first signs of rising tension. The question of escort troops for security would have to be addressed, with perhaps not less than one platoon allocated to each deployed launcher. Range is critical with GLCM based in Britain, and the full 2,500km expected for the ALCM would be essential to cover a reasonable number of Soviet targets of value. Command and control would be simpler than with almost all other systems, however, and vulnerability once the launchers were deployed would almost certainly be low enough to satisfy the criterion that a British independent deterrent should be sufficiently free from the danger of a Soviet first strike to ensure that retribution is certain.

Very close in concept would be sea-launched cruise missiles mounted on some form of fast light naval craft – either a fast patrol boat or a hovercraft. Costs would be significantly higher (£485m at 1977 prices) but such craft would be relatively easy to conceal and quick to disperse from secure bases. Neither type of craft would be vulnerable to Soviet conventional or nuclear counter-action, and both would gain a large measure of additional protection by moving in coastal waters. The prime cost of hovercraft might be somewhat higher, though they would have the additional advantage of being able to run ashore and gain greater concealment. There would be no need for escort, although the crewing requirements of both types of craft would be higher than with GLCM. Any public concerns would be substantially less than with GLCM, but the range requirements would be no less stringent and command and control would be a little more demanding. It must be acknowledged that there would be a threat from shallow-water mining around bases, but surface-effects ships (SES), such as hovercraft, are substantially invulnerable to sea mines.

Adding some SLCM to a large number of naval units designed for traditional naval roles – say destroyers and frigates – would cost £416m at 1977 prices, and the cost of conversion and adding the appropriate command-and-control facilities would be quite low. There is, however, no certainty that the right number of surviving units would be in range of the Soviet Union when they came to be needed in the deterrent role, and sinkings would give rise to targeting difficulties. The main disadvantage in assuming a low pre-launch survivability is that a very large number of cruise missiles would be needed to ensure that enough survived to cover the prescribed targets some days after the start of hostilities. Because the missile cost is a very large proportion of the total, the attraction of this option would depend very much on whether Britain could buy (relatively) cheap SLCM from the United States or whether she had to build her own.

The option of putting SLCM on all fleet submarines is not attractive partly because the same problem of needing large numbers applies, but much more because a significant load of SLCM would so restrict the submarine's torpedo load that its ability to perform its primary role would be severely degraded. There would also be great difficulty in communicating with submarines for the purposes of retargeting and fire control.

Mounting ALCM on dedicated strike aircraft would not be a cheap solution (£625m at 1977 prices), nor would it appear to offer sufficient pre-launch survivability unless the even more expensive alternative of airborne alert were adopted. Airfields – even airfields in Britain – will become increasingly vulnerable to conventional and nuclear attack, and, given the very short flight time of IRBM from the Soviet Union, warning will almost certainly be less than the escape time of the aircraft. The only solution which seems to be worth considering is the use of a number of short take-off and landing (STOL) aircraft. These could be dispersed during times of tension to the large number of existing secondary run ways and there concealed; however, this introduces a problem of security. Even with STOL aircraft, pre-launch survivability would not be high, particularly if the conventional period of

hostilities were prolonged. However, the system has the major advantage that range could be shortened by flying towards the Soviet Union before weapon release, and if there were a big question mark over the usable range of cruise missiles in general this would take on greater importance. On the whole, airborne alert has been discounted as requiring both more aircraft than a ground alert force and also a dedicated tanker fleet which, given the increasing demands on tankers for conventional air defence operations, could add greatly to the cost of the solution. There is one last advantage which may become significant if range limitations on ground- and sea-launched cruise missiles continued. Britain might get 'a free ride' on the fact that ALCM are not, at least for the time being, range-limited in SALT. A sub-option for ALCM would be to use as carriers medium-lift helicopters which could disperse almost infinitely, though they would not be able to shorten the range significantly. This alternative could prove interesting if ALCM range was assured and the capital and running costs of the (greater) number of helicopters compared favourably with the costs of STOL aircraft.

Finally there is the option of the dedicated SSCN. The capital costs per launch vehicle will be very high, and the extra SLCM needed, compared with ballistic missiles, will require 7 or 8 SSCN, each carrying 24 SLCM, compared with 4 or 5 SSBN each carrying 16 SLBM. This would ensure 3 SSCN always on station, with a total of 72 missiles ready to fly, for a total capital cost of £1,164m at 1977 prices. As Ian Smart has noted, this is the one system which will put a considerable, and perhaps insupportable, burden on British shipyards. It is the question of pre-launch survivability that is the most difficult to answer. If Soviet ASW techniques were to improve dramatically and to concentrate on British SSCN, rather than US *Trident* SSBN (because, given their enormously increased operating areas, these remained altogether too difficult to hunt), there could be a serious threat to British boats. However, SSCN also have the ability to shorten the range if SLCM are not able to fly from Britain to the Soviet Union. As with SSBN there is also the possibility of changing from ocean-going boats to much smaller inshore submersibles, and it could be argued that it would be easier to adapt SLCM to a vessel of this type than SLBM, which demand vertical tubes at launch. Here again, it is very

33

much a question of usable range for there would be little chance of the inshore submersible closing on the Soviet Union without detection and destruction by Soviet ASW forces.

In summary, the value of the cruise missile as an *independent* deterrent is dubious. All the same, it has to be admitted that some basing options do look attractive in terms of cost when weighed against the ballistic alternatives – especially if relatively cheap US missiles can be procured. However, it is unlikely that the United States would again enter an agreement similar to the Nassau Agreement, not least because she was then under a moral obligation to make good the cancellation of *Skybolt* and will not be under similar pressures in future. One of the very high costs of independence could well be that of having to pursue unassisted development or, at best, shared development with one or more European allies.

It is at this point that the possibility of Anglo-French co-operation should again be raised. It is understood that France is in the early stages of a cruise missile development programme, but it is much more likely that she will view the cruise missile as an adjunct to a future force of strategic aircraft, thus giving her a stand-off capability and complementing the seaborne deterrent. It does not seem likely that a first-generation French cruise missile will have the range or the accuracy of American systems – and without these attributes cruise missiles are unattractive alternatives for Britain. Over the longer term, France may be in a position to acquire terrain data from her own reconnaissance satellite, but it would seem that inertial guidance will be used at first. For all these reasons, it would be unwise to count on a collaborative project with France that would produce a system that would probably not be as capable as the first-generation American cruise missiles, and with unit costs that would certainly be higher even if there was some sharing of development costs between the two countries. Nevertheless, it would be prudent to attempt to engage the French in technical discussions, if these have not already started, in order to establish the kind of design criteria that are being used and the sort of characteristics that the French system might be required to have. It is certainly the kind of aerospace project in which both France and Britain could collaborate, though there is a political dimension that cannot

be ignored: France has thus far maintained total independence in all aspects of her nuclear force procurement and would not be likely to place the future of her deterrent in any other hands, even on a collaborative basis.

However, if one views the cruise missile not as a means of providing an independent nuclear deterrent force but as a possible British contribution to an Alliance nuclear force, many of the difficulties and inherent disadvantages tend to evaporate. The criterion of minimum deterrence would no longer have to apply, so that the arithmetic could be done quite differently. There would be no need to analyze British systems under the worst-case conditions of all Soviet defences being directed at a relatively small number of British cruise missiles, and no need for the British missiles to be certain of penetrating to twelve targets. The approach would be more along the lines of Britain undertaking to provide (say) 64 cruise missiles – a number calculated as a maximum on the basis of the number of *existing* SLBM, so satisfying the arms-control criterion of not increasing the number of British nuclear systems that could threaten the Soviet Union. At the same time, American misgivings about transferring the technology for an independent deterrent that might be used against American interests could be set at rest, because, whether or not dual key arrangements were instituted, there would be *de facto* negative control through the continuing American monopoly of targeting information. Even the implicit threat that the British nuclear forces might, at some time in the future, be withdrawn from the Alliance could be dismissed, for without targeting data they would have to rely solely on inertial guidance and would cease to constitute a significant threat to anyone. On such a basis, it is possible to envisage the United States being much more willing to sell cruise missiles or enter into licensing arrangements. As with the *Polaris* system, it is assumed that British nuclear warheads would be fitted.

It can also be said that the uncertainty over cruise missile limitations will be less important because assurance of the continuity of the British deterrent will no longer be overriding. If a decision were taken now that independence would cease to be the prime requirement when the *Polaris* system came to the end of its natural life, this would take a great deal of the pressure off the British Government, and might even transfer some of it to the United States, to 'buy back' the range limitations on GLCM and SLCM. With the possible exception of the SSCN basing mode, the lead time for the construction of the cruise missile carriers is likely to be less than 8 years, and this makes it possible to defer a decision on procurement until about 1982, by which time the future of the cruise missile will be much clearer. It would be the case of declaring an intention now to take out an option on the US cruise missile if it comes available, which would have to be construed as an intention to eschew independence after *Polaris* and to integrate Britain's theatre nuclear forces completely with those of the Alliance.

Such a decision would not appear on the surface to satisfy the need to multiply the centres of nuclear release, but the Soviet Union would be in no position to know whether British cruise missiles were ready to fly or not; and would, in prudence, have to assume that they were and could therefore be flown on British orders. From the Soviet perspective, they would *appear* to be as independent as *Polaris* even if the Alliance – specifically the United States – could have a high degree of assurance that the missiles could only be flown with terrain data provided by the United States.

Renunciation
Earlier in this Paper, a distinction was made between total independence and integration. Renunciation here is not taken to mean just the renunciation of a measure of independence, but renunciation of theatre nuclear weapons altogether. Should Britain give up the capability?

There are three main groups of imperatives that might cause Britain to decide to renounce weapons with which to strike the Soviet Union – non-proliferation concerns, cost and utility. Although there are sectors of public opinion that will take their stand on moral or conscientious issues, it is not anticipated that these will weigh heavily. More insistent will be those who argue that Britain has an opportunity to serve as an example to threshold nuclear states by unilaterally surrendering a nuclear capability. Undeniably, the example of forgoing what has once been possessed would be greater than the example of a state which might possess nuclear weapons but has never done so. Britain's renunciation would be more potent than that of Canada, as Canada's is more potent than that of Somalia.

But there are no grounds for believing that a British example would affect the decision of a threshold state one way or the other – there will be far more compelling reasons for a state to decide for or against embarking on a nuclear weapons programme. Britain's example would be applauded by the converted and ignored by the determined. Furthermore, it is extremely difficult to see how a decision to renounce a theatre nuclear capability on non-proliferation grounds could be taken without also renouncing a tactical nuclear weapon capability – and that would imply a denial of the flexible response doctrine of the NATO Alliance, which could be very divisive. It is also likely that others would not believe that no weapons remained, and in any case it is impossible to unlearn what was once well known.

Renunciation on the grounds of cost alone is hard to sustain if Britain is to remain committed to European defence. Certainly cost should modify the choice, but Britain would find it hard to deny that she should make a *pro rata* contribution to Alliance nuclear defence. The size of that share could be assessed (and, undoubtedly, argued over) in the Nuclear Planning Group (NPG), but Britain's allies would be very unlikely to accept that the whole cost of a theatre nuclear system could be counted against Britain's contribution to NATO so long as there remained a substantial *national* justification for the force. What will have to be examined most carefully is the inroads that nuclear renewal might make on Britain's conventional contribution to NATO.

The third possible ground for renunciation might be a feeling that there was no need for theatre nuclear forces in the spectrum of deterrence, or, to take a most extreme view, that the possession of nuclear forces was likely to damage Western interests as a whole and British interests in particular. The thrust of the remarks in the earlier part of the Paper is that this is the one area of competition where the Alliance has lagged considerably behind the Warsaw Pact, with the inevitable consequence that proportional response is now in doubt. Something like a consensus seems to have been reached that a programme is needed to restore credibility at the theatre level. For Britain to renounce nuclear weapons, at a time of substantially heightened threat would inevitably be interpreted as a sign of weakness and lack of resolve – both by her allies and by the Soviet Union. Renunciation of independence in favour of integration, however, could allow Britain to amass some political capital. Complete renunciation without either extracting a *quid pro quo* from the Soviet Union or raising conventional force levels would invite accusations of unilateral disarmament and appeasement. The British theatre nuclear forces at present have distinct value in any negotiations with the Soviet Union and they should not be surrendered without Soviet concessions. To indicate an intention to discontinue the deterrent at the present time would also be counter productive in arms control negotiations. If one of the long-term Western aims is to curb Soviet intermediate-range nuclear programmes, it would be foolish to discard the *Polaris* system or the promise of a successor system before negotiations even get underway.

Conclusions

The preceding examination leads to the following conclusions: Britain should maintain her capability for strategic nuclear deterrence against the Soviet Union. If there ever was a case for giving up this capability, it has been seriously weakened by two developments: the new emphasis in Soviet military programmes on weapon systems which cover targets in Western Europe including Britain; and a general trend towards nuclear proliferation, which a decision to 'opt out of a nuclear game' will not arrest.

The requirements for the destructive capability of the British deterrent – in order to maintain its relevance and credibility – are sufficiently defined by present capabilities. There does not seem to be any need to increase this significantly to provide the limited-deterrent functions of the existing forces. However, because there is a serious possibility that the major nuclear powers may, by the 1990s come close to deploying an effective ballistic missile defence, Britain ought at least to consider ways of increasing the number of deliverable warheads or penetration aids in order to maintain her *present* deterrent capabilities.

The basic options are either to continue to base British deterrent capabilities on ballistic missiles (from submerged platforms) or on non-ballistic nuclear systems, such as the long-range cruise missile. Yet the arguments for an alternative to the present technological structure of British deterrent forces, while not negligible, seem insufficient to warrant a major departure from the pattern and the infrastructure established over the past two decades.

The decision on whether and how to maintain the present deterrent capabilities for the next twenty years will have to be taken shortly. While there is some leeway, it cannot be extended indefinitely if the validity of *existing* deterrence forces is not to be undermined. There is, however, no precise deadline; the time available should be used to consider the options *now*, rather than postpone decision to a time when British nuclear deterrent capabilities will have been reduced with the passage of time, and when major options might have been foreclosed. Britain cannot afford to reserve her position for much longer.

It is becoming clear that the British Government is very interested in acquiring the *Trident* C4 missile from the United States. Such a missile would clearly increase Britain's capability substantially even if only deployed in the same numbers as *Polaris* A3. The thrust of this Paper is that it is doubtful whether Britain needs to be able to deploy more warheads of substantially increased accuracy on missiles with close to twice the range. Rather, the analysis points to the conclusion that the *Polaris* A3 will remain an adequate missile even if new platforms have to be built to carry it. Clearly aging of this missile will be a matter for concern, but there do not as yet appear to be any absolute barriers to prevent Britain taking the necessary steps to assure the reliability of the system into the next century.

[1] See *Twelfth Report from the House of Commons Select Committee on Expenditure (Nuclear Weapon Programme) 1972–73*, July 1973; *Second Report ... 1975–76*, January 1976 (especially the Ministry of Defence memorandum submitted to the committee on 9 May 1975); *Sixth Report ... 1978–79*, April 1979; Geoffrey Kemp: *Nuclear Forces for Medium Powers: Parts I–III*, Adelphi Papers 106 and 107 (London: IISS, 1974); James Bellini and Geoffrey Pattie, *A New World Role for the Medium Power: the British Opportunity*, (London: RUSI, 1976); John Baylis (ed.), *British Defence Policy in a Changing World*, (London: Croom Helm 1977); Julian Critchley, *Contemplating a French Nuclear Connection: The Future of the British Independent Deterrent, Round Table*, April 1978. Also Ian Smart, *The Future of the British Nuclear Deterrent: Technical, Economic and Strategic Issues*, (London: Royal Institute of International Affairs, 1977). There have also been a number of more recent articles in the *New Statesman* and *The Economist*, and a small number of relevant research theses in universities.

[2] See, by way of recent example, the letter signed by J. O'Connell and others, in the correspondence columns of *The Guardian*, 27 April 1979.

[3] D. W. Healey, *Britain and NATO*, and Klaus Knorr, (ed.), *NATO and American Security*, (Princeton, N. J.: Princeton UP, 1959), p. 225.

[4] The best general accounts of the development of British policy and doctrine remains, A. J. Pierre, *Nuclear Politics* (Oxford: OUP, 1972): very well written, as well as very well informed. See also R. N. Rosecrance, *Defence of the Realm* (New York: Columbia UP, 1968), pp. 158, et. seq.; and L. W. Martin, 'The Market for Strategic Ideas in Britain: The Sandys Era.' *American Political Science Review*, vol. LVI, (March 1962): the carry over from the debate begun in 1955 about the new importance of thermo-nuclear weapons was an important element in the movement that, in 1958, led to the establishment of the IISS.

[5] See P. E. Buteux, *The Politics of Nuclear Consultation in NATO, 1965–74*, (London Ph. D. Thesis, 1978), especially p. 6.

[6] Although the size of any inventory of major weapon systems – ICBM or battleships – is related to the purposes that they are required to fulfil, it seems probable that the nature of missiles makes it more likely that the numbers will be 'topped up' because of their ostensible relationship to artillery bombardment. It is also probably inevitable that in a bilateral bargaining process, like SALT, numbers come to matter more. Conversely, it is difficult to determine how few would be needed to perform even a limited range of purposes, especially if the need to ride out a successful surprise attack is taken into account. McGeorge Bundy in his article, 'To Cap a Volcano' (*Foreign Affairs*, October 1969), argued that even a relatively small force embodied horrendous power.

[7] To be fair to the super-powers, it is not only a question of reducing the size of their armouries. Some types of reduction might, paradoxically, be seen to make them more vulnerable to a surprise attack, and therefore more likely to resort to the use of nuclear weapons early in a conflict.

[8] The most easily available reference is Ian Smart, *op. cit.* in note 1, pp. 18–19.

[9] Cf. Aaron Wildavsky, in *The Politics of the Budgetary Process*, (Boston: Little Brown, 1974, second edition), p. 4: 'if one looks at politics as a process by which the government mobilizes resources to meet pressing problems, then the budget is a focus of these efforts'. The comment is made about the US budgetary process, but it is true, *ceteris paribus*, of the British system too.

[10] A commitment by the Labour Party to extend its previous election manifesto pledges about a future generation of strategic nuclear weapons, was apparently a matter of debate before the General Election in May 1979 (see *The Guardian* 6 April, 1979). See also the House of Commons debate on defence (26 March 1979): especially, the speech by Frank Allaun (*Hansard*, vol. 965 no. 79, cols. 71–72).

[11] See the discussions on this point in *Sixth Report from the Expenditure Committee Session 1978–79. The Future of the United Kingdom's Nuclear Weapons Policy* (London: HMSO, 3 April 1979), pp.187–203.

[12] Dr Perry, US Under-Secretary of Defence for Research and Engineering has stated that the power for cruise missile ECM will be only 'of a few watts' and could either take the form of noise jamming or deception (*Flight*, 13 January 1979).

[13] *Flight*, 13 January 1979.

[14] R. V. Jones, *Most Secret War*, Hamish Hamilton, London, 1978, pp. 427–8.

[15] *Ibid.*, p. 428.

[16] *Ibid.*, p. 429.

[17] Jones, *Op. cit.* p. 427.

[18] Statement by the Hon. Cyrus R. Vance, Secretary of State, to SALT II Hearings before the Committee on Foreign Relations, US Senate. Part I, 9–12 July 1979, p.175.

[19] Testimony of the Rt. Hon. Frederick Mulley, Secretary of State for Defense, in *Sixth Report from the Expenditure Committee, op. cit.*, in note 11), p. 7.

[20] In May 1972 the Soviet Union made it clear in a unilateral statement that any attempt by America's allies to go above the number of SSBN in service (or under construction at that date) would entitle the Soviet Union to increase the number of her SSBN *pro rata*.

[21] Memorandum by Walter Schütze, Defence Planning Staff, Bonn, in *Sixth Report from the Expenditure Committee* (op. cit., in note 11), p. 218.

[22] Memorandum by Senator Jean Lecanuet, *Ibid.*, p. 270.

[23] Memorandum by Klaas G. de Vries and Harry J. van den Bergh, *Ibid.*, p. 264.

[24] See WEU Paper 787: 'The Limitation of Strategic Arms', 31 October 1978, p. 10, para. 42.

[25] For detailed calculations see *Sixth Report from the Expenditure Committee*, (op. cit., in note 11), pp. 89–92

[26] *The Times*, 10 January 1980.

[27] *Op. cit.* in note 11.

2 Nuclear Weapons in Europe
GREGORY TREVERTON

INTRODUCTION

Events in the last few years have re-awakened an old concern among the NATO Allies: the role of nuclear weapons in Europe, especially those of continental range. The immediate objects of that concern are the new Soviet nuclear weapons deployed against Western Europe – in particular, the SS-20 intermediate-range ballistic missile (IRBM) and the *Backfire* bomber, often loosely referred to as weapons in the 'grey area' between tactical and strategic.[1] The anxiety is sharpened by the emergence – and clear recognition – of parity between the United States and the Soviet Union in central strategic nuclear systems. SALT II, even if still unratified, codified that parity, and added fuel to the growing debate about the future of strategic deterrence; it also left the Soviet SS-20 and similar weapons unconstrained while restricting, as so many on both sides of the Atlantic feared, possible Western counters to those weapons.

The issue of continental nuclear weapons in Europe is nearly as old as the NATO Alliance. It runs back to the debates in the 1950s over American medium-range ballistic missiles (MRBM) based in Europe. That debate subsided, rather than ended, with the withdrawal of those MRBM – the *Jupiters* and *Thors* – and with the demise of the so-called Multilateral Force (MLF) in 1965.[2] The strategic rationale for those actions was that land- and sea-based missiles from the central American strategic arsenal could by then cover all targets of interest deep in the Warsaw Pact, including the Soviet Union. Psychologically and strategically, America's clear nuclear superiority over the Soviet Union was crucial: it did not seem to matter much that Europe became, in some sense, 'hostage' to Soviet missiles targeted against it so long as the United States retained her unquestioned superiority.

However, the situation was never entirely comfortable, either for Europe or America. Both the introduction and the withdrawal of the *Thors* and *Jupiters* seemed haphazard. The role of NATO's theatre nuclear forces (TNF) has always been vague. For Europeans who live in the potential battleground, 'pure' deterrence has been the key; hence they have emphasized the surest and quickest resort to central American strategic nuclear weapons as the way to ensure that the Soviet Union is not tempted to begin *any* war in Europe. By contrast, Americans have tended to stress the importance of presenting Moscow with credible forces at each level of violence through to a central strategic response.

It did not serve NATO purposes to be too precise about TNF doctrine. Europeans could emphasize TNF as a link to American central systems, while Americans could stress TNF as a complement to conventional defence if need be, and both could reiterate that American nuclear systems remained the ultimate deterrent. Longer-range TNFs were, and remain, hardest to conceptualize in military terms: at what point would such weapons be used and against which targets? They are also the most sensitive politically, for they mean striking the Soviet Union from Europe.

Today, doubts whether the United States would initiate a nuclear attack on the Soviet Union in Europe's defence have again come to the fore, impelled by strategic parity and the increasing Soviet nuclear threat to Europe. It is the credibility of deterrence, and the role of continental weapons in Europe, that are at issue. For that reason, it should be clear that the issues are ones which confront Europe and America alike. To speak of 'grey area' weapons or a 'Eurostrategic' balance is thus to court confusion, by suggesting that the problem is

38

somehow restricted to Europe and that it has nothing to do with the central balance

The NATO Allies decided, in December 1979, to deploy in Europe a force of cruise and ballistic missiles capable of striking the Soviet Union, and they proposed at the same time arms control discussions of continental weapons. Those decisions are important. They became, largely through NATO's own actions, a test of Alliance resolve. Not to follow through would be to portray an image of irresoluteness much worse than the result of the neutron bomb affair.

Yet those decisions are not permanent solutions. They are as much a beginning as an end. Most obviously, the ground-launched cruise missiles (GLCM) and *Pershing* II ballistic missiles which NATO decided to introduce will not even begin to be deployed in Europe before 1983 and deployment will not be complete before 1988. NATO must hold firm to its decision through that period. That will not be easy, particularly with the uncertainty over SALT II and the generally uncertain future of nuclear arms control. Moreover, the NATO decision will be subjected to pressure from without and within. The Soviet Union maintains that the decision implies a fundamental shift in the strategic situation to which she will respond; and public opinion in Europe, particularly on the left of the political spectrum, is instinctively opposed to the new weapons and will seek in Soviet arms control initiatives the evidence that the programme is not necessary.

This Paper examines the array of factors that bear on European and American choices over the next few years. Chapter I sketches the outlines of the strategic balance in the 1980s, as background to considering nuclear weapons in Europe. Chapter II looks at the Soviet nuclear threat to Western Europe and how it has changed, and speculates about Soviet objectives. The third Chapter asks how much sense the abstract calculations of nuclear strategists would make if NATO's leaders ever faced the unthinkable – using nuclear weapons in Europe. Chapter IV examines the arms control considerations that will bear on NATO choices in the years ahead. The final Chapter focuses on the political implications of TNF both for the Western Alliance and the state of East-West relations.

I. THE STRATEGIC BALANCE IN THE 1980s

The issue of nuclear weapons in Europe does not arise in isolation from the general strategic balance. A 'Eurostrategic' balance simply does not exist. The point, from the perspective of West Europeans, is that Moscow should be deterred from attacking Western Europe with nuclear weapons, or from deriving political influence from some presumed ability to launch such attacks; and that NATO should not be self-deterred from carrying out its own strategy of using nuclear weapons first if need be. Those purposes may, but need not, require nuclear weapons in Western Europe capable of striking the Soviet Union. They certainly do not necessarily require Western capabilities in Europe somehow matched to, or 'countering' given Soviet weapons.

The Central Soviet-American Strategic Balance
Even with its uncertain prospects, SALT II provides parameters for strategic competition between the United States and the Soviet Union.[3] Even if it remains unratified, both super-powers may continue to observe those qualitative provisions of it, such as limits on warheads per missile, whose breach would be irrevocable. SALT II's terms would not actually constrain the strategic programmes of either much before 1985. In any case, SALT II will be the basis for any subsequent strategic negotiations even if the Reagan Administration presses forward with efforts to drastically reshape the treaty. Table 1 (see Appendix) lists current Soviet and American central strategic forces, and projections for 1985. Table 2 (see Appendix) sets out the theatre nuclear forces of the two powers, again with projections. Table 3 (see Appendix) gives NATO and Warsaw Pact theatre nuclear forces, excluding the two super-powers but including British and French independent forces, and lists what little is known about Chinese nuclear forces.

SALT II codifies parity in aggregates. Yet even with SALT, the momentum of Soviet programmes would ensure that the Soviet Union maintained, and increased her 'lead' over the United States in most indicators of nuclear strength – in throw-weight, in yield, and in equivalent megatonnage. The United States will retain a lead in the most important denominator – warhead numbers – although that lead will become less pronounced between now and 1985, after which it is likely to increase again, given projected American programmes. Whatever the implications of 'parity', in analysis or image, for the perception of threat in Western Europe, those will be aggravated, at least until new American programmes like MX and *Trident* begin to count heavily in the strategic balance.

Minuteman Vulnerability
By the early 1980s the Soviet Union will pose the theoretical threat to destroy 90 per cent of all American land-based intercontinental ballistic missile (ICBM) forces in a first strike using only a fraction of her own ICBM. By the end of the 1980s the United States could acquire a similar capability against all Soviet ICBM, primarily from the projected force of 200 MX missiles. Vulnerability would be a greater problem for the Soviet Union than for the United States, given the former's heavy reliance on land-based ICBM. Yet ICBM vulnerability will afflict the United States first (although it is worth remembering that Soviet ICBM were vulnerable into the 1970s).

American vulnerability is essentially a problem for deterrence in Europe. That fact has intruded only slowly into both the 'grey area' and the *Minuteman* debates over the last few years. Whatever the elaborate analytic constructs that strategic theorists create, it is hard to see that ICBM vulnerability threatens the United States' ability to deter Soviet nuclear attack *on herself*, even one directed solely against ICBM. A Soviet strike against ICBM, even with more accurate and smaller-yield weapons than those in the current Soviet inventory, would create enormous devastation in six states and kill from a few million to more than twenty million Americans. No Soviet leader could believe that the American President would not respond by inflicting commensurate damage with its submarine-based missiles and bombers, never mind the resulting nuclear

'exchange ratios' as some theorist might calculate them.[4].

In that sense, super-power deterrence is quite robust, and American ICBM vulnerability does not make much difference. Rather, the problem arises with American nuclear guarantees to other countries, especially to Western Europe. It does so in two respects. First, in an escalating nuclear exchange, the United States may want to make selective strikes against military targets in the Soviet Union. ICBM forces, in spite of their potential vulnerability, are attractive for this role given their accuracy, flexibility and relatively secure control. Yet their use for such missions competes with the need to withhold warheads of all types for the ultimate deterrent – assured destruction of the Soviet Union. ICBM vulnerability sharpens that conflict of interest, and an American President might, therefore, be reluctant to spend these forces for a European contingency, especially early.

More generally, assuming the vulnerability of land-based strategic delivery systems, the United States might be reluctant to resort to the use of nuclear weapons based in the continental US, lest Moscow retaliate by destroying (remaining) ICBM. That poses the risk that the United States might try to contain a nuclear war in Europe without committing her central strategic forces, or that NATO might never use American nuclear weapons at all, even in a losing conventional war.

How much and how soon the vulnerability problem is diminished for the United States will depend in part on how quickly MX, the planned successor missile to the *Minuteman* force, is deployed, and how. On current plans, X deployment will not begin until 1986, to be completed in 1989,[5] and there remain doubts about that timetable.

Morever, by the mid-1980s the two superpowers must anticipate the general balance of vulnerabilities a decade hence. Through the 1980s Soviet anti-submarine warfare (ASW) capabilities do not seem likely to pose a significant threat to American ballistic missile submarines. Soviet submarines on the other hand are likely to remain relatively more vulnerable, though longer-range missiles (the SS-N-18) will give more patrol options and so make them harder to track.

The Soviet Union could be the first to face quite general vulnerability: her ICBM will be threatened by American MX warheads and other accurate US delivery systems (while American ICBM will once again be becoming less vulnerable), Soviet submarines will still be quite vulnerable, and there will be only a small bomber leg to the Soviet triad. How the Soviet Union will respond is hard to know, but neither American-style response – a complex, expensive mobile basing system for ICBM or greater reliance on sea-based systems – seems likely. She might instead opt for missile defence, or, perhaps more likely, continue to rely on increases in numbers of missiles and warheads, including those targeted on Western Europe. This is another link between the strategic balance and the European theatre.

Third-Country Nuclear Forces

The progress of China's nuclear forces is very uncertain. Through the 1980s she is likely to pose the Soviet Union a relatively minor threat and virtually no threat to Soviet missiles, unless the pace of Chinese programmes accelerates remarkably. Yet the Soviet Union cannot expect to be able to pre-empt all Chinese nuclear weapons in a crisis: that fact, in the face of great uncertainty elsewhere, will make the Soviet Union sensitive to China's nuclear forces, perhaps well beyond the real threat.[6] Something like a quarter of the existing Soviet SS-4 and -5s are deployed against China. A third of the SS-20s are also deployed in the Soviet East, with a third in the West and a third in central Russia, presumably able to target both China and Western Europe. Some SS-11s in MRBM fields were presumably targeted against China in the past, and some may still be.

The Soviet negotiators argued in SALT that they should be permitted a larger number of missiles because of the need to cope with the Chinese threat. The credibility of that claim should recede with the deployment, outside SALT constraints, of the SS-20, but the Soviet Union will continue to seek 'compensation' for her need to deal with several opponents. And the Soviet 'two-front' problem will complicate any effort to negotiate constraints on the SS-20 and other medium-range Soviet systems in Europe.

Britain will continue to possess four *Polaris* missile-carrying submarines during the 1980s, but the *Chevaline* warhead programme, now finishing deployment, will improve the penetration of the warheads and may add additional warheads (perhaps six instead of three per missile). The successor *Trident* force, due to begin deployment in the early 1990s, will give Britain a total of 512 warheads on four boats, and those warheads will be independently manoeuvrable (MIRV).[7]

French forces will improve more rapidly than British. The silo-based SSBS S-2 IRBM, vulnerable to the SS-20, seem unlikely to be replaced when their useful service ends, in about 1990. France will soon replace her existing MR-60 SLBM warheads with lighter and more accurate MR-61 warheads of the same yield (1 MT); she has also decided to build a sixth missile submarine, and is developing an SLBM, presumed to be MIRVed, the M-4. It is expected to have six or seven warheads, each of 150 KT and as much range as the longest of existing French SLBM: it will be retrofitted into existing submarines from the mid-1980s.

By the end of that period France would then have some 756 SLBM warheads, perhaps with some limited utility against military targets and not just against cities. It is hard to see the rationale for French counterforce capability, except that it may, in Soviet perception, make the force more usable, hence increase the likelihood that it would in fact be used. In any case, the French force will by 1990 constitute more than the present 'minimum massive retaliation' capability it now has. While it will change the strategic situation only at the margins, it will make the Soviet Union more reluctant to exclude French forces from future strategic arms limitation efforts.

What emerges from this brief survey of the strategic balance during the 1980s? Nothing that would dramatically upset the basic balance of deterrence is likely, either in numbers or the qualitative relationship. At the same time however, the creeping decline of secure second strike forces, as a result of the gradually spreading vulnerability of intercontinental nuclear delivery systems, toward a more ambiguous notion of stability is clearly underway and will become more pronounced during the latter part of the decade, for *both* super-powers. That will affect European nuclear concerns in a number of ways: the readiness of the American President to use nuclear weapons first may decline; the Soviet Union may respond to her own vulnerability problem with a greater emphasis on the nuclear threat against Western Europe; and imbalances in the theatre nuclear category may become increasingly more disturbing in political terms.

II. THE SOVIET NUCLEAR THREAT TO EUROPE

Since the early 1960s the Soviet Union has had a large number of continental weapons targeted on Western Europe: some 440 SS-4 and -5 ballistic missiles, plus, presumably, some 'central' system missiles – 100 or so SS-11s placed in MRBM fields in the early 1970s – plus a growing array of frontal aviation. Yet, for most of the 1960s and 1970s this threat received little attention and seemed to cause little concern. Why has this changed at the beginning of the 1980s?

Contrasting US and Soviet Rationales

In the 1950s the United States gave nearly equal emphasis to IRBM for deployment in Europe, ICBM for deployment on American soil and submarine-launched ballistic missile (SLBM). By contrast, the Soviet Union, facing technical problems, evidently decided to deploy a large number of IRBM rapidly and wait until the late 1960s for a second-generation ICBM, thus consigning herself for a decade to gross inferiority in intercontinental systems.

For America the initial decision was driven by technical factors in another sense: the IRBM programme provided a hedge against difficulties in the ICBM programme. Implicit in that logic was that the sooner ICBM could cover all the Soviet targets of interest, the sooner the need for IRBM would fade. The debate at the time recognized some of the arguments for deploying IRBM – it would increase the dispersion of retaliatory forces and provide more flexibility for limited wars. However, the counter-arguments seemed over-riding: politically, the desire for centralized command and control seemed imperative; effective ICBM were at hand; and a second-generation of more survivable IRBM seemed years away.[8] Deployment of IRBM was eventually confined to 60 *Thor* missiles in Britain (manned by the RAF but with warheads in US custody) and 45 *Jupiters* in Italy and Turkey (all US-manned and controlled) and all had been withdrawn by the end of 1964.

By contrast, Soviet actions from the start suggest that IRBM were not for them just a temporary stop-gap until a sufficient arsenal of ICBM had been built up. Rather, the Soviet Union seems always to have had an interest in targeting both the United States and Western Europe. That implied the need for two different kinds of weapons; ICBM and M/IRBMs. The West's tendency to see Soviet strategic doctrine as a mirror of its own has led it to underestimate the continuing Soviet interest in targeting Western Europe, even *after* parity in intercontinental systems had been achieved.

In contrast to American strategic thought, the Soviet Union views her continental weapons as another instrument of strategic military power; like the intercontinental systems, they belong to the Strategic Rocket Forces. Strategically, this makes sense from the Soviet perspective. In case the American 'nuclear guarantee' for Western Europe holds firm, Soviet superiority in continental strategic systems can at least make an American decision to employ intercontinental weapons for a European contingency more difficult. If over the long term the guarantee appears to be in doubt, Soviet continental forces can deter the use of, and perhaps even dissuade the procurement of, European nuclear weapons.

Politically, continental weapons served to remind Europe, especially the Federal Republic of Germany, of Soviet power. The Soviet Union attempted to reap gain from those weapons during the Berlin crises of 1958-61, hoping thereby to put pressure on the weaker or more exposed members of the NATO Alliance. That attempt failed, not least because of America's unquestioned strategic superiority at the time.

But the American superiority is a thing of the past. Once the Soviet Union had an ICBM force that could threaten the United States while maintaining her advantage in continental weapons, this opened up the theoretical option that the Soviet Union might use M/IRBM against Europe but not fire ICBM against the United States provided Washington similarly exempted Soviet territory. That posed the enduring European nightmare: a nuclear war limited to Europe. How real this theoretical possibility was, and is – and thus how much political significance it acquired – is a question addressed later in the Paper.

The introduction in the late 1970s of a new Soviet IRBM, the SS-20, must be seen against this background. The SS-20 may not then seem less menacing but the problem is less new. It may be less surprising that the SS-4s and SS-5s have been supplemented by more modern systems than that it has taken so long. Again, part of the reason must be technical. In the late 1960s the Soviet Union worked on several solid-fuel continental-range variants of the SS-13 ICBM, designated SS-14, which would have had the range of the SS-20. However, the SS-13 was evidently not a successful programme, and the failure rubbed off on the SS-14. In effect, the Soviet Union waited another generation, using the first two stages of the solid-fuelled SS-16 (successor to the SS-13) to form the SS-20.

China has served as an additional, and powerful, inducement to build missiles with ranges to target all opponents. That inducement has been particularly strong since the late 1960s. About a quarter of the SS-4s and SS-5s were transferred east, mostly in 1968 and, when the SS-14 failed, some 120 SS-11 variable range missiles were deployed in M/IRBM fields as an interim measure. The SS-20 may have been given its relatively long-range (3-4,000 miles vs. 1-2,500 for the SS-4s and SS-5s) in order to be able to target all of China from deep inside the Soviet Union.

The Soviet Threat in the 1980s.
There is more continuity to the Soviet continental threat than is implied by public discussion of the SS-20. What makes a difference now is the new Soviet continental capabilities in combination with changes in the strategic balance and developments at other levels of TNF. Unquestionably, the most important change is the emergence, and clear recognition, of something like strategic parity between the United States and the Soviet Union. Parity has raised starkly the credibility of the coupling of the American strategic deterrent to the defence of Europe.

The United States could be counted upon to fire missiles from her strategic arsenal – thereby putting her cities at some risk – in response to a Soviet nuclear strike on Western Europe so long as the United States possessed clear nuclear superiority. Now, it is argued, Europe cannot be sure of the American response. The fear is of long standing; parity has sharpened it, and ICBM vulnerability gives it additional analytic justification. SALT is less a cause of the current concern than a precipitant. It has directed attention to nuclear deterrence in general. By emphasizing what aspects of the nuclear balance are being negotiated, it also underscores what is being excluded, especially Soviet 'medium' range weapons.

The second set of changes from the mid-1960s is the new continental weapons that the Soviet Union has now begun to deploy against Western Europe (and China), primarily but not exclusively the SS-20 mobile IRBM and the *Backfire* bomber. Militarily these weapons give the Soviet Union new kinds of options in attacking Western Europe. Each SS-20 has 3 MIRV, and is both mobile (and so less vulnerable) and more accurate than the SS-4s and SS-5s it supersedes: its accuracy has been reported to be as good as 440 feet over a 2,500 mile range, and its range is over 3,000 miles. [9] This yield of an SS-20 warhead is still large – 150 KT, the same as *Minuteman* – but it is much lower than the megaton yield of the SS-4s and SS-5s. Hence it is somewhat more selective and so more credible as a theatre weapon for attacking military targets while reducing collateral damage. Some 220 were deployed in mid-1981; and the annual rate of increase is between 50 and 60. Two hundred would provide as many warheads as the existing force of SS-4s and SS-5s. With an allowance for new targets, and assuming the phasing out of the older missiles, that would suggest a force in the neighbourhood of 300, a number the Soviet Union would reach by the end of 1982.

A third change – and one too little discussed in the current debate – is the modernization of Soviet shorter-range TNF. The Soviet Union has some 1,300 nuclear missile launchers among her forces in Eastern Europe, with ranges from 10-85 miles for the *FROG*, 50-185 miles for the *Scud* to 500 miles for the *Scaleboard* (all the names are the NATO terms). None of those systems is of recent vintage; the first *Scud* were deployed in 1957, and the most recent, the *Scaleboard*, in 1969. The Soviet Union is developing and deploying successors for all three missiles – the SS-21 for *FROG*, the SS-22 for *Scaleboard* and the SS-23 for *Scud*. Moreover, the Soviet Union is now deploying nuclear-capable artillery, a NATO monopoly in the past, and has an impressive array of modern nuclear-capable strike fighters and medium bombers with range/payload characteristics to cover Western Europe, mostly at low level.

All these new Soviet shorter-range weapons are more accurate, more mobile and have a wider choice of range than their predecessors, and they are also likely to have lower yields. The problems this Soviet modernization poses for NATO are somewhat different to those raised by the SS-20, but the effect may be much the same: targets in Western Europe are now threatened by a whole series of Soviet nuclear systems, not just the SS-20, the *Backfire* and the older M/IRBM. That may give rise to the possibility that NATO would either be deterred from using nuclear weapons in a losing conventional conflict, or no less disturbing, that NATO's existing nuclear delivery systems would be destroyed before they could be used.

So long as NATO was clearly superior to the Soviet Union in shorter-range TNF, Soviet leaders could never be sure that NATO would not use tactical nuclear weapons first, almost irrespective of uncertainties about the balance of nuclear force at higher levels of escalation. Now, the prospective ability of the Soviet Union to respond effectively at shorter ranges in a nuclear war that might be limited to Europe may deter NATO from using nuclear weapons at all.

Geography imposes another asymmetry, to NATO's disadvantage: West Germany (or Holland or France) understandably may feel that any nuclear weapon that can strike them is 'strategic', whether the weapon is an SS-20 fired from the Soviet Union or an SS-21 fired from a short distance inside the East German border. By contrast, none of NATO's current European inventory of land-based missiles can reach beyond Eastern Europe into the Soviet Union and few of NATO's nuclear-capable aircraft combine the necessary range with a sufficiently high assurance of penetration.

Do the Changes Matter?

However, despite all the changes, if Western Europe is in some impressionistic way 'hostage' to Soviet continental weapons, it is still only slightly more so than a decade ago. The United States no longer has clear superiority over the Soviet Union in central nuclear systems, but as long as a decade and a half ago America lost any credible threat to 'disarm' the Soviet Union in a first strike. The United States had by then become vulnerable, and the Soviet Union had achieved a kind of 'minimum deterrence'. Then, as now, deterrence rested on the confidence that the United States would respond. Are there clear military reasons for thinking that can no longer apply?

Strategic parity does not imply that the Soviet Union has more and more military targets which the United States lacks warheads to cover. That is not the case; quite the contrary. As Chapter I indicated, the United States now has something like 9,200 warheads, including the 400 or so *Poseidon* warheads assigned by the US to NATO and targeted by the Supreme Allied Commander, Europe. [10] That number will increase as bombers carrying cruise missiles and the new *Trident* C-4 submarine missiles replace obsolescent *Polaris* missiles. The problem is not that there exists a set of Soviet military activities relative to Europe that cannot be targeted for lack of warheads in America's central strategic arsenal. Rather, the central question for NATO has been and will remain, how America's strategic forces are related to nuclear threats and contingencies in Europe.

Since its inception NATO has been compelled to contemplate two kinds of nuclear contingencies in Europe. One, a first use by the West, contemplates a resort to nuclear weapons in response to a Warsaw Pact conventional attack when NATO defences begin to fail. The second contingency is that the Soviet Union might threaten or employ selective nuclear strikes against Western Europe, either alone or as part of a conventional attack. The two contingencies are linked by the notion of escalation, but their particular implications are somewhat different.

In both cases, the current concern derives from a worry that the changes mean that NATO – that is, the United States – would not use nuclear weapons because it lacked escalatory options or, what amounts to the same, feared that escalation would leave it worse off *vis-a-vis* the Warsaw Pact. In the first contingency, NATO might be self-deterred from a resort to nuclear weapons to stave off conventional defeat because it would know that the Soviet Union could not only now respond in kind to NATO first use of short-range weapons but could, in any subsequent escalation by the West to strikes deeper into Eastern Europe or the Soviet Union, dominate that exchange. Furthermore, the United States could be reluctant to escalate to the use of American central systems (including the *Poseidon* warheads assigned to NATO) for fear of inviting strikes against herself, a fear now aggravated by the vulnerability of *Minuteman.*

In the second set of contingencies, the Soviet Union might threaten or employ limited nuclear strikes, presumably from the SS-20 or shorter-range systems, against major military (or civilian) targets in Western Europe. That prospect, it is argued, is an invitation to Soviet political pressure. NATO would in that case be 'self-deterred' because it would have only a limited capability to launch similar counter-strikes against Soviet targets from European soil. NATO's choices would be restricted to American or allied aircraft capable of delivering nuclear weapons based in Britain or central Europe – 'forward-based systems' – British and French missile systems or, most likely, American *Poseidon* warheads assigned to NATO.

There are grounds for technical doubt about these options. Aircraft, even on fifteen minute alert, are vulnerable to pre-emptive attack, and will have increasing difficulty penetrating Soviet air defences. Yet NATO's existing aircraft – land-based in Europe and on carriers in the Mediterranean – cannot simply be dis-

missed, certainly not from the perspective of a Soviet planner. The use of *Poseidon* SLBM contains some technical problems, but these are perhaps not over-riding. Most important, command and control is less secure and slower for SLBM than for land-based missiles. *Poseidon* missiles carry between 10 and 14 warheads which makes 'small' attacks difficult, and single missile launches could give away the location of the submarine. Existing *Poseidon* missiles do not have the accuracy imputed to the SS-20, but they are certainly accurate enough to strike 'soft' military targets in the Soviet Union, like airfields, of which there are a great many.[11] The D5 *Trident* missiles, to be deployed in the late 1980s, promise to be much more accurate than current SLBM and hence it may have more counterforce potential.

However, the military issues become primarily political rather than technical: would the President of the United States authorize *Poseidon* strikes if they were NATO's most effective military responses? By the elaborate logic of strategic analysis, an affirmative answer is doubtful. For the United States to respond with *Poseidon* strikes on the Soviet Union would be, in this logic, to jump two rungs on the escalation ladder: use of a central strategic system and a strike on the Soviet homeland.

That logic is hard to assign a value to, and is easy to caricature, but it has some force. On the face of it, if the President *were* in fact more likely to authorize an attack on the Soviet Union from GLCM based (say) in Germany rather than *Poseidon* strikes, that would imply that he regarded the Soviet Union as likely to retaliate against the location of the missiles and not against the territory of their owner, thus exempting American territory. Europeans logically should fear that state of affairs, since it hints of 'de-coupling' between Europe and America, a 'limited' nuclear war in Europe.

These fears have existed since the beginning of the nuclear age. The advent of strategic parity between the two super-powers has sharpened but not caused them, as has the emergence of more usable Soviet continental nuclear systems. The fears are inherent in any form of 'nuclear guarantee', hence they cannot be allayed by military hardware. For those who believe that the United States will intervene with her nuclear forces in an East–West war over Europe and that limited nuclear war is unlikely, current American strategic forces should also deter the new missiles that the Soviet Union has been targeting at European soil. For those, on the other hand, who are convinced that no realistic Western strategy can assume that an American President would risk intercontinental nuclear war for the sake of Europe, even American strategic superiority was insufficient to deter Soviet nuclear threats against Europe once the Soviet Union came to possess invulnerable retaliatory nuclear systems with intercontinental range.

However, to state these two poles of the argument does not change the fact that the conditions of nuclear deterrence have evolved. There remain good reasons to believe in the extended deterrent effect of American strategic forces even at a time of parity and growing Soviet continental capability; yet it is also clear that these changes still make more difficult for any American President the agonizing decision of nuclear release in a European conflict. It is in this respect that the changes matter, and that answers will have to be found.

Soviet Objectives

What the Soviet Union seeks by her nuclear deployments against Europe is, in the nature of things, impossible to know with any precision. We are left to speculate from what hints we have – weaponry plus the evidence of manoeuvres plus Soviet writings on nuclear strategy, virtually all of them by military officers. What is most likely to be true is that the Soviet view of nuclear weapons differs from our own. They look nuclear to us, but so must we look nuclear to them: after all, it is NATO's strategy that explicitly contemplates the first use of nuclear weapons.

We focus on the analytics of deterrence, and decry gaps in 'ladders of escalation'. By contrast, the Soviet Union is probably serious when she says that any weapon that can hit her is 'strategic'. Her vision must be dominated by the number of her nuclear opponents, especially China, and by the sheer weight of nuclear attack that could come down on her. The fact that French nuclear forces are independent of NATO, or that British *Polaris* forces are too inaccurate for the hard-target counterforce missions that NATO feels it lacks, or that Chinese forces are both independent and uncertain are all things that worry the West: none of them is likely to be comforting to the Soviet Union.

The record of the last two decades clearly suggests that the USSR accords high priority to targeting Western Europe, probably a higher priority than most in the West have believed. The SS-20 underscores that priority. It demonstrates a traditional objective of Soviet efforts: to deter NATO's resort to nuclear weapons in war, to deter escalation if NATO goes nuclear and to have some chance of avoiding destruction on Soviet territory. In peace, Soviet deployments serve as reminders of Soviet power to Europeans and as instruments to divide NATO countries. More important, as the Soviet planners look toward the 1990s, they may see the nuclear balance with America again turning against them. Nuclear deployments directed at Europe are at least a hedge against that possibility, if not suggestive of a return to a strategy of holding Europe as nuclear 'hostage'.

For much of the nuclear era, Soviet statements asserted that any major conflict in Europe soon would go nuclear and, in turn, quickly become all-out war.[12] Whether the Soviet Union regarded that as sensible strategy, or merely doubted that any conflict could be contained, is again hard to know. In any event, as a declaratory policy it made a certain kind of sense: what better way to deter a first use by NATO than to assert that it would touch off Armageddon? NATO, after all, uses much the same kind of argument to deter a Warsaw Pact conventional attack.

The emphasis on Soviet statements has, however, shifted over the last decade or so. Both the assumptions that conventional war would automatically become nuclear and that nuclear war would inevitably become all-out have been qualified. It is possible to read that evidence – plus improved nuclear delivery systems, especially in terms of accuracy – as an indication of a Soviet commitment to nuclear war-fighting in Europe, if not to the possibility of selective, pre-emptive nuclear strikes against Western Europe.[13]

Yet Soviet actions can also be interpreted as denying options to NATO as much as providing them to Moscow. Given the unpredictability of war, especially nuclear war, it would be surprising for the Soviet Union to leave the initiative to NATO at lower levels of nuclear use. If continental-range forces, like the SS-20, may deter NATO from escalating, replacements for *FROG, Scud* and *Scaleboard* may deny NATO the choice of going nuclear at all, by providing responses in kind to the first use of short-range systems.

There is no question that new Soviet weapons are more capable than their predecessors, and that improvements in accuracy will over the long run cause changes, perhaps basic, in the nature of war in Europe. Yet given the urban sprawl in Western Europe and the degree to which military targets lie within that sprawl, the collateral damage of 'limited' nuclear strikes would not be all that limited.[14] Nor, despite all the recent analysis, is it clear that the Soviet Union cares much about limiting collateral damage. SS-20s do not carry small warheads. Even given her theoretical emphasis on war-fighting in military writings, the Soviet Union may reckon that the prospect of large scale destruction, from conventional as well as from nuclear weapons, will help win wars by dividing the West or deterring it from responding. But she cannot be sure – and base her strategy on such an assumption – that a major war in Europe could be isolated from the strategic nuclear forces of the United States.

From the Soviet perspective therefore, the new medium-range capabilities are no departure from the traditional strategic concept, and that may help to explain why the Soviet Union has been so slow in understanding Western, and particularly European concerns. The SS-4s and SS-5s *are* obsolete: they take a day or more to prepare for firing. Simple logic, military necessity and bureaucratic momentum could all have suggested that they be modernized. Once that disposition was clear, it is only natural that the new system(s) would have more capability than those replaced; that is familiar enough in the West. A final decision to deploy the SS-20 would have been taken in the early 1970s, or about the time that it became clear such systems, along with American forward-based systems (FBS) would not be limited by SALT I. At that point the military argument for proceeding would have been

straightforward and compelling: a new system was ready, old systems needed replacing and SALT left the issue unconstrained. The Soviet Union could modernize her continental missile force (as well as Frontal Aviation) and thereby consolidate her advantage, in the absence but perhaps in the anticipation of later negotiated restraints. Concern over countering Chinese, French and British nuclear efforts would have added strategic weight to these considerations.

This attitude also explains the strong Soviet reaction to NATO's December 1979 decision to introduce 572 new American continental missiles into the European theatre over the decade. No doubt *any* Western military effort would have been severely attacked by the Soviet Union. But on this occasion there has been a different tone, exemplified by Mr Brezhnev's warning in October 1979 that the Western step would fundamentally change the strategic balance between East and West.[15] From the Soviet perspective, these new American weapons represent more than just a European-based capability to respond to Soviet strategic threats against Western Europe; rather, they are an *additional* American strategic option against the Soviet Union, on top of America's strategic triad, and one which might allow the United States to wage nuclear war against the Soviet Union without involving her own territory.[16] It is only logical, from this Soviet perspective, to insist that any negotiations should not be limited to continental range missiles alone but also include American forward-based nuclear facilities, as it is only logical to see these negotiations essentially in a bilateral Soviet-American context.

In the short run, the Soviet Union is certain to try to block NATO's deployment of the new continental systems decided in December 1979. She will try to do that without curtailing her own programmes, especially the SS-20. If she cannot block new NATO deployments, the Soviet Union will feel compelled to make a military response. That could take a variety of forms: there have already been hints that the SS-20 will be followed by a new, more capable system that can target all of Western Europe from east of the Urals, that there are plans to deploy 'more' SS-20s than seem to be envisaged in the current programme and that increases in

Soviet intercontinental strategic forces might be an option to pursue.

For both the West and the Soviet Union, one fact stands out: theatre nuclear weapons, particularly those of longer ranges, cannot be disassociated from concerns over the strategic balance as a whole. Assessments of how that balance will evolve determine for both parties the relevance of their own TNF and the reaction to those of the other side. For NATO, however, there is an additional factor: deterrence for an alliance can never be disassociated from the state of political relations within that alliance. That compounds the technical and strategic complexities of the issue since politics, even more than strategic analysis, cannot rely on clear-cut assessments; the imponderabilities of politics will thus weigh heavily on all decisions – of arms or of arms control – in the theatre nuclear field.

III. TOWARDS A REALISTIC DOCTRINE FOR NATO

Americans and Europeans inevitably approach the TNF question, like other nuclear issues, from very different perspectives. The various slogans – 'deterrence through defence' (or 'war fighting') versus 'pure deterrence' – evoke rather than describe those differences. Underlying them is a more fundamental difference. American thinking about nuclear weapons is rooted in a twenty (or even, arguably, thirty) year tradition of strategic analysis based on concepts derived from economics. Those who developed that analysis left powerful insights about how to begin to think about weapons that are different from all other weapons mankind has known. Yet we have been living for too long on that intellectual inheritance from the 1950s and early 1960s, and strategic analysis has, as a result, often become dangerously mechanical and abstracted from political realities.

Analytic Fallacies

Most of the presumptions of strategic analysis, as it is now practiced, overlook the considerations that would be foremost in the minds of the Western leaders who were confronted with the choice of using nuclear weapons in a European conflict. For leaders on both sides, a step across the nuclear threshold will have implications that will appear literally incalculable. What will be foremost in their minds is the chance – even the expectation – that nuclear exchanges will quickly run beyond anyone's control. 'Selective nuclear options' or planning for 'intra-war deterrence' may offer some hope that nuclear crises can actually be limited, but no rational leader would have much faith in any of that should nuclear weapons actually be used. It is not least on this uncertainty that deterrence continues to rest.[17]

That means that most presumptions about how nuclear weapons would be used in Europe may have theoretical but little prophetic value. Explicit in NATO's flexible response strategy and implicit in most discussions is the notion of an escalation ladder: the first nuclear weapons to be used would be short-range battlefield systems; these would be followed by deeper-strike theatre systems if need be; and eventually, in the extreme case, American central systems would be used.

Yet, to put it starkly, what would ensue if NATO were actually losing a conventional war, and its leaders decided that the time had come to face the great abyss of nuclear use? First, there would be no automatic decision, and great emphasis would be given to those nuclear systems which are most controllable. The US President would certainly want to approve every release of a nuclear weapon and every single target; he could hardly do less. Yet that suggests that he would be extremely reluctant to release short-range weapons for battlefield use at the subsequent discretion of commanders on the scene.

A German Chancellor (or any other European leader) who agreed to an American use of nuclear weapons – and it is hard to conceive that the United States would use them, at least initially, without such agreement – would surely add two conditions: not, by any means, on German territory, West *or* East: and not launched from German (or perhaps even British) territory. That is reasonable enough: who wants to use nuclear weapons on their own territory when any immediate advantage would be cancelled or turned negative by a Warsaw Pact response in kind? Or who would invite nuclear retaliation on their own heads, even if there were grounds for doubting that the Soviet Union would be as discriminating in her response as NATO was in its choice of firing locations?

So where would that leave NATO a few minutes after its leaders began to face nuclear war? A strike on the Soviet Union herself would be ruled out for the time being as too escalatory and NATO leaders would be likely to insist instead on looking at military targets in Eastern Europe.[18] And they would quickly move to the discussion of 'offshore' systems as the best launch vehicles. Thus, a limited *Poseidon* strike against targets deep in Eastern Europe could turn out not to be one of the last rungs' on some notional escalation ladder, but the first.

NATO's customary assumptions may be more tenable in the contingency of a selective Warsaw Pact nuclear strike on military targets in Western Europe. In that case, NATO would want to have a broad range of response options and to select the most limited option commensurate with the attack. Yet given the fact that even a 'limited' Soviet attack would cross the nuclear threshold, it is hard to imagine such a strike except as part of, or as an immediate prelude to, a Soviet conventional attack. NATO might then want to respond with nuclear weapons based in Europe, but the same inhibitions on the use of short-range weapons would apply.

Making Sense of TNF

Trying to make sense of TNF, especially by incorporating realistic political considerations, will not be easy. The strongest argument for reassessment is that NATO can no longer afford to be so vague about why it has TNF.[19] Yet the process of re-thinking carries uncomfortable implications for NATO nuclear doctrine and practice. The first of these is that the thought of nuclear defence strategies, however tempting in technical terms, should be laid to rest. Since its inception, NATO could logically have solved its defence dilemma by acknowledging frankly that no fully convincing conventional defence of Western Europe is possible within foreseeable levels of

NATO spending, given Soviet conventional capabilities. The Alliance would then have built its defence around a threat to use tactical nuclear weapons very early in any conflict; its forces would be structured accordingly, and might be much smaller and cheaper than at present.[20]

The Alliance has never accepted such strategies, and they were specifically abandoned when the doctrine of flexible response was formulated in the early 1960s, but the notion persists. Yet the growing Soviet arsenals of shorter-range nuclear systems make such strategies even less attractive. It is widely recognized that, given the way forces are currently configured, NATO could well be worse off after an exchange of battlefield nuclear weapons. On that score, a decade and a half of NATO studies of low-level TNF have made a difference. It is true that a nuclear defender dispersed for nuclear combat could retain some of the advantages of the defence, and a variety of means of making the early use of nuclear weapons credible have been suggested, for instance by creating or preparing to create in time of crisis a depopulated border zone on the intra-German frontier.

However, responsible political leaders in the West simply will not authorize the use of nuclear weapons early in a conflict (unless the other side fires them first), or delegate responsibility for weapons to *anyone else* (much less to field commanders). Moreover, nuclear defence strategies are by their nature de-coupling. After all, their aim is to deter attack by presenting unacceptable odds on the ground, not by the risk of escalation. Politics in NATO Europe are strained enough by current nuclear issues. It is hard to believe they could bear the weight of strategies that relied on the early and extensive release of nuclear weapons.

The second implication is the need to reassess NATO's existing TNF arsenals. It is hard to conceive of why NATO should have anywhere near the number of short-range and battlefield nuclear systems it now possesses, or anything like 6,000 nuclear warheads in Europe (after the withdrawal of 1,000 US warheads announced in December 1979). Many of the warheads are obsolete. And for the reasons set out above, the use of shorter-range weapons is not very credible in precisely the scenario where

NATO strategy contemplates it – as the escalation of a losing conventional war.

Moreover, most of these tactical warheads are stored at some fifty sites; NATO presents no more than about 70 TNF targets in peacetime, and only 200–300 once weapons are dispersed in preparation for war.[21] Procedures for securing release of weapons, dispersing them from stockpiles and applying the codes to unlock the weapons would take hours, even days. Much of the current NATO posture does, as one analyst puts it, beg the Soviet Union to pre-empt, and perhaps even make it possible for Moscow to do so with conventional weapons.[22] Yet because short-range nuclear weapons will continue to look attractive as a compensation for conventional force deficiencies, it will be difficult to wean some parts of the NATO military establishment, notably the American Army, away from them.

This is not to argue for a complete dismantling of short-range nuclear systems but rather for a shift in emphasis toward longer-range weapons. Longer-range systems are attractive on two grounds. First, they are less vulnerable to pre-emption because they can be based further back in NATO Europe, even if their intended use is near the NATO front-line. And, second, they provide a capability for selective strikes well into Warsaw Pact territory, which should prove a more credible deterrent than battlefield first use. NATO might consider a declaratory policy making clear that its first resort to nuclear weapons, if need be, would be strikes well into Eastern Europe.

Longer-range TNF can be deployed on both land and sea. From a purely military perspective there are strong arguments for sea basing: mobility, hence relative invulnerability to pre-emptive destruction, and the lack of obvious retaliatory options against European territory inherent in land-based systems. Command and Control would remain a serious problem, but there is no reason why sea-based cruise missiles should be less accurate against military targets than ground-based versions, and next generations of SLBM will be more accurate than current systems. Moreover, some of the political controversy which surrounds the stationing of nuclear weapons on European territory could be avoided, and the escalatory distance to strategic sea-based systems would be reduced.

However, NATO's December 1979 decision excluded sea-based continental systems, apparently for three main reasons. Land-based missile technologies seemed to be more readily available. Cost was also crucial; sea-based systems would be more expensive, either directly if new submarines (or fast surface craft) were built as launch platforms, or indirectly if existing attack submarines were converted to the cruise missile role. Second, several NATO governments, especially the Norwegian, opposed sea-basing for fear that NATO submarines would seek the protection of Norwegian inland waters for their operations and thus expose Norway to Soviet retaliation.

Finally, there was a widely held view that only the visibility of deployment on land could demonstrate NATO's resolve to the Soviet Union, reassuring Europeans that the US President would not be tempted to fail to respond to a Soviet nuclear attack on Europe. Not all of these arguments are convincing. There is more than a hint that Europe and America were caught in a game of mirrors, with America arguing that only ground-basing would assuage European fears and West Germany in particular sensing a US preference for land-based systems. If sea-based systems are attractive on technical and strategic grounds, they will have to be considered more seriously in the future.

A third implication is that *any* NATO nuclear strategy will put a tremendous strain on arrangements for command, control, communication and intelligence (C^3I). In the customary scenarios, it is not clear that NATO would be able to use nuclear weapons effectively at all; the imperative of control collides with the requirements of timely use for military purpose. By the time the American President authorized release and approved targets, and the weapons were physically prepared and triggered, they could well have been overrun or their use have otherwise become inappropriate. Soviet strikes on some ten C^3I centres in Europe could 'blind' the Alliance.

Incorporating realistic political considerations only increases the problem. NATO leaders will first need to communicate with each other, and to do so fast, in the middle of a war raging in Europe and without the Soviet Union intercepting the communications. The

50

more that political leaders, especially the American President, insist on complete control of weapons release and targeting – and they *will* so insist – the greater the need for a C³I system that provides many and rapid choices of weapons and targets.

Given the short distances in Europe, command and control installations are likely to remain vulnerable no matter what NATO does. It may be made tolerably adequate for most war purposes, but it is not easy to imagine that political leaders, in a crisis, would feel confident that they could execute and control the sophisticated, limited nuclear exchanges against military targets in Europe that are conjured up by current strategic scenarios.[23] This again argues for a doctrine which relies less heavily on nuclear forces, and for nuclear forces which combine a greater degree of flexibility with missions that make military sense under realistic conditions of European warfare.

No Alternative to Conventional Strength

Finally, and most important, all of this discussion underscores the importance of conventional forces. Shifting toward longer-range nuclear forces, with declaratory policy to match, can make nuclear threats more credible than they are today. But *any* threat to use nuclear weapons first will inevitably become less and less credible. There is no alternative to investing more heavily in conventional forces. Of course, the obstacles are also considerable. NATO has preached its inferiority in conventional forces for so long that it has come to believe it. Beneath the surface of that debate other factors are at work, especially the abiding reluctance of Europeans to contemplate a conventional war in Europe. Finally, improvements in conventional defence are not only costly but they also run up against the shortage of personnel which most Western armed forces are likely to experience during the latter part of the 1980s.

There is no question that the Soviet conventional forces in Eastern Europe are impressive and growing more so. Yet the situation is hardly as bleak as it is often portrayed, and probably never has been. If the Warsaw Pact attacked without prior massive mobilization, NATO could field almost as many men in the central region as the Pact. The Pact's numerical advantage during the first several months of mobilization would peak after about two weeks, but still be less than 2-1, hardly happy for the West but not appealing to a conservative Soviet military planner.[24] Moreover, despite continuing Soviet force improvements, NATO's position should look better in a few years, given the improvements undertaken in the Long-Term Defence Programme (LTDP). The debate over the impact of new weapons, such as precision-guided munitions (PGM), rages, but it is hard to believe that on balance it does not favour the defence.[25]

There is no question that reliance on more conventional defence would require more defence effort, especially in Western Europe, but the increases need not be so large as to be completely out of the question. If it is correct, as this Paper has argued, that NATO can no longer rely on a doctrine which assumes an early use of nuclear weapons, and if it is also true that the credibility of nuclear employment is becoming more circumscribed, then there is no alternative to strengthening the capability of conventional forces for the sake of effective deterrence. This will require more than just additions to present forces; it will need careful study of the deterrence capability of conventional forces, the ways to improve it, and the force structures that will respond to the task.

To recognize that NATO's traditional theatre nuclear doctrine is becoming obsolete and that the threat of a first use of nuclear weapons against conventional attack is losing its credibility is only the first step for a much wider exercise: to incorporate a realistic notion of the use of theatre nuclear forces into a doctrine of deterrence in which conventional forces will have to play a greater role. That will have consequences for both conventional and nuclear forces. For the latter it will mean that the primary task of nuclear weapons in deterrence will be to deter the Soviet first use of these systems, and that Western TNF must both be survivable against a Soviet strike and capable of destroying Soviet nuclear installations and other facilities of similar military value. But whatever the details of a new NATO doctrine, one thing seems clear. Only if the doctrine for Europe is credible in itself will US nuclear weapons stationed there be able to continue to perform that task which is essential to all Alliance deterrence: to demonstrate convincingly the risk of nuclear escalation to the strategic nuclear level.

IV. OPTIONS FOR ARMS CONTROL

The immediate prospects for arms control in the realm of TNF are bleak, but at the same time negotiations seem imperative if NATO is to move toward implementation of its December 1979 decisions. NATO is in the position of negotiating its potential systems against modern Soviet weapons, like the SS-20, that are deployed and increasing rapidly in number. Moreover, with the future of SALT uncertain, the fate of the continental talks, begun in preliminary form in Geneva in October 1980, is similarly unclear, and where to negotiate is itself in question.

Beyond the immediate prospects lie fundamental questions about what, if anything, TNF arms control can contribute to Western security, and how it relates to both force planning and arms control at other levels of military force. There will continue to be the problem of keeping military decisions tolerably in step with politics. For instance, the cast the continental range issue has acquired in public perception – 'countering the SS-20' – will continue to hang over NATO's actions, making the Alliance vulnerable to Soviet manipulations of SS-20 deployments and running the risk that even successes on the continental range issue will only underscore problems at shorter ranges of TNF.

NATO's TNF decisions in December, which grew out of the Alliance LTDP, combined new deployments with an arms-control initiative to the Soviet Union. 572 new missiles of continental-range are to be deployed in Western Europe beginning in 1983–84 to be completed, if there are no delays, by about 1988. 108 of these are extended range (about 1,000 miles) *Pershing* IIXR ballistic missiles, which would replace the *Pershing* IA missiles currently deployed with American forces in Germany. The *Pershing* IIXR, with a radar terminal guidance system, is extremely accurate, about an order of magnitude more so than the *Pershing* IA.

The rest of the new missiles will be American ground-launched cruise missiles (GLCM),
160 in Britain, 96 in the Federal Republic, 48 each in Belgium and the Netherlands, and 112 in Italy. With a range of about 1,500 miles, they will be deployed in peacetime on mobile transporter-launchers on American airfields; they would begin to move off the bases only in times of crisis. GLCMs, with a terrain-matching guidance system (TERCOM), are also highly accurate. As part of the decision, NATO committed itself to reduce the number of its warheads in Europe by 1,000. In effect, the new deployments will modernize NATO's TNF by shifting the centre of gravity toward continental-range systems.

Steps Towards Negotiation

NATO accompanied its deployment decision with an American offer to negotiate with the Soviet Union over continental nuclear weapons, presumably in SALT III. That offer, made in the December communiqué, sets out the following objectives: negotiations should be conducted between the United States and the Soviet Union, thus dealing with American and Soviet delivery systems only; they should in the first instance concentrate on longer-range land-based missiles, not on aircraft or sea-based systems; the principle of parity should apply to continental-range systems; and any agreed limitations must be adequately verifiable.[26]

For the West, as these proposals indicate, the NATO decision to expand its continental weaponry is essential to respond to the Soviet build-up and to correct imbalances in the overall spectrum of nuclear deterrence. Once the programme is implemented or once arms control has reduced its need by setting lower limits for Soviet continental weapons, a tolerable balance will be re-established, sustaining the credibility of NATO's strategy for deterrence.

The Soviet perspective is different, as major Soviet statements suggest. The first was President Brezhnev's major speech in East Berlin on 6 October 1979, when he tried unsuccessfully to halt NATO's impending decision. The main pointers to Soviet thinking were contained in one explicit statement and one implicit premise. '. . . the implementation of [the NATO] schemes', Brezhnev warned, 'would essentially change the strategic situation on the continent. [The] objective is to break down the balance of forces . . . and to attempt to achieve military superiority for the NATO bloc'.[27] In spite of the worries in the West over the Soviet SS-20, however, the Soviet President refused to offer the one concession which was likely to have undermined the NATO decision: a halt to the SS-20 programme. By Soviet premises, that was not called for. Moreover, stopping a major weapons programme in mid-stream would have run directly against ingrained Soviet habits. Soviet leaders may also have calculated that NATO would fail to agree on a programme even without a major Soviet move.

For the Soviet Union, the introduction of new American continental missiles in Europe is not a correction of the balance but a new challenge to the existing force relationship. In fact, as Soviet commentators have repeatedly stated since, the *Pershing* II and the cruise-missiles are seen as an *additional* American strategic option, the means to conduct nuclear war against the Soviet Union without employing central strategic systems. The Soviet focus remains the homeland, a concern that runs back to the beginning of SALT. That is why, in the Soviet perspective, the NATO programme would alter, not confirm the balance. By contrast, the SS-20 missiles constitute, in the Soviet presentation, no change in that balance since they are not directed against the United States and since they are merely the technological upgrading of the existing Soviet continental systems which the West had accepted as outside the central strategic relationship. The initial Soviet reaction to NATO's December 1979 decision was, in the light of these views, not surprising: negotiations, so Soviet representatives underlined repeatedly, would not be possible unless the West first renounced, or at least formally suspended its own programme.[28]

While perhaps logical in Soviet eyes, that position was hardly politically tenable. If the Soviet Union truly was concerned about the introduction of new US weapons into Europe, then negotiations offered the only way to halt or hinder that programme, either by appealing to European public opinion (through demonstrating Soviet readiness to talk) or, if need be, by agreeing on mutual constraints around the negotiating table.

In early July 1980, during Chancellor Schmidt's visit to Moscow, the Soviet leadership moved away from its earlier rigidity. It agreed that negotiations could start 'without waiting for ratification of the SALT II treaty' by the US Senate, 'but any accords that might be reached' in the separate talks 'could be implemented only after the entry into force of this treaty'. Negotiations should be conducted between the Soviet Union and the United States alone, with French and British nuclear forces deferred to the central SALT III talks.[29] However, the Soviet Union also returned to a demand she had made periodically since the beginning of SALT I by saying that the talks should deal with issues 'relating to both medium-range nuclear missiles in Europe and the existing American forward-based nuclear weapons' – American nuclear-capable aircraft (or even shorter range nuclear systems) based in Europe or on aircraft carriers around it – the two issues to be discussed 'simultaneously and in organic connection'.[30]

In February 1981 the Soviet position moved somewhat further. In his report to the 26th Party Congress Brezhnev finally offered a moratorium on the construction of deployment of new medium-range nuclear missiles – thus including the SS-20 – to begin as soon as negotiations started.[31] Yet the call for a moratorium came late, as the SS-20 programme neared completion and with the NATO deployments still several years away. Moreover, the moratorium appeared limited to those systems deployed *in* Europe, thus apparently leaving unconstrained the third of SS-20 deployments east of the Urals but within range of Western Europe.

By mid–1981, after preliminary talks in Geneva, the starting points for negotiations had thus become clearer. NATO had spelled out its objective – parity – and the Soviet Union had insisted on widening the negotiations beyond continental missiles to include forward-based systems (FBS). These differences will be central difficulties in the negotiations.

53

However, there are nevertheless two important points on which both sides seem agreed: that continental missiles in Europe should be a major issue of the talks and that the two super-powers should conduct them bilaterally.

What Objectives for NATO?

Yet political, conceptual and military issues connected with the immediate future of the negotiations remain. The most obvious is political and concerns the parlous fate of SALT. But there are also hard questions of precisely what objectives the West should pursue in negotiations and of how to deal with two particularly thorny issues: FBS and verification.

The Soviet agreement to *start* talks even in the absence of a SALT II ratification removed a procedural obstacle but not the underlying political and technical ones. With the election of President Reagan, if not before, SALT II died as a treaty to be ratified by the United States Senate. The Reagan Administration has stressed its commitment to the SALT process, but even under the best of circumstances it will be some time, perhaps years, before a SALT treaty is in place, though the two sides may agree to continue abiding by the qualitative restraints in SALT II during the interim.[32]

It is not clear whether European political patience can last that long. If political opinion on the centre and the left of the political spectrum became convinced that SALT was going nowhere, then the support for NATO's nuclear modernization programme could rapidly erode. The incentives for serious negotiations would erode with it: for the Soviet Union since she would have obtained what she wanted without paying a price; for America since she would find herself with little to offer to obtain Soviet restraint. The political underpinning for the continental negotiations would then be lost.

To the long-term Western objectives, the guidelines in the December 1979 communiqué are no more than a rough sketch. Indeed, as so often in the past, the West knows where to begin but not where to arrive in arms control. Is the primary objective to restrain the Soviet SS-20 programme, to protect nuclear delivery systems in Europe against pre-emptive destruction, or to complement the SALT agreements by making circumvention more diffi-cult? The West does not seem as yet to have made up its collective mind. The objectives need not be entirely incompatible with one another, but which ever is emphasized in negotiations will lead to different outcomes.

If, for example, curbing the SS-20 programme is the main objective, as much of the official justification provided for NATO's TNF modernization suggests it is, then NATO would forego all or part of this modernization for a limit on the number of SS-20s. This is the clear implication of the language used in the NATO communiqué of December 1979. Not only would this put the West in an unfavourable bargaining position when attempting to restrict existing Soviet missiles in exchange for not building American ones, but it would also put the Western programme at the mercy of Soviet SS-20 moves. Should the Soviet Union decide, as early as 1981, that she had accumulated enough of these weapons, she could try to undermine the Western modernization effort by going beyond Brezhnev's February speech to propose that, even without negotiations, she would build no further systems provided the West abstained from deploying new continental weapons on its side of Europe. This is all the more likely since the Soviet Union may be nearing the end of SS-20 deployments in any case. With 220 in place by mid–1981, that would imply that work would have begun on around 250 – the number often presumed in the West to be the target for Soviet deployments.

If, by contrast, the principal Western objective is protecting NATO's nuclear delivery systems from pre-emptive destruction, that would indicate a very different negotiating strategy. First, it would imply much less preoccupation with numbers of SS-20s. If the NATO programme is based on the premise that the Alliance needs survivable weapons of continental range in order to carry out its strategy, that need is not very sensitive to how many SS-20s there are. By this logic it is more important to deploy most or all the GLCMs and *Pershings* than it is to wrest ten or twenty per cent reductions in numbers of SS-20s. That would suggest that any quantitative limits would be fairly high, not really constraining the Soviet Union while providing incentive for NATO to build toward its planned total of 572.

54

That objective might also indicate other negotiating approaches. One, hardly promising given the current technologies and deployment patterns of the two sides, would be to argue that cruise missiles are less menacing than ballistic missiles as continental weapons since they are slow and thus less suitable for first strikes, especially of the pre-emptive nature. After all, once NATO made its December 1979 decision, the Soviet Union singled out *Pershing* IIs on the argument that their deployment would reduce the flight time of American 'strategic' weapons to the Soviet Union from several tens of minutes to several minutes. There is something to that argument, since the *Pershing* IIs would pose a particular threat to time-urgent command and control centres in a massive American strategic strike. Yet the argument seems mostly to have been propaganda, too handy to pass up. Soviet leaders are probably reconciled to *Pershing*; they are less of a departure since something called *Pershing* already is deployed in Germany and because, given the rather high cost, NATO is unlikely to deploy more than the planned 108. By contrast, in Soviet eyes the cruise missile threat must look open-ended.

Protecting NATO's theatre weapons from pre-emptive strikes would also suggest considering measures in the realm of nuclear confidence building. One proposal has been for NATO to deploy only GLCM launchers in Europe, with the missiles stored in the United States during peacetime, provided the Soviet Union will similarly store SS-20 missiles out of range of Western Europe.[33] That notion is intriguing but probably impossible to verify, a point developed below. More promising might be to be recognize that some shorter-range Soviet TNF deployed in Eastern Europe pose the same pre-emptive threat to NATO theatre weapons as do the SS-20s. It might be possible to agree that both sides, in peacetime, would deploy short-range TNF, including launchers, out of range of the other. That might involve fewer verification problems than schemes which tried to separate missiles from launchers (though it would depend on accurate range estimates), but it would also raise awkward issues for the current NATO strategy that contemplates the pre-emptive use of nuclear weapons.

Finally, if NATO sought primarily to shore up SALT agreements by constraining weapons left out of the central SALT negotiations, that would carry two somewhat contradictory implications. Politically, it would argue for a tight link between the continental negotiations and SALT, lest the theatre balance were to become 'de-coupled' from the central American deterrent. Moreover, SALT strategies do carry implications for theatre negotiating approaches. For example, common wisdom holds that the more aggregate limits on central systems are reduced, the more salient theatre systems, and particularly continental weapons, become. That is surely true in perception.[34] (In fact, even on the basis of limits of 1,000 on strategic launchers, 800 on MIRVed strategic launchers and 500 on MIRVed strategic land-based launchers, and SALT II limits on fractionation, both sides would be able to field up to 10,000 total warheads on their central systems, depending on precise rules about replacing old systems with new.) Further deep reductions in central system aggregates, as the Carter Administration proposed in 1977, would surely make Europe and the US more sensitive to the 'balance' at other levels, particularly of continental weapons

At some point, the 'complement SALT' objective might dictate including continental weapons under expanded SALT totals. For instance, the SALT II aggregate of 2,250 might be raised to 2,650 to include continental weapons, with both sides given freedom to determine the precise mix between continental and central systems.[35] Constraints on warhead numbers might be achieved by including continental systems under the SALT II sub-ceilings on MIRVed launchers, perhaps expanded somewhat. This approach would not eliminate the formidable problems associated with continental negotiations – different structures and paces of deployment, FBS or verification – but it would mean that what are at present considerable asymmetries in continental capabilities would become less dramatic in talks comprising both central *and* continental weapons. More important, it would underscore the unity between NATO's continental weapons in Europe and the central US deterrent.

However, the other implication of this negotiating objective runs in a somewhat different direction. Just as SALT II dramatized the SS-20 by excluding it, so continental talks, whether separate from or fully integrated with SALT, could underscore the threat posed by the shorter-range Soviet systems they left out. NATO could find it had 'solved' its SS-20 problem only to have it replaced by an SS-21, SS-22 and SS-23 problem. Shoring up SALT by preventing circumvention would thus argue for including or somehow constraining shorter-range TNF as well.[36]

Specific Issues: FBS and Verification

However and wherever continental weapons are discussed, what to do about FBS will complicate the talks. From NATO's perspective there are grounds for scepticism about including FBS but not for outright opposition. At a minimum, if NATO seeks to include the Soviet *Backfire* bomber under continental constraints, it will have to offer some FBS in return. Doing so could provide an additional reason for NATO's nuclear modernization because it would free nuclear-capable aircraft for badly-needed conventional missions and reduce the ambiguity inherent in dual-capable aircraft, an interest the Soviet Union may share.

Soviet FBS objectives remain unclear. In part, the Soviet Union's interest in FBS represents a residue of her traditional 'homeland-to-homeland' SALT definition. On the one hand, for continental missiles the USSR has accepted the symmetry between Soviet missiles that can strike Western Europe and American missiles in Western Europe that can strike the Soviet Union. Yet FBS is a different category; almost by definition no Soviet aircraft are forward-based, and are therefore liable for inclusion. Other objectives may lurk in the background. For instance, American carrier-based A-6s and A-7s can reach the Soviet Union only if the carriers are deployed well towards the Eastern end of the Mediterranean. Soviet leaders may thus harbour hopes of achieving back-door constraints on US carrier operations by arguing that A-6s and A-7s could be excluded only if the US at the same time gave a pledge to restrict the operating areas of the carrier task forces. Even if the USSR fully accepted the principle of symmetry in aircraft as well as missiles, FBS would remain a problem. Table 4 shows why.

No matter how FBS is defined, the balance is heavily tilted in favour of the Soviet Union. As more FBS are included the situation becomes worse. Moreover, range is inadequate as a criterion for aircraft because it is arbitrary, depending on mission profile, bomb load, refuelling and basing. Worse, as the range threshold is lowered, the numbers are dominated by shorter-range aircraft whose status as theatre-nuclear weapons clearly is more questionable than for longer-range systems. With both missiles and aircraft there is the problem of how to count Soviet systems deployed against China. About a third of the SS-20s are out of range of Western Europe and about a quarter of Soviet nuclear-capable aircraft are deployed facing China. But SS-20s can be moved, perhaps even by air, and aircraft could be rapidly deployed westward, so NATO will be as reluctant to exclude China-oriented Soviet systems as the Soviet Union will be to include them. That might be handled, at least for the SS-20, with a combination of a global ceiling on all SS-20 and a sub-ceiling on those based in range of Western Europe. A further negotiating problem will be what to do with Soviet aircraft assigned to the Naval Air Force – in 1980, 280 *Badger,* 40 *Blinder* and 70 *Backfire* aircraft.

Verification will also be a serious problem, the implications of which analysts have been slow to grasp. SALT standards must apply in a much more complex context since the systems concerned are smaller and more mobile. For instance, on the SALT model, nuclear-capable aircraft constrained under a treaty would have to be distinguished from non-nuclear versions of the same type by some so-called 'functionally related observable differences' (FROD); that is, something visible by satellite and clearly related to the nuclear/non-nuclear distinction. But FRODs will be hard to design for, let us say, aircraft that can carry bomb loads internally.

Whether particular proposals make sense will frequently turn on the question of verification. For instance, Western intelligence is said to determine that a particular SS-20 base is operational by the level of activity observed there, without actually having sighted an SS-20 launcher by satellite. If so, that means that no proposals would be verifiable which required

56

the United States to keep cruise missiles in the United States while deploying only the launchers in Europe, and the Soviet Union to take comparable measures. Similarly, proposals to ban or limit missile reloads for the SS-20 or cruise missiles would take a degree of intrusive verification, such as on-site inspection, that is hard to imagine the Soviet Union accepting.

An Approach to Negotiation

It is tempting to look at the prospects for continental nuclear negotiations and dismiss the endeavour as folly. The signs are not encouraging: NATO starts with few chips and the Soviet Union with many, while the history of arms control is scarcely replete with negotiations that have produced parity, as opposed to merely ratifying a pre-existing parity; what is to be negotiated will itself be a prime subject of negotiation; and the whole question of verification hangs over the talks. But in the case of continental TNF it is not good enough to say that negotiations are unpromising. European politics alone compels an effort. NATO must try to square the circle, and the Reagan Administration early on pledged to continue the TNF talks even though it remained far from a defined approach to SALT.

For the years immediately ahead, NATO's interests are best served by a limited continental negotiation closely linked to the SALT process, which although not the best of the negotiating alternatives, is better than others. It would seek to put some (relatively high) limits on the most politically visible of the Soviet systems, perhaps just the SS-20 if the Soviet Union would pledge to dismantle the SS-4s and SS-5s. Not that this approach is without problems – quite the contrary, the most obvious difficulty being the uncertain future of SALT itself – but it is better than the alternatives. There are clear limits to how far TNF negotiations could progress if separated from SALT, even if the will to move were there. To use the most stark example, it would make little sense to formalize limits on the SS-20 if limits on Soviet ICBMs were in doubt. TNF negotiations thus presume *some* shape to SALT, and early in its tenure as the Reagan Administration committed itself more and more tightly to TNF talks, it was sliding toward SALT.

Looking at the programmes of the two sides, there are several points at which a crude parity might be ratified.[37] By about 1985, with NATO perhaps halfway through its programme, both sides would have about 250 modern land-based continental launchers assuming that the Soviet Union does not go beyond the projected figure. 'Parity' at that point would require the Soviet Union not to build beyond 250 or, alternatively, for NATO to exclude the one-third of the SS-20s whose operating bases facing China are out of range of Western Europe. This would also be a parity in launchers, not in warheads as NATO has insisted, for the Soviet Union would have three times as many warheads given that each SS-20 carries three warheads. Moreover, even equality in warheads will not be attractive to NATO's military planners who will not regard one cruise missile as the equal even to one SS-20 *warhead*.

A rough parity in warheads could only exist by the end of the decade if NATO deployed all its planned 572 systems, the Soviet Union stopped the SS-20 at 250 and NATO were willing to exclude the China-oriented one-third of those. That 'parity' might be extended to include FBS, if the United States continued to have 156 F-111s in Britain and counted them all (2 warheads each). On the Soviet side only *Backfire* might be included, with, say 135 of those counted (3 or 4 warheads each). (By 1988 the Soviet Union might have some 375 total *Backfires,* with the half devoted to the Naval Air Force and the quarter or so of the remaining based in the East excluded from the continental agreement. The 66 American FB-111s based in the United States that are part of the Strategic Air Command and the other F-111s in the US might also be excluded as the basis for a compromise.) This would also mean excluding the *Badgers,* which might be phased out by the end of the decade in any case, and the *Blinders,* which probably will not be.

In any case the elements of a compromise will be rough indeed, but might not be out of the question. An agreement which merely ratified the programmes of the two sides would hardly be attractive either to Western Europeans as arms control or to the Soviet Union as a reduction in NATO's plans. However, NATO might trade a small reduction in its planned deployments for a firm cap on the SS-20, thus

57

striking a deal which left the US with more launchers but the Soviet Union with more warheads.

As a fall-back, if delay in SALT threatens to erode European support for the December 1979 decision, NATO might consider tacit restraint instead of formal negotiations. It might offer to limit its deployment plans in exchange for Soviet restraint on the SS-20. Tacit restraint would, however, invite the Soviet Union to interfere in Western force planning by manipulating the pace of her SS-20 deployments. Postponing all or even part of the deployment of new weapons allocated to given NATO countries in December 1979 could also reopen political issues better left closed. More to the point, now that Soviet SS-20 deployments exceed, in warheads, the projected total of the NATO programme, there is little sense in restraint on NATO's part.

Negotiating approaches over the next few years need to be framed in the light of long-term NATO interests. At a minimum, the next steps taken should not further distort the public cast of the issue, or foreclose more general negotiating strategies that NATO may want to retain. Over the long run, for instance, integrating continental weapons under expanded SALT ceilings may come to seem attractive; that time is not yet, not least because of SALT's dim future. Yet it is important in making decisions about how to define FBS to keep in mind that NATO may want later to incorporate those definitions of continental range systems, including FBS, into SALT.

Perhaps more pressing is the need to think now about what it left out of the continental negotiations. There is a real danger that the focus of public concern will shift from long-range TNF like the SS-20 to shorter-range systems not projected to be covered by negotiations. To reduce that risk while not committing NATO to a comprehensive TNF negotiation, the Alliance might, for example, propose a carefully-defined freeze on the deployment of shorter-range systems in Europe while the continental negotiations proceeded. The problem, of course, is that the existing balance is again sharply in the Soviet Union's favour. For weapons over 100 miles in range and excluding continental weapons (Soviet SS-4, SS-5 and SS-20 and *Backfire* and American F-111), the Soviet advantage in warheads is about 1,280 to 270 and 460 to 80 if qualitative factors are taken into account.[38]

Yet some kind of freeze need not be ruled out. European NATO members contribute much more to NATO's nuclear assets than do the non-Soviet Warsaw Pact members, so the Soviet-US shorter-range balance tends to exaggerate the Soviet advantage. Moreover, the USSR has a range of new systems – the SS-21, SS-22 and SS-23 – for deployment. A freeze would at least lessen the risk that even successful management of the continental issue would dramatize the nuclear 'threat' at shorter ranges.

V. TNF: THE POLITICAL CONDITION

As the preceding discussion makes clear, there are no final solutions to the issue of nuclear weapons in Europe. NATO will continue to face nuclear dilemmas that cannot be made to go away. One of these is obvious: Europe is dependent, finally, on the American strategic deterrent, most of which is on the other side of the Atlantic from the point of attack. That geographic dilemma cannot be resolved for political reasons: for Germany to have nuclear weapons of her own is not on the cards; the remedy would be worse than the problem, at least for the foreseeable future.

For NATO there is no escaping some nuclear paradox. The task is to manage it. Weapons

matter, but politics will be decisive. In particular, the general state of the trans-Atlantic relationship will bear on the political adequacy of nuclear arrangements as much as on the specifics of military hardware. When Europeans are tolerably confident of American purpose and leadership, nuclear matters will be less salient; when they are not, specific issues, like the SS-20, will emerge as surrogates for concern about the ultimate reliability of the American nuclear guarantee. Crudely put, what Washington does about the dollar may matter nearly as much to confidence in nuclear arrangements as what it decides to do about the SS-20.

Moreover, it is a mistake to conceive of the nuclear issues themselves too narrowly. That has been the unfortunate thrust of public discussion thus far. Yet it is not, or ought not to be, a question of building Western weapons to 'counter' the SS-20. NATO's needs should shape NATO forces, not a feeling that the West should match the Soviet Union weapon for weapon. It is the credibility of Western deterrence and the role of nuclear weapons in Europe that are at issue, matters of concern to Europe and America alike.

NATO's concerns at the level of continental weapons must be seen in the light of the requirements of deterrence at other levels. For the United States to do something about the vulnerability of her *Minuteman* ICBM force is probably as important, in both military assessment and European perception, as deploying new NATO missiles capable of striking the Soviet Union. By the same token, the Soviet modernization effort also comprises shorter-range TNF, many of which could perform the same missions against the West as the SS-20. As suggested earlier, too much preoccupation with continental-range systems now will lead to excessive concern with shorter-range systems in the future once the implications of their modernization are 'discovered'.

For all these reasons, the NATO decision to deploy continental cruise and *Pershing* II ballistic missiles in Europe is more a beginning than an end. Even with other improvements in NATO, and American, nuclear forces, America and NATO will not acquire a nuclear superiority that is psychologically reassuring, let alone militarily significant.

The history of nuclear weapons in Europe emphasizes that there cannot be a military solution to the dilemma. There were European doubts over the reliability of America's nuclear deterrent even in the 1950s at a time of undisputed US strategic superiority over the Soviet Union, and there would be those doubts even if the United States were prepared to match the Soviet SS-20 and *Backfire* system for system in Europe. Nuclear weapons and nuclear decisions serve in part as political symbols for the Alliance; they cannot by themselves provide the substance of cohesion. It is clearly important for NATO to arrange its nuclear forces in a way that makes military sense, and much

remains to be done in this respect. But to pretend that any of these measures will provide a solution is to misunderstand the problem: America's support for Western European security is rooted in political cohesion more than in military arrangements. General de Gaulle was correct in saying (although he was careful not to put it that way) that America's security commitment to Europe depends in the first instance not on military integration but on continuing political interest.

Nuclear issues will, therefore, tend to be most prominent in the Alliance when confidence in political cohesion is weakest, and they will be most sensitive for that country which must fear most for its security from a decline of the American involvement – the Federal Republic. All nuclear disputes in the thirty years of Alliance history, from the MLF to the neutron bomb and TNF, have also been disputes about the specific role of West Germany in the Alliance and about German–American relations.

A German Problem

The 'German problem' is bound up with the fact that NATO and Europe's major power and the nation most exposed geographically is a non-nuclear-weapons state. The Federal Republic touched off the recent round of discussions over the continental nuclear threat to the West. At his Alastair Buchan Memorial Lecture in London in October 1977, Chancellor Helmut Schmidt called explicitly for a recognition of the need for parity at all levels – strategic nuclear, theatre nuclear, and conventional.[39] Herr Schmidt urged that the United States and the Soviet Union negotiate over long-range theatre nuclear systems in SALT III when he met Mr Brezhnev in Bonn in May 1978 and he pressed the point on President Carter again at the Guadeloupe Summit in January 1979. Throughout discussions of SALT II within the Alliance, West Germany was the ally most sceptical about US assurances on non-circumvention provisions, most concerned about cruise missile restrictions, and most eager that the US commit herself, in the SALT III principles section of SALT II, to some negotiation of 'grey area' weapons in SALT III.

This unusual nuclear persistence by West Germany was due, at least in part, to the

59

strained relations between Bonn and Washington. There were serious differences over central issues in the Carter Administration's foreign policy, from nuclear proliferation to the role of human rights in East–West relations. The resulting sense of uneasiness surfaced in the nuclear issue, as it did in exaggerated reactions to reports from Washington over Presidential Review Memorandum 10 in 1977, which suggested the possibility that NATO forces might in the event of war have to fall back across West German territory to regroup for defence.

Moreover, Carter's policy in the instance of the neutron bomb, and to a slightly lesser degree on continental TNF, forced the West European governments to share responsibility in the decision to produce nuclear weapons, not just the subsequent decision to deploy them. That was a departure from past practice which seemed logical on the American side since these weapons were after all to be used in Europe, yet it could not but raise concern in the over-sensitive German perspective: would not greater German involvement in the nuclear decision-making of the Alliance lead to less American involvement in the security of Germany?

The issue of continental nuclear weapons will continue to be sensitive in Germany. It evokes the rawest nerves in the Federal Republic's relations with both West and East, for it concerns both the credibility of the American nuclear guarantee and the state of detente with the Soviet Union and Eastern Europe. It is a barometer of relations in both directions, and is thus bound to provoke division within Germany. That was obvious in the early stages of the debate that took place during 1979 when it became clear that NATO might deploy new continental weapons. On the one hand, the Christliche Soziale Union/Christliche Demokratische Union opposition taunted the Chancellor over his lack of nerve in the neutron bomb episode and argued that NATO should deploy new continental weapons. On the other, the governing Sozialistische Partei Deutschlands was divided within itself, with its left (for want of a better term) emphasizing the dangers to detente of new weapons and arguing that negotiations should be tried first. In that context it was for a long time easier for Bonn to say what it would not do than what it would: it would not agree to have NATO deploy new continental weapons in Germany alone.

For Germany, as for the other NATO states, the needs of domestic politics sometimes interfere with sensible management of nuclear issues among the Allies. Part of Chancellor Schmidt's successful handling of the TNF issues in internal politics in late 1979 was due to Bonn's stated refusal to be the only European state to deploy new continental weapons: Germany would not be alone. This came to be known as the 'non-singularity' principle. Yet within the Alliance that ran two risks – of creating just the impression of German-American bilateralism that it was intended to prevent, and of putting too much pressure on particular small European NATO members. NATO was spared the former in part by the eager involvement of Britain's new Conservative government and the latter by the surprising willingness of Italy to accept new weapons. Yet the continuing problems encountered in Belgium and the Netherlands over the NATO programme cannot be divorced from the way the issue was handled.

Similarly, it is tempting for European politicians, particularly Herr Schmidt, to say that negotiations with the USSR might reduce the need for new NATO deployments of continental weapons, or altogether remove it. This became known as the 'zero option'. Yet to leave that impression goes against military logic, and is at best unrealistic. It runs the risk that public support for deployment will be undercut by Soviet negotiating offers. During the early stages of the 1980 German election campaign, Schmidt made several statements which looked, to Washington at least, like proposals for a freeze on new continental deployments. That was just the notion NATO had resisted before December 1979, and a sharp German-American row ensued.

The Federal Republic will continue to play a greater role in nuclear matters but shrink from taking too obvious a lead. For the Government, inbred caution was reinforced by the neutron bomb affair. Chancellor Schmidt no doubt felt he had been lured into more explicit support for neutron bomb deployment than he felt comfortable with only to have President Carter pull the rug from beneath him at the eleventh hour.[40] Bonn will continue to look to its European partners to give any new deployments a NATO-wide flavour, and so make Germany a smaller target for Soviet anger, and will continue to stress the importance of negotiations.

Thus, the particular conditions of German security contribute to the general political problem which is to sustain the credibility of America's nuclear-based security commitment to Europe when the Soviet Union is the equal of the United States. Yet while in the past West Germany was less representative of European attitudes as a whole, this appears to be changing. Nuclear issues have acquired a new sensitivity in most of the smaller European NATO countries, and even in Britain they are becoming unexpectedly controversial again. What distinguishes the Federal Republic in these developments is not just the controversy but the simultaneous sharpness of the security concern: nuclear weapons are both necessary and undesirable for most European countries but Germany is as aware as Britain or France, if not more than either, of the necessity.

Politics and Process

If the problem is essentially political, two major consequences follow. The first is that it can never be solved once and for all since political dynamics and political perceptions cannot be frozen. To deal with the problem does not mean solving it but making it politically manageable. That requires a constant effort on both sides of the Atlantic, along with a recognition that the precondition for its success is political cohesion and political trust.

Second, nuclear issues must be handled with care. The continental TNF case is so far a success, but hard won and fragile as it is, that success could turn to failure later. It became a test of Alliance will, with the neutron bomb fiasco hanging over the deliberations: military analysis was far less important than the realization by NATO leaders that they could not afford to flinch twice. In large measure, the United States herself created the SS-20 problem in Europe. SALT underscored the SS-20 and *Backfire* by excluding them while including – albeit in the Protocol – continental-range ground and sea-launched cruise missiles. Europeans outside defence establishments care

much less what the nuclear balance is than that Americans are tolerably comfortable with it, so the American debate about the state of the US deterrent was bound to be replayed in Europe, and to find particular expression in concern over continental weapons.

Once official discussions began in NATO, the United States was ambivalent about the merits of the issues. In the Spring of 1978, the Defense Department was prepared to embrace the NATO consensus in favour of deploying some new continental systems based in Europe. However the American Government backed away from that consensus and attempted to remain neutral, to the distress of some Allies. The United States' initial reaction was dominated by two concerns: a desire that the continental issue should not further complicate SALT II, and a strong sense that the Alliance was not ready to reach decisions on issues that touch the centre of NATO nuclear doctrine and practice.

The natural inclination to respond to allied concerns thus mixed with a temptation to wish the whole issue away, perhaps by arguing that after all nothing had really changed in the Soviet threat to Western Europe. Amidst official open-mindedness, bureaucratic momentum developed in Washington, and various parts of the Government said different things to Europe. At the same time as the American State Department attempted to dampen enthusiasm over cruise missiles and so reassure Europe about the SALT II protocol, Pentagon officials were singing the virtues of cruise missiles to their European colleagues. By 1979 the official United States view moved toward accepting the apparent NATO consensus of the previous Spring, as much as a sign of its seriousness in addressing allied concerns as an indication of clear preference.

The ingrained habit of looking for an American lead prevented European governments from taking the initiative themselves, apart from insisting on the need for arms control. If, in future, nuclear matters in the Alliance are to be decided in a way that strains political relations less, both the United States and West European governments will have to find more satisfactory procedures to cope with them. This is all the more so in the light of the emerging issues. In the United States, continuing concern over ICBM vulnerability could lead to increasing doubts over the feasibility of extending deterrence to Europe and scepticism over a NATO doctrine which implies a first use of nuclear weapons in a European war. That in turn would again raise European doubts over the credibility of the American commitment.[41]

At the same time, Soviet concern over NATO's modernization programme and the possibility that the Soviet Union may respond to new American strategic developments by a return to the 'hostage Europe' strategy of the late 1970's will increase Soviet pressure on the European consensus, through threats and through arms control initiatives. If the Alliance can learn from the experience of the past years, it has a chance of meeting these challenges with confidence; if not, then the prospects for the successful management of nuclear issues and of the political questions they imply for the Alliance are bleak.

Nuclear Consultation

Concepts of the TNF issue have been shaped by the ways it has been handled. Inter-allied discussion of the 'grey area' issue began with European interest in 1977 in a weapons system – the cruise missile – and was responded to by the United States in the first instance in an arms control context, SALT II. The issue then became part of the Long-Term Defence Programme and was taken up in a force planning context by the so-called High Level Group (HLG) of the NATO Nuclear Planning Group (NPG). During 1978 there was periodic interest within NATO in analysis of arms control possibilities, but with scant result. Then, in the late Spring of 1979 NATO formed a foreign office counterpart to the defence ministry HLG – the Special Group, so-called – to look systematically at arms control and political considerations.

At the same time, inter-allied consultations on SALT continued, both within NATO and in bilateral contacts between European NATO members and the United States. Those consultations were meticulous in detail and supplemented by so-called 'reinforced' meetings of the North Atlantic Council (NAC) with experts from capitals present.

Yet it is far from clear that this range of procedures was adequate. Many Europeans,

for instance, remain disturbed by the sequence of events in 1977 which led to the firm inclusion of cruise missiles in SALT II. Nor will existing practices meet the needs of the years ahead. The HLG engaged in a full discussion of both the technical and political implications of various new continental systems for deployment in Europe. However, force planning in the HLG first lagged behind then ran well ahead of arms-control thinking. By 1979 there was the impression, most telling in the Federal Republic, that NATO was on the verge of deploying new weapons in Europe capable of striking the Soviet Union with little evidence of having analyzed the arms-control prospects or the impact of the new Western weapons on East–West relations.

In the case of TNF modernization, the careful HLG review played an important role in building support for new deployments. More generally, while the central purpose of the NPG has been political rather than military – reassuring by informing – it did at least compel Americans and Europeans alike to think about nuclear strategy in Europe. The low-level study processes in NATO during the early and mid-1970s also appear to have made some progress in framing TNF doctrine.

Yet in other cases the limitations of existing structures have been more apparent. The neutron bomb, for example, proceeded happily through the Alliance at the technical level, buried within the NPG and so within defence ministries. Neither the NPG nor any other Alliance instrument served as the place where a warning of the possible political impact was sounded, early, and pressed on political leaders of allied governments. By the time the issue emerged from the NPG for decision, opportunities to shape the domestic politics surrounding it had been lost. However compelling the NPG's technical analysis, it counted for little.

The reasons why the NPG seems unlikely to play a political role are not hard to find. First, it is not a body where decisions can be taken. Second, it is, as noted above, a defence ministry operation. Its ministerial participants may share with their bureaucracies an interest in not raising warning signals that would derail new weapons proceeding through national budgetary politics. Lastly, the NPG's emphasis on security, appropriate enough, has limited the range of officials in any government who know about the issues that come before it, with the inevitable result that political evaluation comes either too late or not at all.

On the arms-control side, however meticulous American consultation with Europe during SALT II, those consultations still amounted to Washington stating its intentions and giving Europe a chance to object. When European interests come to be even more directly affected by a future SALT or by TNF discussion outside SALT, 'old' consulting practices will not suffice, however well executed. TNF negotiations offer the Soviet Union abundant opportunities to try to divide Europe from America by targeting their proposals where the interests of the two seem to diverge.

New forms of prior consultation will be required even for limited negotiations about continental weapons. If a TNF negotiation, in SALT or elsewhere, is to touch Europe's interest directly, must the Europeans participate at the negotiating table? If Europe is not at the table, the argument runs, it will always depend on American assessments of the tactical situation, and tactics may matter a great deal (as, for instance, in deciding when to suggest to the Soviet Union a compromise on non-circumvention during SALT II). At some stage direct European participation will probably be necessary, and an American government should surely not oppose it. Yet Europe will not want to take part soon, preferring negotiations to be limited to US and Soviet systems.

However, in any case some issues – such as what limits to accept or propose on cruise missiles, both nuclear and conventional – will require NATO decisions, with American negotiators constrained by the outcome. MBFR provides a model to avoid, since, given the importance of the issues, it would only add layers to decisions taken elsewhere. In 1980 the United States resisted European pressure, perhaps largely *pro forma,* to adopt a consensus procedure on the model of MBFR for TNF negotiations. NATO's decision to convert the Special Group into the Special Consultative Group, a standing body composed of senior representatives from capitals, makes more sense. Operating on the basis of American leadership, it should serve both to keep experts

from capitals close to any SALT negotiations and to lay the basis for Alliance-wide decisions on TNF issues that affect NATO. Those decisions would be taken, as they are now, in capitals at the appropriate level, with the North Atlantic Council ratifying them if need be.

The pre-1966 NATO Standing Group in Washington, is another model, though one that would smack of *directoire* to NATO's smaller members. The Standing Group was the executive agent of the Military Committee and consisted of representatives of the military chiefs of staff of the US, Britain and France. After 1964 it had an international planning staff, by custom with a German director. But in spite of the anticipated sensitivity of the smaller countries, some kind of special nuclear consultation group that is closer to the American decision-making process than the Special Consultative Group may be in order; it would only be a recognition of the fact that the smaller states prefer to leave these issues to their larger partners anyway.

There is also a need to improve NATO's procedures for making choices about nuclear weapons procurement, and for ensuring that force planning and arms control stay together. At a minimum, the NPG – itself the product of the last period of great strain in NATO nuclear arrangements, the MLF episode of the 1960s – needs to be broadened and opened more to foreign policy considerations.[42] Since crucial nuclear decisions will inevitably be made by Heads of Government, there might be a case for infrequent summit meetings of NPG members, perhaps in tandem with NATO summits.

However, the problem is less one of ensuring that attention is paid to nuclear issues at the top of government than of getting that attention at the right time and in the right form. In the case of the neutron bomb, attention at the highest levels came too late. In the instance of continental weapons, high-level attention – in this case Chancellor Schmidt's speech at the IISS – came too early, before staff work began to pose the issue coherently.

NATO already has more institutional baggage than it can use, but there may still be a case for new nuclear machinery – for example, a nuclear planning body directly under the NAC, meeting occasionally in ministerial session with both foreign and defence ministers present, and with more joint staffing. That might be complemented by an independent NATO assessments staff, perhaps attached to the Secretary General. That staff need not have a mandate restricted to nuclear matters. It would be designed to make European NATO members less dependent on US assessment, especially in an area like nuclear matters where European national capabilities are particularly weak – though they will still remain dependent. (For instance, the 1977 US paper for NATO on cruise missiles was regarded among European defence establishments as more a brief for SALT II than a full analysis of cruise missiles).

This range of suggestions for better processes of nuclear consultation and joint decision-making can be extended; it is listed here not as an organizational blueprint but rather to suggest the possibilities that the Alliance has at its disposal.

Conclusion

The political caveat must be reiterated here as in the earlier discussion: even if the Alliance developed and made use of more appropriate procedures, the underlying problem will not disappear as long as Europe remains dependent on the American deterrent. All that can be done is to manage the ambiguity. Some ambiguity is inevitable, and necessary, for the sake of both America and Europe. If for the United States the security commitment to Europe meant the certain destruction of American cities in the event of war, that commitment would scarcely be given unreservedly; some ambiguity sustains American support for Europe's security. Conversely, if for Western Europe the agreement to link her security to American nuclear weapons were to mean the destruction of Europe, the search for alternatives to the NATO Alliance would be well under way; ambiguity allows for the integration of European and American concerns precisely because it avoids the artificial clarity of extremes.

To manage this ambiguity is, in the final analysis, a task of political will, confidence and skill, more than procuring specific weapons or achieving arms-control agreements. Ambiguity must continue to exist, but it cannot be merely camouflage for confusion. In an era of nuclear parity, ambiguity cannot be an excuse for evading hard military choices on the argument that somehow the Soviet Union will be deterred if she is at least as uncertain about NATO's plans as the Alliance itself. The Alliance has to show it is serious, in both the conventional and the nuclear realm. It has to seek answers to the nuclear ambiguity in the full recognition that there can be no definitive solutions. It must remain credible to an opponent and satisfying to all members of the Alliance. This is a formidable task, but for the Western Alliance nations it should not seem daunting as they have coped relatively well in the past. If they learn the right lessons, they should also be successful in the future.

NOTES

[1] The terminology can be confusing. By 'continental' nuclear weapons is meant those based in the Soviet Union capable of striking Western Europe – but not the United States – and vice versa. That includes weapons classified by the IISS as both 'medium' range (500–1,000 miles) and 'intermediate' range (1,000–4,000 miles). 'Medium' range is often used loosely to refer to both medium and intermediate range weapons, and this is occasionally done here, but only as shorthand because that term does not fully evoke the nature of the threat.

[2] The MLF was to be a fleet of NATO surface ships, manned by sailors of different nations, carrying medium-range nuclear weapons whose firing would have been controlled by the United States. It was pushed by the United States in the early 1960s before being killed by President Johnson.

[3] For discussion of SALT and for a reprint of the Treaty itself, see Survival, September/October 1979. For detailed discussion of the Treaty's provisions and their effects, see Jan M. Lodal, 'SALT II and American Security', in Foreign Affairs, Winter 1978/79.

[4] A number of studies have estimated the American deaths caused by a Soviet attack on ICBM. They range from 2 to 20 million immediate deaths, and from about 5 to 40 million dead including longer-term effects. US Congress, Office of Technology Assessment, The Effects of Nuclear War (Washington, 1979), pp. 83-84. In his 1980 Defence Report, Secretary of Defense Harold Brown said 'I myself continue to doubt that a Soviet attack on our strategic forces whose collateral damage involved "only" a few million American deaths could appropriately be responded to without including some urban–industrial targets in the response'. Department of Defense Annual Report, Fiscal Year 1980 (Washington, 1979), p. 75.

[5] The SALT II limits on MIRVed launchers are the following:

1,320 for missiles and for bombers carrying air-launched cruise missiles (ALCM); 1,200 for missiles, both SLBM and land-based ICBM; and, most important, 820 for land-based ICBM. MIRVS per missile are limited at their current numbers for existing missiles, and at 10 and 14 for new ICBM and SLBM, respectively. For an outline and assessment of the calculations of Soviet threat on which the MX is based, see Desmond Ball, 'The MX Basing Decision', *Survival*, March/April 1980

6 For a discussion of China's nuclear forces and their possible impact on Soviet–American deterrence, see my 'China's Nuclear Forces and the Stability of Soviet–American Deterrence', in *The Future of Strategic Deterrence. Part I*, Adelphi Paper No. 160, London: IISS, 1980.

7 For a detailed discussion of British choices with respect to a *Polaris* successor, see Peter Nailor and Jonathan Alford, *The Future of Britain's Deterrent Force*, Adelphi Paper No. 156, London: IISS, 1980.

8 The now classic discussion is Albert Wohlstetter, 'The Delicate Balance of Terror', *Foreign Affairs*, January 1959. For a strong argument that NATO's planning about nuclear weapons in Europe during the 1950s and 1960s was incoherent and its policies unwise, see Uwe Nerlich, 'Theater Nuclear Forces in Europe: Is NATO Running Out of Options?' *The Washington Quarterly*, III, 1 Winter 1980.

9 These and other figures in this and the next paragraphs are from *The Military Balance 1980–1981*, (London: IISS, 1980).

10 President Eisenhower proposed earmarking American *Polaris* submarines to NATO in December 1960, and the proposal was put into practice in 1963 when three submarines were assigned to NATO for planning purposes. For background, see Robert Hunter, *Security in Europe* (Bloomington, Indiana: University of Indiana Press, 1972), pp. 105-106. Of course with these, as with other US nuclear systems assigned to NATO, the assignment is transparent, since SACEUR could not fire them for NATO purposes without the authorization of the American President.

11 The American Single Integrated Operational Plan (SIOP) divides Soviet nuclear targets into four categories: opposing nuclear forces and other 'hard targets'; economic and recovery targets; political control mechanisms; and other military targets (OMT). OMT is the largest of the four categories, some 20,000 comprising half the SIOP targets. See Desmond Ball, 'Soviet ICBM Deployment', *Survival*, Vol. XXII, No. 4, July/August 1980, pp. 167-170. On the uses of submarine-launched missiles against OMT, see Desmond J. Ball, 'The Counterforce Potential of American SLBM Systems', *Journal of Peace Research*, 1, 1977, pp. 23-40.

12 The debate over Soviet doctrine, or even whether there is one in our terms, is a lively one. For recent contributions, see Robert Legvold, 'Strategic Doctrine and SALT: Soviet and American Views', *Survival*, Vol. XXI, No. 1, January/February 1979, pp. 8-13; Raymond Garthoff, 'Mutual Deterrence and Strategic Arms Limitation in Soviet Policy', *International Security*, Vol. III, No. 1 (Summer 1978), pp. 112-147; and Fritz W. Ermarth, 'Contrasts in American and Soviet Strategic Thought', *International Security*, Vol. III, No. 2, Autumn 1978, pp. 138-155.

13 For analyses along that line, see Joseph D. Douglass, Jr.,

and Amoretta M. Hoeber, 'The Nuclear Warfighting Dimension of the Soviet Threat to Europe', *The Journal of Social and Political Studies*, Vol. III, No. 2, 1978, pp. 107-146; and Joseph D. Douglass, Jr. 'Soviet Nuclear Strategy in Europe: A Selective Targeting Doctrine', *Strategic Review*, Autumn 1977, pp. 19-32. Occasionally, however, the logic seems almost tautological, assuming Soviet intentions and then inferring what *must* be the capabilities of Soviet weaponry. For example, the emphasis on accuracy and the options it could – and by implication, will – give the Soviet Union is pronounced in the writing of Pierre M. Gallois. See his 'The Future of France's Force de Disuasion', *Strategic Review*, Vol. VII, No. 3, Summer 1979, pp. 34-39.

14 See Paul Bracken, 'Collateral Damage and Theater Warfare', *Survival*, Vol. XXII, No. 5, September/October 1980, pp. 203-207.

15 President Brezhnev's speech is excerpted in *Survival*, Vol. XXII, No. 1, January/February 1980, pp. 28-30.

16 See, for instance, the article in *Pravda* by Soviet Defence Minister Dmitriy Ustinov, 25 October 1979.

17 McGeorge Bundy's comments on the incalculability of the nuclear war and the effect of that realization on political leaders are to the point. See his paper to the IISS Conference in September 1979, reprinted in *Survival*, Vol. XXI, No. 6, November/December 1979, pp. 268-272.

18 Alton Frye, 'Nuclear Weapons in Europe: No Exit from Ambivalence', *Survival*, Vol. XXII, No. 3, May/June 1980, pp. 98-106.

19 For parallel discussions, both of them more sanguine about the possibility of reaching rough agreement on TNF doctrine, see J. J. Martin, 'Nuclear Weapons in NATO's Deterrent Strategy', *Orbis*, Vol. XXII, No. 4, Winter 1979; and Michael Higgins and Christopher Makins, 'European Theater Nuclear Forces and "Gray Area" Arms Control', Paper presented to the Sixth Annual National Security Affairs Conference, National Defense University, Washington, pp. 23-25, July 1979. See also A. Philip Hughes, 'Cutting the Gordian Knot: A Theater-Nuclear Force for Deterrence in Europe', *Orbis*, Vol. XXII, No. 2, Summer 1978, pp. 309–332.

20 W. S. Bennett, R. R. Sandoval and R. G. Shreffler have done the most work on such proposals. See their 'A Credible Nuclear-Emphasis Defense for NATO', *Orbis*, Vol. XVII, No. 2, Summer 1973.

21 These estimates are from Anthony Cordesman, *The Evolution of US Strategic Capabilities and the Validity of Extended Deterrence*, Adelphi Paper forthcoming.

22 Jeffrey Record, 'Theatre Nuclear Weapons: Begging the Soviet Union to Pre-empt', *Survival*, Vol. XIX, No. 5, September/October 1977, pp. 208-211.

23 As John Steinbruner put it '... regardless of the flexibility embodied in individual force components, the precariousness of command channels probably means that nuclear war would be uncontrollable, as a practical matter, shortly after the first tens of weapons are launched – regardless of what calculations political leaders might make at the time'. 'National Security and the Concept of Strategic Stability', *Journal of Conflict Resolution*, Vol. XXII, No. 3, September 1978, p. 421. For a careful argument pointing in the same direction, see Desmond Ball, *Control and Nuclear War*, Adelphi Paper forthcoming.

24 The most comprehensive assessment of the conventional

65

balance is that by Robert Lucas Fischer, *Defending the Central Front: The Balance of Forces*, Adelphi Paper No. 127, (London: IISS, 1976). His analysis is still apt, and numbers have not changed enough to alter his basic conclusions.

[25] For a debate on the implications of precision-guided munitions, see John J. Mearsheimer, 'Precision-guided munitions and Conventional Deterrence'; and Daniel Gouré and Gordon McCormick, 'PGM: No Panacea', both in *Survival*, Vol. XXI, No. 1, January/February 1980, pp. 15-19, respectively.

[26] NATO Communiqué, M2 (79) 22, 12 December 1979.

[27] See Note 15.

[28] See, for example, Foreign Minister Gromyko's statement of 18 February 1980, reproduced by Tass. An excerpt is printed in *Survival*, Vol. XXII, No. 2, March/April 1980.

[29] At his press conference on 25 July 1979, Foreign Minister Gromyko seemed clearly to foreshadow such a Soviet position: 'Success [in SALT III] is possible only when the talks cover the question of the American forward-based facilities, i.e. both US military bases, of which there are enough, both in Europe and outside Europe, and which are known to be trained in the military-strategic respect on the Soviet Union'.

[30] *Pravda*, 15 July 1980.

[31] Brezhnev's report is excerpted in *Survival*, Vol. XXIII, No. 3, May/June 1981.

[32] This would in effect continue the current situation with respect to SALT II. Both sides would agree to abide by those provisions, whose breach would be irrevocable under the terms of the treaty itself. For instance, SALT II permits a maximum of ten warheads for the Soviet SS-18. By the treaty's counting rules, every missile is presumed to carry the maximum number of warheads with which *any* missile of that type *ever* has been tested. Thus a single test of an SS-18 with eleven warheads would be an irrevocable violation of SALT II. By contrast, no-one expects the Soviet Union actually to dismantle the systems as required under SALT II before the treaty is ratified, and that dismantling could in any case be done later.

[33] See, for example, Alton Frye's proposal in 'How to Save SALT', *Foreign Policy*, No. 39, Summer 1980.

[34] See, for example, the discussion by Richard Burt in Christoph Bertram, ed., *The Future of Arms Control, Part I: Beyond SALT II*, Adelphi Paper No. 141, (London: IISS, 1977), p. 11 ff.

[35] This idea had been suggested earlier by some German and British analysts. For an interesting proposal along those lines, see Lawrence Freedman, 'The Dilemma of Theatre Nuclear Arms Control, *Survival*, Vol. XXIII, No. 1, January/February 1981, pp. 2-10.

[36] Higgins and Makins make an argument for a comprehensive TNF negotiation, perhaps multilateral, *op. cit.* in note 19, p. 28 ff. Former British Foreign Secretary David Owen suggested that Europeans, including the Federal Republic, should be included in future SALT negotiations. See *Survival*, Vol. XXII, No. 3, May/June 1980, pp. 120-124.

[37] This discussion owes much to Freedman, cited above.

[38] Derived from *The Military Balance 1980-1981* (London: IISS, 1980), pp. 118-119.

[39] His speech is printed in *Survival*, Vol. XX, No. 1, January/February 1978, pp. 2-10. At one point, he said: 'SALT neutralizes . . . strategic nuclear capabilities. In Europe this magnifies the significance of the disparities between East and West in nuclear tactical and conventional weapons'.

[40] For a description of the neutron bomb affair, see Alex A. Vardamis, 'German-American Military Fissures', *Foreign Policy*, No. 34, Spring 1979, 87-106. For discussion of the alliance politics of the issue, see Lothar Ruehl, 'Die Nichtentscheidung über die "Neutronenwaffe" ', *Europa Archiv*, No. 5, 1979, pp. 137-150.

[41] See, for example, William Kaufmann, 'Defense Policy', in Joseph A. Pechman, ed., *Setting National Priorities: Agenda for the 1980s*, (Washington: The Brookings Institution, 1980).

[42] For general description of the NPG and its functioning, see Richard E. Shearer, 'Consulting in NATO on Nuclear Policy,' *NATO Review*, No. 5, October 1979, pp. 25-28.

Table 1a: American and Soviet Strategic Forces: 1979 and 1985

System & Type	No. of Warheads	No. of Launchers 1979	1985[a]	System & Type	No. of Warheads	No. of Launchers 1985[a]
Inter-continental Ballistic Missiles						
United States				**Soviet Union**		
Titan II	1	54	54	SS-9	1	120	–
Minuteman II	1	450	450	SS-11	1	215	–
Minuteman II	3 MIRV	550	536	SS-11	3 MRV	455	60
				SS-17	4 MIRV	140	200
				SS-18	10 MIRV	188	308
				SS-19	6 MIRV	280	312
				New Missile	1	–	300

System & Type	No. of Warheads	No. of Launchers 1979	1985[a]	System & Type	No. of Warheads	No. of Launchers 1979	1985[a]
Inter-continental Ballistic Missiles							
United States				**Soviet Union**			
Titan II	1	54	54	SS-9	1	120	–
Minuteman II	1	450	450	SS-11	1	215	–
Minuteman II	3 MIRV	550	536	SS-11	3 MRV	455	60
				SS-17	4 MIRV	140	200
				SS-18	10 MIRV	188	308
				SS-19	6 MIRV	280	312
				New Missile	1	–	300
Submarine Launched Ballistic Missiles							
United States				**Soviet Union**			
Polaris A-3	3 MRV	160	80	SS-N-6	1	254	–
Poseidon C-3	9 MIRV– (average)	352	336	SS-N-6	3 MRV	272	352
				SS-N-8	1	268	268
Poseidon C-4	8 MIRV	144	160	SS-NX-17	1	12	–
Trident C-4	7 MIRV	–	168	SS-N-18	3 MIRV	144	–
				SS-N-18	7 MIRV	–	176
				New Missile	14 MIRV	–	180
Long-range Bombers							
United States				**Soviet Union**			
B-52 (bombs and SRAM*)		340	225	Bear		113	30
B-52 (ALCM†)		–	120	Bison		43	–
FB-111		66	66	New Bomber		–	60

[a] These figures assume SALT II limits are in force.
* SRAM: short-range attack missile
† ALCM: air-launched cruise missile

Table 1b:Illustrative Totals

	1979		1985 with SALT II		1985 without SALT II	
	US	USSR	US	USSR	US	USSR
Delivery Vehicles	2,116	2,504	2,214–2,223	2,250	2,298–2,842	2,650–3,000
Total Weapons[b] (RVs & bomber weapons)	9,200	5,000	11,500–12,000	10,000–12,000	12,000–13,000	14,000–17,500
Throw-weight[b] (million lbs.)	7.2	11.3	8.5–8.6	14.4–15.0	10.0–13.1	16.6–17.5

[b] Operational systems only.

SOURCES: This and the following tables are derived from information on the public record, especially *The Military Balance 1979–1980*; American government estimates in 'Illustrative US and Soviet Strategic Forces Through 1985', released in July 1979; data presented by Paul Nitze to the American Senate, *The SALT II Treaty*, Hearings before the Committee on Foreign Relations, 96 Cong., 1 sess., 1979, Part 1, pp. 452–75; and Robert Metzger and Paul Doty, 'Arms Control Enters the Gray Area', *International Security*, Winter 1978/1979, pp. 17–52.

Table 2: American and Soviet Theatre Nuclear Systems, 1979 & 1985

System & date first deployed	Number of Launchers 1979	Number of Launchers 1985	Range[a] (miles)	Warheads	Yield	CEP (nm)
Ranges over 1,000 miles						
Missiles						
United States						
Poseidon C-3 (1971)						
SLBM	48	48	2,500	9 (avg)	50KT	0.25
Pershing IIXR MRBM	–	108	1,000	1	100–200KT	0.02
Ground–launched cruise missile	–	464	1,500	1	1–500KT	0.01
Soviet Union						
SS-20 (1977) IRBM	120	300	3–4,000	3	150KT	0.05?
SS-5 (1961) IRBM			2,100	1	1MT	1.5
SS-4 (1959) MRBM	450	100?	1,200	1	1MT	1.0
SS-N-8 (1972) SLBM	6	–	4,800	1	1–2MT	0.8
Aircraft						
United States						
F-111 E/F (1967)	156	156	2,925	2		
Soviet Union						
Tu-22M *Backfire* (1974)	60[b]	200	3,000	5		
Tu-16 *Badger* (1955)	300[b]	300	1,650	4		
Tu-22 *Blinder* (1962)	135	135	1,750	2		

Table 2 continued

System & date first deployed	Number of Launchers 1979	1985	Range[a] (miles)	Warheads	Yield	CEP (nm)
Ranges 100–1,000 miles						
Missiles						
United States						
Pershing 1A (1962) SRBM	108	–	450	1	60–400 KT	0.2
Soviet Union						
SS-22 SRBM	?	150?	500?	1	KT range	–
SS-12 (1969) SRBM		150?	500	1	MT range	–
SS-1C *Scud* B (1965)	400?					
SRBM			185	1	KT range	–
SS-X-23 SRBM	–	150?	200?	1?	KT range?	–
Aircraft[c]						
United States						
F-4[d]	250	250	700	3		..
A-6E	20	20	320	3		
A-7E	40	40	585	4		
Soviet Union						
Su-19 *Fencer* (1974)	230		400	2		
Su-17 *Fitter* C/D (1974)	640		325	2		
MiG-23/27 *Flogger*		3,500?				
B/D (1971)	1,400		500	1		
MiG-21 *Fishbed* (1970)	1,000		250	1		
Su-7 *Fitter* A (1959)	220		275	1		
Ranges under 100 miles						
United States						
Lance (1972) SRBM	36	36	70	1	1–100 KT	
M-110 203mm artillery (1962)	215	215	13	1	KT range	
M-109 155mm artillery (1964)	300	300	11	1	2 KT	
plus Atomic Demolition Munitions (ADM)						
Soviet Union						
SS-21 (1978) SRBM			65	1	KT range	
SS-16 *Scud* A (1957)	900?	900?	50	1	KT range	
FROG 7 (1965) SRBM			10–45	1	KT range	
M-55 203mm artillery (1950s)	150?	150?	18	1	low KT	

[a] For aircraft, ranges given are estimates of combat radius given normal loads and mission profiles.
[b] Excludes Naval Air Force aircraft. Similarly, some nuclear systems, such as the AS-3, -4 and -6 cruise missiles, are excluded as devoted to naval, not land, missions.
[c] Numbers given are inventory figures for nuclear-capable aircraft, *not* numbers actually devoted to nuclear missions. As a rough assumption, something like one-third of US and one-fourth of Soviet strike aircraft would be available for nuclear roles.
[d] Aircraft based in Europe only.

Table 3: NATO and Warsaw Pact (excluding US) Soviet and Chinese Theatre Nuclear Forces, 1979, 1985

System, Type, Date First Deployed and Countries Equipped	Number of launchers		Range (miles)	Warheads	Yield	CEP (nm)
	1979	1985				
NATO						
Missiles						
SSBS S-2 (1971) IRBM						
France	18	18	1,875	1	150 KT	n.a.
Pershing IA (1962) SRBM						
FRG	72	72	450	1	60–400 KT	0.2
Polaris A-3 (1967) SLBM						
Britain	64	64	2,880	3(MRV)	200 KT	0.5
MSBS M-20 (1977) SLBM						
France	80	96?	3,000	1	1 MT	n.a.
Honest John (1953) SRBM						
FRG, Greece, Turkey	91	–?	25	1	KT range	n.a.
Pluton (1974) SRBM						
France	32	32?	75	1	15–25 KT	n.a.
M-110 203mm artillery (1962)						
Belgium, Britain, Denmark,						
FRG, Greece, Italy,						
Netherlands, Turkey[a]	n.a.	?	13	1	KT range	n.a.
M-109 155mm artillery (1964) –						
(Same countries as M-110						
plus Canada and Norway	n.a.	?	11	1	2 KT	n.a.
Aircraft						
Vulcan B2 (1960)						
Britain	48	–	2,000	2		
Buccaneer (1962)						
Britain	50	–	200	2		
Mirage IVA (1964)						
France	33	33	670	1		
F–4 (1962)						
FRG, Greece, Turkey	175	175	700	3		
F–104 (1958)						
Belgium, Canada,						
Denmark, FRG[a], Greece,						
Italy, Netherlands,						
Norway, Turkey	367	102?	650	1		
Tornado						
Britain, FRG, Italy	–	530	850	2?		
F-16						
Belgium, Denmark,						
Netherlands	–	250	575	1		
Mirage 2000 – France	–	48	930	1		
WARSAW PACT[b]						
Missiles						
SS-1b *Scud* A (1957) SRBM						
all	132	100?	50	1	KT range	
SS-1c *Scud* B (1965) SRBM						
all			185	1	KT range	

70

Table 3 continued

System, Type, Date First Deployed and Countries Equipped	Number of launchers 1979	Number of launchers 1985	Range (miles)	Warheads	Yield	CEP (nm)
FROG 3-7 (1957–65) SRBM						
all	206	150?	10–45	1	KT range	
SS-21 (1978) SRBM?	–	?	65	1	KT range	
SS-X-23 SRBM?	–	?	200?	1	KT range?	
Aircraft						
Su-7 *Fitter* A (1959)						
Poland, Czechoslovakia	115	?	275	1		
Su-20 *Fitter* C (1974)						
Poland	35	?	325	2		
MiG-23 *Flogger* B (1971)						
Poland	3	?	500	1		
CHINA						
Missiles						
CSS-3 ICBM	2	?	3,000–3,500	1	?	
ICBM tested	?	?	8,000	1	?	
CSS-2 IRBM	50–70	100?	1,500–1,750	1	1–3 MT	
CSS-1 MRBM	40–50	30?	600–700	1	1–3 MT	
Aircraft						
Tu-16 medium bomber	90	90?	1,650	2?		

[a] The artillery, like most of the strike aircraft, are dual-capable; few of them may in fact be allocated to nuclear missions, particularly in the case of the M-109. Any that are nuclear are dual-key, with nuclear warheads in the custody of the United States – except for Britain which has her own nuclear weapons. Denmark and Norway do not allow nuclear weapons on their soil in peacetime, and Canada does not have nuclear weapons with her forces.
[b] These are dual-capable systems, and few may be allocated to nuclear missions. Any that are nuclear have warheads in the custody of the Soviet Union.
[c] As for the US and Soviet aircraft, these are inventory figures: not all the dual-capable aircraft would have nuclear missions. As a rough estimate, all the *Vulcans*, half the *Buccaneers* and one-third of the strike aircraft might be assumed nuclear.

Table 4: Soviet–American FBS Balance 1980, under Alternative Definitions

Definition	No. of Launchers US	No. of Launchers USSR	No. of Warheads US	No. of Warheads USSR	Systems Included US	Systems Included USSR
A: Modern land-based continental missiles	0	160	0	480	–	SS-20
B: All ground and air systems over 1,800 km in range	156	1,118	312	2,106	F-111 E/F	A + SS-4, -5, *Backfire*, *Blinder, Badger*
C: All ground and air systems over 750 km in range	540	1,788	756	3,146	**B** + F-4, A-6, A-7	**B** + *Fencer, Scaleboard*

3 Deterrence in the 1980s: American Strategic Forces and Extended Deterrence

ANTHONY H. CORDESMAN

INTRODUCTION

There is nothing new in Europeans questioning the credibility of the American nuclear commitment to the defence of Europe, or the willingness of the United States to risk using her strategic forces to halt a successful Warsaw Pact attack on NATO. Both Europeans and Americans have publicly and privately questioned US resolve to defend Europe since the date when the first Soviet test of a thermonuclear weapon became public.

This questioning has naturally increased in intensity since the Soviet Union began to deploy large numbers of theatre nuclear weapons and intercontinental ballistic missiles (ICBM). Ironically, several European defence experts and commentators expressed strong doubts about US ability to extend deterrence during the year before the Cuban missile crisis. Although the resolution of that particular crisis eased European fears, it scarcely stilled all uncertainty and doubts.

The Multilateral Force (MLF) debate of the mid-1960s was largely a product of continued European questioning of extended deterrence. Although the MLF was never deployed, this was more the result of the vicissitudes of the politics of the day than of European confidence in the assignment of some US submarine-launched ballistic missiles (SLBM) to the Supreme Allied Commander Europe (SACEUR) and the creation of a NATO Nuclear Planning Group (NPG).

Similar European doubts were exposed during the debate over the *force de frappe* and French withdrawal from NATO's military command, during the British debate over the creation of Britain's *Polaris* force, in various German debates over changes in the basing of theatre nuclear weapons on German soil, and during many of the high-level NATO discussions that went into the planning of the

Military Committee document MC 14/3 and NATO's discussion of flexible response. Such fears delayed the conversion of NATO's dedicated nuclear strike aircraft to dual-capable or conventional missions by half a decade longer than was otherwise required.

During the last three years, however, the basis of European uncertainty about the US commitment to extended deterrence has changed fundamentally in character:

- First, it has become obvious that the USSR has achieved full parity with the US in her ability to achieve assured destruction against civil and economic targets;
- Second, it has gradually become clear that the USSR may acquire a temporary superiority in counterforce exchange in the early 1980s if she launches a first strike against US ICBM forces;
- Third, the Soviet Union is acquiring increasingly superior numbers of long-range SS-20 IRBM and *Backfire* medium bombers, and could be moving towards a credible first-strike capability to virtually disarm NATO's land and air forces in Europe;
- Fourth, data gradually becoming public on Soviet nuclear plans indicate that the Soviet military appears never to have accepted mutual assured destruction. Instead, it seems to have focused on developing a doctrine of war-fighting capability which is in part based on disarming nuclear first strikes which will, in effect, achieve a practical decoupling of US strategic forces from NATO;
- Finally, the quality of US leadership during the last few years, and such incidents as President Carter's handling of the 'neutron bomb' have raised serious doubts about US resolve.

Unhappily, many of the doubts raised about America's ability to extend deterrence to Europe are essentially political arguments based on theoretical descriptions of strategy and military capability that are divorced from the reality of the US forces now in being or in procurement. (For a full presentation of these arguments, see Henry A. Kissinger, 'NATO: The Next Thirty Years', and McGeorge Bundy, 'The Future of Strategic Deterrence' both in *Survival*, November/December 1979.) They may well lead Europe to seek the wrong kind of American assurances and American and NATO force improvements. This becomes clear when one looks at the criteria that American and NATO forces must meet to make extended deterrence effective in the 1980s and at how American capabilities for extended deterrence have evolved during the last twenty years.

I. THE CRITERIA FOR EXTENDED DETERRENCE

It is important to note in beginning this examination that there is no hard and fast definition of 'extended deterrence', nor any fixed method of evaluating US strategic forces, plans and doctrine, and saying whether they do or do not provide extended deterrence.

'Extended deterrence' is the result of *Soviet* perceptions of both US and NATO capabilities, and not the result of the relative total size of US and Soviet strategic forces. It is the result of the ability of US strategic forces to contribute to the deterrence of Soviet or Warsaw Pact aggression at the theatre level, to limit the intensity of such attacks, and to terminate them on terms favourable to the US and her Allies. To a lesser degree, it is the result of the ability of theatre forces to contribute to the deterrence of Soviet strategic attacks on the US by increasing the difficulties of launching successful attacks, and by increasing the risk of unacceptable retaliation by a combination of strategic and theatre forces.

In any given scenario, Soviet perceptions of extended deterrence will be largely determined by the mix of strategic nuclear, theatre nuclear, and conventional capabilities on each side as they apply to the particular scenario and objective involved. 'Extended deterrence' thus covers a necessarily broad and uncertain range of force characteristics, contingencies, and United States' national security objectives. It can be applied to virtually any military theatre in the world. For NATO, 'extended deterrence' covers those situations where the Soviet objective would be serious enough to make escalation to theatre nuclear war credible. In other parts of the world, it covers any situation where the objective is important enough for the United States to undertake the risk of using strategic forces.

In both cases, the common element will be that a limited use of US strategic forces could alter the outcome favourably for the West, and that the resulting risk of all-out strategic conflict would be proportionate to the value of the theatre objective being defended. This means that the degree of deterrence extended in any given contingency is shaped by an extremely complex mix of factors. However, it will always depend upon the Soviet perception that US strategic forces have the particular capabilities needed to intervene in a given conflict, and that the required level of force is one that the US has both the incentive and will to use.

This means that extended deterrence can function at very different levels of military capability. If the US has sufficient flexibility to use her strategic forces in limited theatre strikes without degrading her overall ability to attack Soviet countervalue targets, then extended deterrence can be credible, provided always that the US has convincingly demonstrated that she plans to employ her strategic forces, has the will to do so, and values the objective enough to take the risk. Conversely, even a weak US possessing inferior and relatively inflexible strategic forces, might provide a convincing degree of extended deterrence against a massive Soviet theatre nuclear first strike on NATO forces in Europe, simply because of the importance of the objective and the large-scale prior involvement of US theatre forces. Obviously, a vast range of contingencies exist between these extremes where the credibility of extended deterrence will depend entirely on the circumstances.

At the same time, extended deterrence does become steadily more convincing as theatre capabilities and nuclear forces are improved. The credibility of extended deterrence in Europe is not simply a function of US strategic capabilities but of NATO capabilities as well. This is particularly true as NATO theatre nuclear forces improve their range and capability and become more and more capable of attacking those Soviet and Warsaw Pact targets currently covered by US strategic forces. For example, NATO's plans to deploy land-based cruise missiles and *Pershing* II MRBM inevitably blur the distinction between US strategic and NATO theatre forces. This makes it more credible that any large-scale conflict in Europe which involves theatre nuclear weapons will escalate to a level where US strategic forces become involved and that limited uses of US strategic forces would be made to cover any gap in NATO forces, because of the limited levels of escalation involved.

No simple equation exists between the strategic balance and US ability to provide extended deterrence, nor is extended deterrence inevitably tied to the risk of all-out strategic conflict or its outcome. Its extent will be determined by whether the combination of US strategic and NATO (or other) theatre capabilities offers an overall range of military options that makes US willingness to use the required number of strategic forces credible to the USSR. Where both strategic and theatre forces are well suited to the defence of Europe, and where US forces are strong enough to limit any Soviet incentive to escalate to even broader levels of conflict, then the level of deterrence extended is likely to be high.

For similar reasons, there can be no simple definition of the particular US strategic forces or types of strike that may be employed in support of extended deterrence. Bombers, ICBM, SLBM and cruise missiles can all be employed with different degrees of flexibility. The particular mix of targets will be chosen to fit the situation and forces available. It might involve anything from demonstrative strikes on Warsaw Pact air bases in Eastern Europe to counter-city strikes to deter further Warsaw Pact nuclear attacks on urban areas in West Germany. It could involve a strategic strike on the major Other Military Targets (OMT) (i.e.

targets of military significance but excluding strategic weapons) facilities in the Western Military Districts of the USSR, or SSBN attacks on a Soviet fleet operating against Norway.

Finally, extended deterrence does not simply apply to the prevention of war. It also applies to limiting its scope and intensity, and to its termination. Extended deterrence can thus be measured according to a number of different operational standards. The most critical is how far US strategic and NATO theatre nuclear capabilities deter any form of war and eliminate any incentive for the USSR to expand her forces and improve her war-fighting capabilities. The second in priority is how far these capabilities deter large-scale confrontations or attacks. The third is how far the active employment of Western nuclear forces in war can terminate a conflict, once it has begun, on terms acceptable to NATO. For obvious reasons, the least important operational standard is the ability actually to inflict unacceptable levels of massive damage on the Soviet bloc once deterrence of war has failed.

Given this definition, it should be clear why it is difficult to establish firm criteria for measuring the degree of extended deterrence that any given balance of forces provides. Nevertheless, there are at least some criteria that US and NATO forces must meet, and others which, if not essential, are desirable.

Essential Criteria

US and NATO nuclear forces must meet four criteria to make extended deterrence credible to the USSR and to be effective in limited nuclear wars:

– The risk of escalation resulting from the use of US strategic forces, in addition to NATO theatre nuclear forces, must be limited enough to avoid the US running an unacceptable risk of mutual civil and economic annihilation with the USSR. The US cannot afford to rely on extended deterrence options which target Soviet cities and populations, or which expose her strategic forces to massive counterforce strikes. She must have limited nuclear options for her strategic forces which 'blend' into the escalation ladder created by NATO conventional and theatre nuclear forces, and which can pose an unacceptable risk of additional damage to Soviet and East European facilities and military forces without having to rely on a large-scale strategic exchange.

- The US must have sufficient survivable strategic forces so that even large-scale exchanges in defence of NATO will not lead to an unacceptable 'run down' of US strategic capabilities against the USSR, needed as the ultimate defence. There must be no incentive for a Soviet strike against the remaining US strategic forces.
- The US must have the flexibility of rapid targeting capability and ability to control collateral damage. She must have flexibility to tailor her attacks rapidly to the most significant targets in the specific scenario she faces, and to minimize the height of each step in escalation. The more flexible, rapid-reacting, accurate and limited the US options for response, the greater the credibility of use and conflict termination on an acceptable level.
- US determination to use any combination of strategic and theatre nuclear forces in the defence of Europe must be credible. Once US and NATO forces have met the previous criteria, the US must do everything in her power to convince the USSR that she will not accept a defeat in NATO, and that close links exist between the US strategic forces and the defence of Europe. This linkage is partially assured by the deployment of some 300,000 US forces in Europe and by the deployment in Europe of a substantial portion of the total US inventory of nuclear weapons. However, it is also determined by the explicitness and determination with which the US states her commitment to extended deterrence, by the ability of US strategic forces and war plans to execute limited strikes if deterrence fails, and by the extent to which NATO theatre nuclear weapons provide a smooth and survivable ladder of escalation which couples to the capabilities of US strategic forces.

These four criteria are necessarily somewhat vague in terms of the precise forces and plans required to meet them. Many different mixes of US and NATO nuclear capabilities are adequate to provide a substantial degree of extended deterrence, and there is room for a wide range of legitimate political and philosophical difference over how large and diverse a range of capabilities is required. This is one of the reasons why experts can so disagree regarding the adequacy of US forces to carry out extended deterrence, and it may be a reason why men who think in largely political terms tend to ignore the details of force changes.

Non-essential Criteria

This uncertainty as to the minimum criteria that US and NATO forces must meet has also led many to insist that *additional* force improvements must be provided, or that additional criteria must be met, if the West's nuclear forces are to be capable of extending deterrence. While many of the proposed force characteristics are unquestionably desirable, they are not essential to the success of extended deterrence. This has become clear in many analyses over the last fifteen years, and an understanding of the relative merits of such additional force capabilities is also important to an understanding of the evolution of US forces.

- In strictly military terms, the US does not require strategic superiority. The increase in US strategic warhead numbers to over 9,000, combined with the capabilities of US and Allied theatre nuclear forces, creates a situation where the US can credibly strike large numbers of Warsaw Pact targets using only a relatively few strategic systems. Large numbers of survivable warheads are desirable, however, to minimize any Soviet incentive to launch limited counterforce attacks, or to strike the US in some other limited way. Further, perceptions regarding relative superiority have an undeniable political and deterrent effect.
- The US does not have to have the capability to launch counterforce strikes against Soviet strategic nuclear forces. There are several thousand OMT in Eastern Europe and the Western USSR which the US can strike with her strategic forces, and whose destruction would inflict serious damage to the USSR's ability to fight, while avoiding any major collateral damage to Soviet civilians. The Soviet Union cannot credibly launch coun-

terforce strikes in retaliation for such US strikes without risking an all-out exchange. Similarly, there are large numbers of key Eastern European economic or 'counter-value' targets which the US can hit without striking the USSR. The East European population associated with such non-Soviet Warsaw Pact (NSWP) targets varies from negligible to levels high enough to give the US the ability to enforce equivalent population damage to the Warsaw Pact for any damage to Western Europe without striking at the USSR. Putting it bluntly, Eastern Europe's human and economic survival are now inevitable hostages to Western nuclear power. There are also a significant number of key economic targets on Soviet territory, distant from population centres which are inevitably in the same hostage category.

The US therefore has many options between 'assured destruction' (counter-city) targeting of the USSR and counterforce strikes. In fact, even the desirability of a large-scale first-strike counterforce attack capability is questionable, given the risk of Soviet launch under attack to protect the Soviet ICBM force. However, many argue that, since the USSR also possesses a counterforce capability, such a threat by US and NATO nuclear forces would have a deterrent value and an impact on Soviet perceptions worth its war-fighting risk.

– Although it is semantically something of a contradiction in terms, the US does not need a 'war-fighting' capability to conduct and win all-out strategic nuclear exchanges. US strategic and NATO theatre nuclear forces do not have to be able to fight and conclude a war, in the sense of being able to destroy the Warsaw Pact's ability to attack or to remain a military force-in-being. In fact, such a capability is probably impossible to achieve, given the size of the forces on each side and the number of nuclear weapons that would remain after any conceivable strike, and may lead to intensities of conflict which are far more damaging to both sides than a process of politically-oriented strikes and exchanges. The US can instead extend deterrence by threatening to inflict high levels of damage, by being in a position to terminate conflicts on terms favourable to NATO, and

by demonstrating her willingness to increase the damage she inflicts until the Warsaw Pact in a war accepts NATO's terms for a cessation of hostilities. This may well involve strikes against the Warsaw Pact military forces which are threatening to defeat NATO, since this may be the least escalatory response in many contingencies. However, modern nuclear forces can nevertheless deny the Warsaw Pact 'victory' by threatening to inflict damage to any aspect of its existence as a set of modern industrialized states.

– The US does not have to have large numbers of highly accurate, low-yield, or long-range strike systems. While such force characteristics are unquestionably desirable, she can use relatively inaccurate and high-yield systems like *Poseidon* to strike at Warsaw Pact other military and economic targets, and to inflict carefully escalated and controlled levels of damage. She can do the same with existing NATO theatre systems. There are plenty of targets in the Warsaw Pact for the use of high-yield weapons in air bursts with relatively low-accuracy and reliability. Many of these targets are not time sensitive.

– There is no requirement for the US to have flexible and survivable C³I, targeting, damage assessment and retargeting capabilities. Again, these force characteristics are desirable, but attack options which are relatively insensitive to the detailed dynamics of a given conflict can be pre-planned. There is also considerable doubt as to how rational or sophisticated nuclear bargaining can be in the real world. Moreover, it is not clear whether NATO gains from a Warsaw Pact perception that it will use nuclear forces highly flexibly and surgically nor whether NATO and the US can in fact buy such capabilities at any reasonable price.

– The US and NATO do not need a clear strategy for the threatened use of US strategic systems in extended deterrence. Experts are sharply divided over the relative merits of an explicit strategy compared with uncertainty, and of rational compared with irrational action in a crisis, whether as a means of improving deterrence in peacetime or of encouraging Soviet willingness to terminate a conflict. At least one former Commander of US Strategic Air Command has argued privately that the US should have many options but no strategy; that the US and NATO must in any case react to the Warsaw Pact; and that the USSR will be most deterred if she has no way of predicting how the US would use strategic weapons.

- The use of US strategic forces does not need to be guaranteed. It is obvious that extended deterrence benefits in credibility both from being a declared US strategy, and from every improvement in the capability of the US to execute such a strategy. At the same time, however, there is no obvious need for a NATO finger on the trigger nor for some kind of automatic US response in order to render US forces highly threatening to the USSR.

There is obviously a large gap between the four *essential* criteria discussed earlier and these merely desirable force characteristics, and this gap has been endlessly debated both inside and outside the United States. The advocates of stronger nuclear forces have often vehemently stated the absolute necessity of some, or all, of such desirable characteristics. In practice, however, they are optional, and each United States' Secretary of Defense and every set of nuclear planners since the early 1960s has had to consider the fact that providing the desirable characteristics would involve billions of dollars of expenditure which must be traded off against other United States' force capabilities.

II. EXTENDED DETERRENCE AND MUTUAL ASSURED DESTRUCTION: 1950–1968

The rather slow evolution of Western capabilities to meet these criteria was not the result of a failure to perceive what kinds of forces might be necessary or desirable. Several senior US military officers and civilians raised many of the same points about extended deterrence in the late 1950s, and similar ideas were extensively debated and analysed within the Office of the Secretary of Defense and in NATO from at least 1962 onwards. Rather, the development of capabilities for extended deterrence has been slowed by other factors. These have changed significantly over time, but they have included a US concentration on maintaining strategic superiority, the search for arms control, a focus on other NATO problems and priorities, and the rate at which the technology could be made available to implement the more sophisticated concepts of using strategic forces to support extended deterrence. The history of these changes still shapes the state of extended deterrence today, and a knowledge of it is essential to understanding both current Western capabilities and the West's potential capabilities in the 1980s.

From the 1940s to the Cuban Missile Crisis

The US has always been faced with the need to formulate four different types of strategic doctrine and plans which affect her ability to extend deterrence. First, a declared doctrine for public debate and to provide messages to the Soviet Union. Second, a weapons acquisition or force development doctrine which shapes her future capabilities. Third, an internal doctrine which the Department of Defense can use for planning. And, fourth, a targeting or warplan doctrine which translates current capabilities into strike plans.

All four of these doctrines involve different groups of US planners and different levels of political sensitivity. As a result, each can differ, broadly or in detail, although in theory they are co-ordinated by the National Security Council and the Office of the Secretary of Defense. This range of difference can be particularly great in the case of declaratory doctrine. Declaratory doctrine has often been manipulated to meet the needs of American foreign policy and domestic politics, and has often departed very significantly from operational doctrine and war plans.

This gap between declared doctrine and the reality of US war plans and military capabilities has been particularly important in the case of extended deterrence. During the late 1940s, for example, the US had virtually no capability to launch successful nuclear attacks on the Soviet Union. The operational US stockpile then consisted of less that 80–120 weapons, most of which were of doubtful reliability and even potentially defective. Moreover, the US lacked all-weather accuracy and combat-ready and experienced bomber forces. The *only* US strike option then would have been to strike at the major Soviet cities, and the outcome would have been highly uncertain because of the total inability to predict the resulting damage to the USSR. Yet most historians now feel that the *image* of American nuclear strength exercised a powerful deterrent force in limiting Soviet action during this period.

During the early 1950s, crash efforts to improve the US strategic forces reversed this situation. When Secretary of State Dulles announced the doctrine of massive retaliation on 12 January 1954, the US had a virtual strategic monopoly. Although the Soviet nuclear effort had received extensive publicity, and the Soviet Union had deployed significant theatre nuclear forces, the US could have extended deterrence in terms of almost any mix of damage she could threaten to inflict upon the Soviet Union and Eastern Europe without a major risk to herself. Further, the bomber forces of the day gave her a long period in which to react. She could have had days in which to pick a mix of OMT or other limited targets without the complications or time pressures inherent in the 15–25 minute flight times of the ICBM and SLBM of today.

The US also increased her relative strength in the late 1950s because she initially overestimated the rate at which the USSR could deploy new bombers and ICBM. This, and the relative vulnerability of the Soviet strategic forces at this time, had the effect of moving the US towards a true counterforce capability. During the Cuban missile crisis she had approximately 1,500 B-47s and 500 B-52s, and had already deployed over 200 of her first generation of ICBM. In marked contrast, the Soviet strategic missile threat consisted of a few token ICBM whose unreliability was so great that it was uncertain exactly whom they threatened. Soviet long-range bomber forces consisted only of 100 Tu-20 *Bear* and 35 Mya-4 *Bison*, whose range and flight characteristics forced them to fly at medium and high altitudes where they were extremely vulnerable to US fighters and surface-to-air missiles. Although the USSR also had over 100 Tu-16 *Badger*, these medium-range bombers were largely a threat to Europe and Japan.

Once Secretary of Defense McNamara finished evaluating the notorious 'missile gap', he found that the US was so superior that she did not need to rely on massive retaliation and, during 1961–2, he briefly shifted her to a declared counterforce strategy. In practical terms, this shift in strategy had several effects. The Single Integrated Operational Plan (SIOP) was adjusted to emphasize Soviet strategic systems and OMT. The US developed 'limited war' options in the form of a number of preselected strike options that so far as possible avoided Soviet cities and population centres, although they still involved the release of at least several thousand US and NATO nuclear weapons. In Europe, US and NATO planners at least examined the possibility of using US and NATO forces to launch a pre-emptive disarming first strike against Warsaw Pact theatre nuclear forces that were then uprotected and slow to react.

The first three years of the 1960s can thus be described as the zenith of extended deterrence – at least in the sense that the US could have put the SIOP and NATO Nuclear Strike Plan (NSP) into operation to defend Europe with near impunity. It is extremely doubtful whether the combined use of strategic and theatre nuclear forces could in fact have protected Europe, in the sense of avoiding the use of nuclear weapons against European targets, but until late in 1961 they did have a significant damage-limiting capability. This gave the West overwhelming strength in terms of its overall mix of strategic and theatre force capabilities.

McNamara and Extended Deterrence

However, McNamara's somewhat tentative delaration of a counterforce strategy was quickly overtaken by political and military events. The USSR had solved most of the initial teething problems which had limited her ICBM capabilities by late 1963, and in the mid-1960s she began rapidly to build theatre and strategic forces which the US then had no way of successfully attacking. Even though the Soviet ICBM forces were not originally sheltered and so were very soft targets, and although they had very long reaction times in preparing for flight, the counterforce capabilities of contemporary US ICBM were even more limited and uncertain. The US had her own reliability problems: severe C³ limits, poor missile accuracy and missiles with only one re-entry vehicle (RV) each. She was also limited by her ability to launch restricted numbers of missiles at one time, and was thus faced with the prospect that the USSR could increase her ICBM forces faster than the US could expand her capability to target and destroy them. The growth of the Soviet ICBM threat also meant that US air defences could now no longer limit the damage it could do to US cities, and that the warning time in which US civil defences could implement a shelter and evacuation programme had vanished.

The trends and interactions involved are shown in Table 1, as is the growth in Soviet capabilities against Europe. This shows that, by 1965–6, the US began to face a significant assured destruction (counter-city) capability from the USSR, and that Europe faced a similar threat from Soviet intermediate- and medium-range ballistic missiles from roughly 1961 onwards. These trends obviously presented serious problems for both overall US strategic planning, and for extended deterrence. Long before the US faced anything approaching strategic parity – which did not occur until the early 1970s – she faced both a major Soviet strategic threat to herself and a Soviet capability which could destroy virtually all European population centres, large-scale industrial complexes and major NATO military targets.

These same shifts also made NATO's theatre nuclear posture increasingly vulnerable (and so destabilizing) and put pressure on the link between US strategic forces and the long-range NATO theatre systems based in Europe. By 1963, the US had phased out her unreliable *Thor* and *Jupiter* missiles, and – with the advent of jet tankers – stopped basing B-47 bombers in Europe in an attempt to reduce the vulnerability of her strategic forces. NATO's only long-range strike capability then consisted of a limited number of British bombers, some ineffective and totally unreliable US cruise missiles, and a large number of NATO strike fighters dedicated solely to nuclear attack missions.

However, the Soviet SS-4s and SS-5s increased the vulnerability of NATO fighters on their airfields. This meant that any fighters which were not on Quick Reaction Alert (QRA) (i.e. able to take off within minutes) would probably be lost. NATO had less than 200 main operating bases at this time, and only 70 of these were suited for the basing of nuclear strike fighters. The number of US nuclear weapons storage sites for these fighters was far smaller (less than a third) and many of these sites could in any case have been destroyed or disabled by a large-yield attack on the associated airbase. Moreover, several of the central nuclear weapons storage sites contained large numbers of weapons and they were known to the USSR. They were also located where they would in addition cause massive damage to other NATO military targets.

In practical terms, NATO's growing vulnerability forced SACEUR to plan on the basis of a pre-emptive strike, using all nuclear alert forces, under attack warning conditions. This gave NATO's nuclear forces a 'hair trigger' character and, although no one used the term at the time, it was clear that they could only survive if NATO launched its weapons on warning of impending attack. At the same time, such NATO plans meant that the SIOP had to be based upon the assumption that *any* major NATO nuclear conflict would involve the initial release of over 1,000 long-and medium-range theatre nuclear strikes. These had to suppress and interdict Warsaw Pact conventional and theatre nuclear forces as effectively as possible in the first day of conflict, and NATO therefore had little or no ability to avoid massive collateral damage to Warsaw Pact civilians or economic facilities.

The result of this was to make any restraint by the US in shaping her extended deterrence options almost impossible, and to give both the SIOP and NATO's NSP an automaticity which was highly undesirable. Both NATO and the Warsaw Pact faced a situation where there was an extremely strong incentive to strike first, where both sides had to launch their initial strikes in such large numbers that they were likely to cause strategic escalation, and where any restraint might well lead to a catastrophic increase in damage. While this led NATO Headquarters to become increasingly concerned about the risks inherent in any delay in nuclear release caused by NATO's political authorities, it had the opposite effect in

Washington. It convinced many Americans that reliance on nuclear strike aircraft in Europe to provide extended deterrence was unacceptably dangerous to both the United States and to Europe.

From 'Countervalue' to 'Assured Destruction'
The US reaction to these trends in Soviet strategic and theatre nuclear capabilities was to adopt the declaratory strategy of assured destruction and to reduce NATO's vulnerability by reducing her QRA forces and emphasizing conventional options as an alternative to reliance on theatre nuclear weapons.

Secretary of Defense McNamara examined a wide range of other options. These included both changing US strategic forces to provide more sophisticated strike options in support of NATO, and deploying a large and less vulnerable long-range theatre nuclear missile force in Europe to provide a sounder linkage between US strategic forces and NATO theatre nuclear capabilities.

There were many political and budgetary reasons why the Secretary rejected these options, but there were also some important technical considerations. The command-and-control capability of US strategic forces was then comparatively primitive in its ability to implement limited nuclear options. Every aspect of conflict management, from retargeting to damage assessment, took too long, and the information that planners could count on was so limited as to make it almost impossible to manage nuclear forces in anything other than large-scale predetermined attack options. Long bomber flight times, and low ICBM and SLBM numbers – plus low accuracies and yields – also restricted what the US could do with her strategic forces. It is certain that the US could then have developed a much better capability for extending deterrence to Europe, but it would have been extremely costly to create and it would still have had serious limitations.

Similar technical problems affected any attempt to upgrade NATO's long-range theatre nuclear strike forces. The US was already in the process both of deploying the *Pershing I* missile and attempting to develop options for a NATO Multi-lateral Force, but neither option seemed likely to solve NATO's vulnerability problem. Any extended-range missile with accuracy and reliability superior to the *Pershing*, with its range of 450 nautical miles (nm), would then have been as costly as additional US ICBM. It would also have presented serious command-and-control, nuclear safety and basing problems for the technology was not available to provide effective and survivable C^3I support for a mobile missile, and any land-based missile which could be used flexibly in a wide range of strikes would virtually have had to be silo-mounted, again raising its cost to the ICBM level.

The problems inherent in deploying a mobile missile are illustrated by the *Pershing* I. This could only strike at a very limited range of pre-selected targets and could only be fired from predetermined sites. Co-ordination of strikes for the entire *Pershing* missile force and aircraft took months. Even with this pre-planning there was a good chance that the Soviet forces could locate the *Pershing*, for the road movement of the system was so visible that Soviet agents could track individual missiles to their sites. The reliability and accuracy of the missile was also sharply degraded by road movement for this affected both the guidance platform and missile frame. *Pershing* I had to carry warheads with yields of 100KT and above and could only attack soft area targets.

The basing problem was even worse. An adequate NATO force had to consist of at least several hundred missiles in order to provide a useful range of attack options. (The relevant Soviet target base then consisted of about 500 Soviet missile sites, up to 400 Warsaw Pact airbases, and some 200 additional facilities.) In the case of silo-based missiles, Europe would have had to accept several hundred silos, and there was no guarantee that these could be made hard enough to ride out strikes by the SS-4 and SS-5 force. The cost of silos would have been very high, and there would have been substantial manpower and sub-system costs. The situation was no better for mobile missiles. The missiles could only solve the vulnerability problem if they were not concentrated in bases in peacetime – as was *Pershing* – because NATO could not count on sufficient warning for dispersal. This meant that any mobile missile force would have had to be scattered around 200–300 sites in Europe, giving rise to great cost and serious security problems.

Although the MLF offered an alternative solution to some of these problems, the accuracies of the proposed surface-ship-mounted missiles were substantially worse than those of the already inadequate land-based mobile missile option. Although the MLF could have reduced vulnerabilty to pre-emptive missile attack, it opened up other equally serious vulnerabilities to Soviet Naval counteraction. It would thus have lacked true survivability, and would have been even less flexible for actual employment in a NATO conflict than US SLBM.

Secretary McNamara ultimately chose a fundamentally different set of options. On 18 February 1965 he announced that the US would rely on 'assured destruction' to deter any Soviet strategic strike against the US. In effect this meant that the US had decided to seek a stable strategic balance with the USSR by convincing her that no conceivable action she could take would eliminate the US capability to devastate the USSR, and that extended deterrence would be effective because the risk that any nuclear conflict in Europe would start a process of escalation which would ultimately trigger such a US attack on the Soviet population and economy.

This new declaratory strategy was not based on any very sophisticated military strike plan so much as on the then overwhelming US lead in strategic nuclear delivery vehicles (SNDV). There was then no indication that Soviet ICBM forces would suddenly surge upwards, and the US lead seemed so great that assured destruction hardly required detailed planning. It was clear that the effect of US retaliation would be devastating, inflicting damage on the USSR in greater orders of magnitude than a Soviet strike could inflict on the US. It was also clear that, once the destabilizing aspects of NATO's posture were reduced, the size of the US conventional and nuclear forces in Europe would create a situation where any initial Soviet attack would have to be so large that it ran a severe risk of triggering the SIOP. By the standards of the time, that seemed planning and strategy enough. As a result of these factors, and sharp resistance by the Joint Chiefs of Staff (JCS) and Strategic Air Command (SAC) to any further changes in US war plans, Secretary of Defense McNamara did little to reduce the minimum threshold of attacks in the SIOP. He

concentrated instead on making the ultimate threat to Soviet cities more convincing, and he adopted a procurement strategy for US strategic forces based on maximizing delivery systems and warhead numbers, and reducing the future vulnerability of the triad.

The US solution to NATO's vulnerability problem, following the collapse of the MLF negotiations, was equally simple. The US sought to shift NATO from reliance on a thin screen of conventional forces, designed only to defend against 'incursions and other local hostile actions' and to force the Soviet Union into making an attack sufficiently large to trigger a NATO nuclear response (the 'sword and the shield' concept enshrined in the document known as MC 14/2), to an emphasis on major NATO conventional defence options supported by existing short-range theatre nuclear systems and backed by US strategic superiority. This new US policy became the strategy of 'flexible response', and one of the key elements of this strategy came to be to reduce NATO's reliance on dedicated QRA nuclear strike aircraft in favour of more conventional use of air power. Nuclear-capable aircraft were retained to deter the Soviet Union from launching a massive nuclear first strike on Europe.

The US succeeded in getting NATO agreement to this shift, although it took far longer than simply announcing the shift to 'assured destruction'. NATO's adoption of flexible response involved hard negotiation from 1964, and it was 1968 before NATO ministers agreed to the document known as MC 14/3 and to plans which emphasized conventional options. The reduction of the QRA strike aircraft force took even longer and came only after the US had assigned a large number of *Polaris* SLBM warheads to SACEUR for longer range targeting by NATO to make up for the reduced QRA posture and the failure of the MLF.

Adding 'Mutual' to 'Assured Destruction'

McNamara's adoption of Assured Destruction meant more, however, than simply a rejection of counterforce options and of sophisticated US and NATO capabilities for extended deterrence. Even though it was conceived at a time when its authors believed US strategic superiority would continue indefinitely, assured destruction was founded on the assumption that US superiority would steadily decline in absolute terms and had already lost much of its meaning in terms of protecting the US economy and population. As a result, McNamara and the planners around him began to see less and less value in a massive effort to achieve strategic superiority in a military sense, and became steadily more interested in some form of arms control that would stabilize the balance.

This shift in viewpoint was compounded by the rapid changes in Soviet forces which began to take place between 1965 and 1967. As Table 1 shows, it was during this period that the growth in the number of Soviet ICBM began to really move towards 'parity', demonstrating a rate of growth which previously had been badly underestimated by the majority of the US intelligence community. This confronted McNamara with the fact that the USSR would before long be able to hit over 1,000 US targets, and was increasing its force at a rate where US superiority in assured destruction had already disappeared.

As a result, McNamara added the word 'mutual' to his declared strategy of 'assured destruction' in an interview on 18 September 1967. He did so with several goals in mind. First, he wished to persuade the USSR that the US accepted its vulnerability and would not seek to eliminate it. Second, he wished to place a tighter cap on the cost of US strategic programmes and to set a clear policy goal of not seeking a damage-limiting or war-winning strategy. Third, he wanted to define the number of targets necessary to assure destruction on both sides at so low a level that no conceivable counterforce exchange would ever eliminate either side's retaliatory credibility and no arms-control effort would become tied to large numbers of systems. And fourth, he wished to notify the USSR formally that the US accepted the fact that *any* significant use of either strategic or theatre nuclear weapons could result in a process of escalation that would effectively destroy the Soviet Union.

It seems fair to state that, as he neared the end of his term as Secretary of Defense, McNamara regarded the balance of risk as so high on both sides that he saw no real need for highly sophisticated strike options. While he and his staffs did discuss such options, they had

low priority relative to such pressing issues as the Vietnam War and, once President Johnson had quietly eased McNamara over to the World Bank, no one in the last year of the Johnson Administration had time for nuclear strategy.

Extended Deterrence in 1967
In summary, therefore, the US ended its era of superiority in assured destruction capability without any clear plan for executing strategic strikes in support of extended deterrence. If anything, she regarded the improvement of NATO conventional forces as a much higher priority for ensuring the overall deterrence of Warsaw Pact aggression than any possible action she could take to improve the capability of either her own nuclear forces or NATO's. The US also continued to rely on the risk of strategic nuclear war to deter the Soviet Union without having any limited options in the SIOP beyond demonstrative use.

This had serious implications during the early 1970s as US forces began to deploy warheads equipped with multiple independently targetable re-entry vehicles (MIRV) and the total number of US strategic warheads increased dramatically. While it is true that assured destruction had never meant that the US had no option other than hitting at populations or civil economic facilities, there was a natural tendency, as the number of her warheads increased, to use them to target more and more Soviet military facilities. The United States did stress counterforce targeting in the sense of striking at more and more Soviet military targets; what it did not stress was flexibility and restraint.

It is also relevant to point out that the NATO weakness in the theatre balance, shown in Table 1, and the Soviet shift towards strategic parity, were both relative. By 1967, the US had over 3,000 strategic nuclear delivery vehicles (SNDV), and 7,000 US tactical weapons were deployed in Europe. These presented a massive threat to the Warsaw Pact, even allowing for probable losses resulting from a Soviet first strike. The US also still enjoyed considerable superiority in accuracy, survivability, and many other key force characteristics. While the balance had changed by 1967, it still did not appear to threaten either US superiority in most measures of the strategic balance or the credibility of the assumption that any Soviet attack on Europe would lead to the use of US strategic forces.

III. EXTENDED DETERRENCE IN THE FIRST NIXON ADMINISTRATION

The US did little to improve her plans for extended deterrence between 1968 and 1974, although experts did begin to pay more and more attention to the options for making such improvements. The major concerns of US policy-makers were Vietnam, the overall build-up in Soviet military capabilities, detente and arms control, and the slow pace of NATO's effort to build up its conventional options.

During this period, however, the US and USSR did have to cope with two major changes in the structure of strategic forces: the competition over ABM; and over the introduction of MIRV. These two competitions led the Nixon Administration in very different directions, one of which was to change US capabilities to support extended deterrence radically.

On the one hand, the US lead in ABM technology created at least the possibility that one side or both could create a damage-limiting capability by some time in the early 1980s, and raised the spectre of a trillion-dollar arms race with the USSR to be the first to create such a capability. On the other hand, the number of delivery systems shown in Table 1 came to mean less and less as the introduction of the first US and then Soviet MIRV drastically changed the ratio of delivery systems to strike capability.

The resulting growth in warhead numbers on each side, shown in Table 2, reveals that between 1970 and 1974 the number of US ICBM and SLBM warheads targetable on the Warsaw Pact increased threefold, from less than 2,000 to about 6,000, and they have since risen to about 9,000. The growth in Soviet warheads was much slower, and only began to reach truly significant proportions in 1974.

Table 2 also shows that the US initially used her lead in MIRV technology to deploy large numbers of SLBM warheads with high survivability but limited yield and accuracy. In contrast, once the USSR began to deploy MIRV, she concentrated on ICBM. This initially permitted the USSR higher yields and, as MIRV accuracy increased, also allowed her to move towards a counterforce capability against US ICBM. It should be noted, however, that ICBM represent only 24% of the US ICBM/SLBM warhead mix.

Initial Assumptions about MIRV and ABM
The Nixon Administration initially interpreted these trends in the strategic balance as leading to an increased US advantage in all major contingencies, although it concluded that it would never be in a position to avoid massive Soviet retaliatory damage to the US. As a result, the US went into the first Strategic Arms Limitation Talks (SALT I) with the impression that she held two key cards. The first was MIRV technology – since at that time she grossly underestimated the speed with which the USSR could introduce MIRV – and the second was in ABM, where she had a clear lead in technology, although it was far from certain that she could create an effective defence system for either her cities or her military forces.

This analysis of the balance had several major effects for extended deterrence. First, the perceived US lead again reassured a new Administration that there was no real urgency about further improving either the strategic or theatre nuclear balance, particularly in the absence of any doctrine for making use of the latter capabilities. Second, it reinforced President Nixon's initial view on coming to office that NATO theatre nuclear systems did little more than increase the risk of accidental war or threaten loss of US strategic control. Third, it meant that the Administration felt it was free to concentrate on SALT I and the Vietnam issue.

A practical result of these trends was that US military, which had to write US war plans, was faced with the problem of loading more and more missile warheads into roughly the same set of SIOP strike options. This posed a number of problems. The accuracies of the new missile systems did not permit effective attacks against the 1,500 or so Soviet ICBM, and there were only about 100 Soviet bomber bases and submarine ports that could be attacked with SLBM and ICBM forces. Further, although the number of US warheads steadily increased, the total megatonnage of US warheads (including bomber forces) had dropped by 60%, and the total number of weapons including bombs had gone down by 25% because of cuts in the bomber force. The net effect was that the military had to concentrate on preplanned missile strikes against the target set containing 25,000 targets (excluding Soviet ICBM), while the marginal value of directing yet more weapons against Soviet cities decreased sharply after approximately the first 200–350 strikes.

With her ICBM and SLBM missile force the US could therefore cover more and more Other Military Targets, together with additional military and quasi-military production and research and development facilities distant from large population centres. This focus on fixed preplanned strikes on OMT reached the point where even the ultimate assured destruction option in the SIOP directed nearly 70% of US strategic weapons to non-strategic Soviet and Warsaw Pact military targets.

In theory, therefore, the US acquired both the prompt invulnerable delivery capability and the targeting necessary to support extended deterrence. However, this was not supported by the development of the required command, control, communications and intelligence (C³I) capabilities, by war planning that would have allowed her to use these capabilities effectively, or by any serious joint planning with NATO. In fact, one effect was to thicken up the existing SIOP options by adding more warheads, rather than to improve the range and flexibility of the SIOP by adding new options. According to one Pentagon expert, until 1974 the lowest SIOP attack option (other than 'demonstrative use') involved the release of at least 2,500 weapons and was so closely linked to the Priority Strike Program (PSP) in SACEUR's Nuclear Operations Plan (NOP) that it would have almost automatically triggered an additional 1,000 NATO fighter or missile strikes.

Accordingly, until at least 1974, the ultimate effect of deploying US MIRV and the shift from bombers to missiles, was to raise the level of conflict that would have resulted from *any* attempt to use US forces and to increase the risk of escalation to all-out war. From the European point of view, it is also important to realize that by then the USSR had at least 2,000 relatively high-yield bombs and warheads

threatening Europe, the accuracy of which was not suitable for discriminate strikes against small military targets, and which could launch in the face of a US attack but could not ride out such an attack with any confidence. These facts are generally ignored in talking about extended deterrence and the era of US strategic superiority. They should be remembered before showing any nostalgia for this period.

After SALT I: Soviet MIRV and no ABM

As in 1964 and 1967, however, the US gradually discovered that she was basing her declarations and plans on a major underestimation of Soviet capabilities. Shortly after the signature of the ABM Treaty and SALT I in May 1972, she began to realize that she had seriously miscalculated the trends. Broadly speaking, in the months after the 1972 election US policymakers began to discover that the Soviet Union was modernizing her delivery systems, introducing MIRV and improving system accuracy faster than either US scientists or the US intelligence community were predicting.

This process is a now familiar aspect of the history of strategic planning, but in 1972–4 the failure to predict the growth of this aspect of the Soviet threat still came as a major shock. The Nixon Administration discovered that the USSR could introduce MIRV far more quickly than it had expected. This meant not only that the Administration lost the advantage that it had counted on to preserve the US lead through the late 1970s, but also that the Soviet advantages in ICBM throw-weight suddenly took on a whole new meaning, because Soviet ICBM could carry many more warheads than US ICBM. ·

This interaction between the discovery of the real extent of Soviet MIRV programmes and the growing importance of the qualitative differences in US and Soviet strategic forces is shown when one compares Tables 2 and 3. Table 2 shows that the year 1974 marks a sharp, even dramatic, change in the rate of increase in Soviet ICBM warheads. Table 3, however, shows that, long before 1974, the US had begun to fall behind in such total measures of strategic force capability as equivalent megatonnage and total numbers of delivery vehicles and was soon to fall behind in throw-weight.

The trends shown in Table 3 did not matter so long as the US appeared to have a very marked lead in MIRV technology, accuracy and other aspects of missile technology. However, the sudden Soviet 'break-out' in fitting MIRV created a very different picture. It meant that, although the US could retain a major lead in the number of targets she could attack, the Soviet Union came to lead in assured destruction capability against the US civil and population base, and moreover had delivery systems in being which, if fitted with MIRV, could ultimately launch far more warheads than the United States.

This change in the rules of the game occurred when the second Nixon Administration was just beginning, and made it almost certain that US policy-makers would begin to re-examine US nuclear strategy. This was rein-

forced by the fact that the American withdrawal from Vietnam freed American policy-makers to think about other aspects of defence, and by the appointment of James R. Schlesinger as Secretary of Defense. Schlesinger had stressed the need to improve US capability to employ limited nuclear strike options since 1968. Accordingly, the early 1970s began a steady process of improvement in the way the US thought about extended deterrence and about the need to include options for lower thresholds of conflict in the SIOP, although this thinking initially did little more than improve the co-ordination of the SIOP and SACEUR's Nuclear Strike Plan (NSP) so as to eliminate some conflicts of timing and emphasis.

IV. LIMITED STRATEGIC OPTIONS AND THE RISE OF THE COUNTERFORCE THREAT

The primary catalyst in initiating the new US strategy was the Office of Program Analysis and Evaluation (PA&E), reporting to the Secretary of Defense, which faced the problem of trying to readjust the long-term defence programme for strategic forces to the changes taking place in US policy and in the balance. It conducted several in-house studies which indicated that US forces had become dangerously imbalanced toward large-scale options even before Schlesinger became Secretary. As a result, it began a joint study of new targeting options with the Joint Chiefs of Staff. This study was originally confined to a narrow circle, not only to avoid disturbing the arms-control negotiations going on at the time, but because the defence officials involved were afraid of interference from the National Security Council, the Arms Control and Disarmament Agency and the State Department on political and diplomatic grounds.

By late 1972, however, this planning had reached the point where the JCS had completed a preliminary re-examination of the SIOP, and the whole future of US strategy was beginning to be re-examined on an inter-Agency basis. Soviet progress in MIRV and other increases in Soviet capability, kept this inter-Agency effort going at a comparatively intensive level, and by mid-1973 it had produced a broad consen-

sus in favour of a new US approach to strategic planning.

As a result, Schlesinger began to hint at the coming changes in US strategy in November and December 1973. These changes received the President's approval in January 1974 and were issued in the document filed as NSDM-242. The Administration then approved its public release as declared strategy, and Schlesinger announced the change in his testimony in Congressional hearings in March 1974.

Schlesinger's testimony shifted the United States away from a declared but unimplemented strategy of assured destruction to one which formally stressed the need to seek to destroy the USSR's long-term capability to recover as an advanced industrial economy under her current regime, and the use of strategic and theatre nuclear weapons in carefully graduated responses. The new doctrine emphasized the targeting of Soviet strategic forces, OMT in the USSR, and Soviet or Bloc military targets in other countries.

The words Schlesinger used both in his original March 1974 testimony and on subsequent occasions were often confusing, even to their authors, because of the continuing debate inside the Pentagon as to precisely how the US would implement the doctrine, and because of technical uncertainties affecting US forces. The key message, however, was to communicate to the USSR that the US would develop the capability to use her nuclear forces in limited nuclear options (LNO), so that escalation control would exist all the way from the most limited use up to an all-out exchange.

New Strike Options for Extended Deterrence
The US was, in effect, formally announcing to the USSR that she was ceasing to focus the planning of her strategic forces on deterring large-scale strategic conflicts, and that she was adding a range of lower-level options that could be used to deter or 'win' a wide range of other types of wars. In practice this involved the development of the following kinds of nuclear strike options:

– *Countervalue Options* were strike options against non-military targets. They could be of two kinds: strikes on transport, production and other targets with immediate impact on Soviet ability to fight in the particular crisis or conflict at issue; or strikes at any non-military target in the Soviet Bloc which might be a reasonable exchange for the losses being suffered by the US or its Allies. Consistent efforts were made to find counter-value targets which minimized any loss of life. Although a number of studies performed for the Department of Defense by private contractors which became public presented such options as targeting only the Russian population of the USSR, or 'surgical' strikes against key concentrations of the Soviet leadership and intelligentsia, these reflected little more than the normal tendency of researchers to explore every option, and they were never part of formal US plans to implement the new strategy.
– *Counterforce Options* were strike options against Soviet or Soviet Bloc military targets of any kind. These included strategic forces, theatre nuclear forces, conventional forces and fixed military facilities. One of the key features of the new strategy was that the counterforce target mix should be the one most likely to persuade the USSR to terminate a conflict. That implied options for attacking relatively small numbers of targets or fixed facilities of the kind not previously

used as targets for US strategic forces. Included were options for limited or demonstrative strikes on Soviet strategic forces.

– *Limited Nuclear Options* (LNO) originally meant strikes against carefully selected targets on Soviet territory, but later were often used to describe all limited strike options in most public discussion. They involved both counterforce and countervalue targets in the USSR, but emphasis was placed on counterforce options.
– *Regional Nuclear Options* (RNO) included the entire mix of countervalue and counterforce targets in areas like the Warsaw Pact or Persian Gulf that might be attacked by US strategic and theatre nuclear forces. In many parts of the world, the same type of options were most logically targeted on Soviet territory. Planning again stressed counterforce options, and particularly OMT.
– *Theatre Nuclear Options* (TNO) included all the military targets in the theatre of operations directly involved in the conflicts. They could involve many different types of 'theatre' throughout the world, and they often overlapped RNO when the theatre involved conflicts as large as the entire Central Region. More attention was also devoted to the use of theatre nuclear weapons in TNO than in the other options, although it was clear that theatre weapons could be employed in LNO and RNO as well.

All of these options fit under the broad heading of limited strategic or Limited Strike Options (LSO). They also had the common characteristic that they created a need for new intelligence, targeting, C^3 and damage-assessment capabilities to increase the flexibility with which the US could use her strategic forces in this wide range of options. These capabilities later became lumped under the acronym C^3I (Command, Control, Communications and Intelligence). They also made increases in accuracy desirable, and argued for flexibility of yields and the ability to retarget rapidly.

Other Key Factors
There were several other aspects of the new strategy which deserve careful attention. First, Schlesinger explicitly rejected the notion of be-

ing able to develop a significant damage-limiting capability with US strategic forces. He did so both on cost grounds and on the basis of an almost universally agreed series of inter-Agency analyses which indicated that any advance in strategic defence technology – even if permitted by the ABM treaty – would simply lead to a matching increase in Soviet defensive and offensive capabilities.

Second, Schlesinger accepted the fact that both sides could escalate to a virtually unchallenged assured destruction capability. His references to counterforce targeting did not mean the use of such strikes to develop any kind of 'war winning' capability for all-out strategic exchanges but rather that such strikes could help the US to 'win' at lower levels of nuclear conflict. He stated in effect that both sides had the option of limited exchanges against the other's strategic forces as an alternative to strikes on cities and populations, and declared that this was part of US strategy.

Third, Schlesinger explicitly rejected strategic competition in terms of gross static measures of military capability such as throw-weight, equivalent megatonnage (EMT), counter-military potential, and numbers of delivery vehicles. He established a doctrine based on 'essential equivalence' in terms of the ability to attack the Soviet and Bloc target base allowing for the loss or degradation of US and NATO forces in prior exchanges.

The USSR initially seemed genuinely afraid that the US was seeking to develop a pre-emptive counterforce capability, a fear reinforced by the then superior US accuracy and hardening technology and the fact that so much of the Soviet force was loaded on ICBM and bombers. Yet Schlesinger was simply responding in kind to the fear that the USSR might be able to develop a strike capability that would enable her to destroy a significant portion of the US ICBM force at the cost of as few as 15,000 to 150,000 prompt civilian casualties. Schlesinger was also concerned that, although the ICBM force then only carried 23% of US warheads, roughly 50% of US warheads were vulnerable to pre-emptive attack including those aboard bombers, which could not take off on alert, and submarines in US and foreign ports. Accordingly, Schlesinger was seeking to deter such Soviet limited-strike alternatives to assured destruction by creating strikes options which ensured that US forces could retaliate in kind without escalating to attacks on Soviet cities.

The Counterforce Strategy

US officials and experts also tended to become confused over what Schlesinger was saying about counterforce capability, and this may have been partly responsible for the Soviet misinterpretation. Many confused the distinction between military targets of any kind and civil targets by using the term 'counterforce' to refer only to strikes against Soviet strategic offensive forces. In fact, virtually all of the resulting US 'counterforce' targeting was against non-strategic Soviet and Soviet and Bloc military forces, and this was dictated by the fact that the targeting of Soviet ICBM was both extraordinarily provocative and tended to produce unfavourable exchange ratios in terms of the residual numbers of warheads on both sides. Furthermore, US strikes at Soviet ballistic missile nuclear submarine (SSBN) ports would involve large-scale collateral damage, as would Soviet retaliation in kind. Moreover, OMT strikes do not invite confusion over whether the US is carrying out a first strike against Soviet strategic forces, and this is critical because, although Soviet ICBM silos are now probably hard enough to render impractical a mass US attack with existing ICBM, major uncertainties must still exist for Soviet planners over the actual outcome of such a strike.

The more detailed aspects of the planning for Schlesinger's new strategy were never heavily publicized and did not result in quite the same level of confusion and debate. They included a broad effort to find ways of limiting civil or collateral damage from attacks on military targets, to try to fill the gap between NATO's reliance on short-range theatre nuclear systems and the use of US strategic systems, to reduce the vulnerability of all nuclear forces, to find credible regional LSO for the defence of areas like Iran and South Korea, and to structure US limited strike plans to emphasize counterforce targets, in the sense of striking at mixes of Soviet and Warsaw Pact military forces and facilities rather than 'countervalue' economic and civil facilities such as East European cities or steel complexes.

These were reasonable extensions of a fairly moderate shift in US strategy and policy, although the words used in some policy papers and studies regarding these aspects of the 'Schlesinger Strategy' which reached the press often lacked the pragmatism and restraint of the US officials who actually made the decisions involved.

Deficiencies of US Capabilities

It is one of the ironies of the resulting public debate over Schlesinger's new strategy that comparatively little of it focused on the fact that US forces were in no position to implement it without major improvements. This is partly because many of the key aspects of US strategic forces required to execute LSO had never received much public attention, and partly because changes taking place in strategic forces were then so new that they received only limited attention.

However, the declared strategy of NSDM-242 highlighted the following deficiencies in US capabilities:

– The entire US warning and command-and-control system was oriented around large-scale exchanges. The US warning system could only warn against a mass Soviet attack. It provided very poor and unreliable attack characterization capability for many types of limited exchange and was virtually unable either to assist in identifying and targeting exactly which Soviet forces were used in a given attack – which is highly desirable in limited counterforce retaliation – or to provide precise measures of the level of Soviet escalation involved. The system was particularly bad at analysing Soviet actions at precisely the low levels of escalation where the US strategy sought to control or terminate the conflict.

– US and NATO defence communications systems were unlikely to survive in war, and US systems particularly were poorly integrated between the services, between civilian and military intelligence, between the National Command Authorities and the theatre and at tactical command level. They were also extremely unreliable and too automated. The US communications system had evolved from the assumption that the SSBN,

ICBM and bomber forces would have at least 16 hours to effect any change of targets, and would generally expect to have up to 48 hours. Nor could it provide the President with timely and accurate information on what was happening or allow him to choose a controlled response, consult with allies as necessary, or quickly execute his plan.

– The US and the NATO allies had virtually no means of rapidly directing weapons onto targets more than 50 miles behind the forward edge of the battlefield (FEBA) in NATO, and lacked the ability to direct nuclear weapons in many other regions in less than 48–96 hours. The US also had an extremely poor ability to assess precisely and rapidly the damage done to either side. This gap between the declared strategy and actual capability led to some ludicrous situations during this period. US planners would spend days arguing over very precise strike options and bargaining arrangements with the USSR, or gaming real time exchanges based on perfect knowledge in Washington and the Kremlin, when in fact the US lacked any real ability to obtain virtually any of the required data at anything like the rate required.

– The US emergency command-and-control system for strategic war consisted then mainly of relatively primitive aircraft whose equipment and data handling facilities limited them to the management of large-scale retaliatory attacks. The so-called 'hardened' National Command Authority (NCA) facilities were in fact distinctly vulnerable to attack by Soviet ICBM. This meant that a Soviet attack on her facilities could blind the US at any time, and that she had therefore to assume that the USSR would not attack Washington or nearby installations.

– The bulk of US warheads were survivable. However, while most of the *Minuteman* missiles then took 16–28 hours to reprogramme, the US did not even have a C^3 system for reprogramming her SLBM in a way that suited their use in LSO. Moreover, no real effort had been made to establish a reporting system for the NCA that could check the availability and functioning of particular groups of ICBM, SLBM or bombers. There was therefore a high risk that a limited employment could misfire or give the wrong signal.

Finally, bomber and SLBM system accuracies were relatively poor – much less than the theoretical missile accuracies or systems performance specifications quoted in most literature.
- These technical problems were compounded by the human problems of shifting from mass strikes to politically-orientated LSO. A large organization involving thousands of decision-makers had to agree on such options and transform them into specific plans. It quickly became apparent that practical war planning required the selection of very conservative options which were restricted in number, and which could get broad enough Pentagon and Administration support to avoid constant changes in concept and a high probability of being implemented in a crisis. This process, however, was so agonizing that virtually everyone was unhappy with the result – from the President down to the lowest staff officer involved. It also took years to achieve, and had constantly to be revised to match US capabilities and changes in procurement policy.
- It also gradually became apparent that in the real world there are no 'firebreaks' between TNO, RNO and LNO. The strategic and tactical nuclear capabilities on both sides were then, and are now, so great that either side can retaliate to its potential advantage regardless of the LSO it must respond to. Further, virtually any firebreak between types of systems and targets which is based on American or Allied perceptions not only may, but probably will, be different from the firebreak perceived by the USSR.

None of these factors invalidated the new US emphasis on Limited Nuclear Strikes, but, to return to the minimal criteria for extended deterrence discussed earlier, they meant that when such a strategy was announced in 1974, it was announced with the knowledge that the US could not really have the force to carry it out until the late 1970s or early 1980s.

The Problem of NATO Nuclear Forces
The US announced her emphasis on LSO and conducted discussions within the NATO Nuclear Planning Group (NPG) without having reached any clear recommendations as to what should be done about NATO theatre nuclear forces. Certainly there was much debate on the matter and many ideas were proposed and discussed, but there were a number of reasons why selecting some combination of these ideas and putting them into practice had only limited priority:

- The immediate focus of American attention was to preserve the US troop presence in Europe in the face of major congressional pressures for its withdrawal. The Administration had to emphasize the need for conventional forces and was even prepared, at the Mutual and Balanced Force Reduction (MBFR) talks in Vienna, to offer reductions in US theatre nuclear forces in return for Soviet troop reductions in Central Europe as a means of trying to prove to the Congress that the US could create a significant conventional defence capability.
- The cruise missile was still a concept only, and advances in missile guidance and C^3 technology had not yet reached the point where the broad problems we discussed earlier of long-range theatre missile C^3 basing, accuracy, reliability and vulnerability could be solved. The *Polaris*, and later *Poseidon* warheads allocated to SACEUR seemed to offer better capability than the available theatre systems, and the Soviet long-range theatre threat had not evolved to the point where their lack of visibility on European soil seemed to be a political and strategic problem.
- Any effort in theatre nuclear forces seemed likely to occur only at the cost of improvements in NATO conventional forces. NATO conventional forces were then relatively weak, and this created such vulnerability at the lowest levels of escalation that the US gave priority to their improvement and put her energies into trying to redress the conventional imbalance through negotiations with the USSR.
- Soviet long-range theatre nuclear forces (LRTNF) were still composed of ageing bombers and SS-4 and SS-5 missiles. The US had deployed a limited number of F-111s to Europe in 1969 and had committed more significant numbers of US-based F-111s to SACEUR. This reinforcement capability gave

NATO 'quasi-survivable' long-range forces which were backed by the increase in assigned US SLBM warheads resulting from fitting the missiles with MIRV. Any further US initiatives to improve NATO forces seemed likely to do little more than lead to a Soviet response in kind.

- Schlesinger found it expedient to push a US offer to reduce the number of nuclear warheads in Europe in return for a reduction in Soviet conventional forces. This allowed him more domestic and foreign flexibility in dealing with MBFR, and he preferred to focus on strategic systems where the US had unchallenged control, rather than on NATO forces, where LSO and RSO (NATO SEP, or Selective Employment Plans) required a formal and complex process of agreement by the Alliance.

- The shift in Soviet capabilities that created a near-term counterforce threat to the United States was not yet apparent. Accordingly, the US superiority in warheads seemed so great that a balanced range of escalatory capabilities, including survivable NATO-based long-range theatre nuclear strike forces, did not seem critical to the credibility ·of the new American strategy or to extended deterrence.

The result was that only limited advances were made in the quality of United States' and NATO theatre nuclear war planning, and theatre force improvement plans. The US Army recognized a need to modernize the warheads for its artillery and *Lance* short-range missiles, and to upgrade the *Pershing* longer-range missile to correct some of its severe limitations in targeting and deployment flexibility. Tactical nuclear bomb yields and tactical missile yields were also cut back to levels more proportionate to the size of Warsaw Pact targets. NATO also adopted new Nuclear Operations Plans (NOP) to reduce collateral damage, and changed the Priority Strike Programme (PSP) within the NOP to provide additional lower-threshold strike options. However, no major changes were planned in NATO long-range theatre nuclear forces, and the result was little more than tinkering in the absence of any clear conceptual framework for modernizing them.

The Rise of the Counterforce Threat

During 1975–8 it steadily became clear that the USSR would create a major counterforce capability against the *Minuteman* force by the early 1980s. Virtually every three months during this period the US discovered yet another significant improvement in Soviet ICBM design and deployment, missile accuracy, missile reliability and fractionation capability. As Table 3 shows, by the time Secretary Rumsfeld wrote his FY 1978 *Annual Report*, the US was projecting inferiority in several key measures of the balance and therefore a major risk that the USSR could 'win' a counterforce exchange.

The fact that the Soviet Union could 'win' any kind of exchange with the US came as a major shock to many of the US policy-makers involved. However, the nature of such a 'victory' needs careful qualification. The wargaming of a so-called 'counterforce run-down' depends on the Soviet Union being able to launch her forces with theoretical efficiency and effectiveness in a first strike against 1,054 US ICBM silos. The game goes on to assume that the United States is then forced to launch her surviving ICBM in a retaliatory strike against 1,469 Soviet ICBM silos, an unknown number of which are empty. Not surprisingly, the end result of the game, under these assumptions, is that the remaining American strategic forces are smaller than the remaining Soviet forces, and that further counterforce exchanges against ICBM make this situation still worse for the United States.

Such a war game is definitely a worst-case scenario for the US, in that there is no conceivable reason for her to retaliate for such an attack by striking Soviet ICBM silos, given the range of Soviet OMT that she could attack without significantly running down her residual ICBM forces. It also ignores the massive asymmetries in the triad on each side.

Table 4 shows the relevant differences in the mix of US and Soviet strategic offensive forces. While about 50% of US strategic delivery vehicles are on ICBM, ICBM carry only 24% of US warheads and 33% of throw-weight. Although not shown in the diagrams, ICBM carry 44–49% of megatonnage. Accordingly, the US would retain virtually 75% of her ability to strike at other Soviet targets even if she lost all her ICBM force. In marked contrast,

ICBM represent 56% of Soviet delivery vehicles and carry 75% of warheads, 70% of throw-weight and, although not shown, 85% of mega-tonnage. Any major counterforce run-down of Soviet ICBM immediately threatens the credibility of Soviet retaliatory capability.

Nevertheless, the fact that this contingency was possible began the complex debate over US 'counterforce inferiority' which still continues. It also shifted attention away from how the US could use her strategic superiority to win conflicts at low levels of escalation and to-wards guarding against a worst-case defeat by Soviet limited counterforce first strike. This in turn meant a rapid shift in focus away from the problem of making extended deterrence effective to a concentration on the B-1, *Trident*, MX and cruise missile. While efforts to give US strategic forces a full range of LSO and capabilities did not stop, the high priority that LSO activity had enjoyed under Schlesinger dropped sharply under Rumsfeld, who concentrated more on trying to make qualitative improvements than on planning.

V. EXTENDED DETERRENCE SINCE 1977

While the Ford Administration had sought to continue to compete from strength, President Carter and his closest advisers initially questioned whether such competition would result in anything more positive than larger nuclear forces and even larger defence budgets. As a result, the new Administration concentrated on trying to find some arms control arrangement with the Soviet Union that would produce far lower levels of nuclear forces and halt the trends that were producing a first-strike counterforce capability on both sides. The period 1976–8 was therefore one of drift, in which only limited changes took place in actual US strategy, war plans and procurement strategy. The President did make some major decisions, such as the cancellation of the B-1, but these were prompted more by the budget and problems in the bomber's development programme than by any new concept of how he wished to shape US strategic forces. Most of the other force improvement programmes begun under Schlesinger and Rumsfeld continued, although some major new delivery system programmes were delayed. The new Administration did show more interest in some aspects of C³ capabilities than its predecessor.

Re-examining US Nuclear Strategy
Yet the Administration did start a general review of US strategy in the spring of 1977. Presidential Review Memorandum 10, or PRM-10, received major publicity because of its discussion of changes in US policy regarding NATO and the defence of the Far East. Its major effect on extended deterrence was to call attention to the fact that the US had so far made only limited progress in translating the strategy and targeting policy announced in NSDM-242 into war plans and capabilities. As a result of PRM-10, the President issued a Presidential Directive, PD-18, in August 1977, which called for six major policy studies, including one on nuclear targeting policy which was the key one for extended deterrence.

This broad mix of studies did not lead to any major shifts away from the basic strategy which Secretary Schlesinger had set forth in NSDM-242, or in the basic structure of SIOP 5, which had grown out of NSDM-242. The work on the nuclear target policy review did, however, lead to the development of a highly complex matrix of 'building block' options that could be flexibly combined to suit a given crisis or war. It also led to the development of strike option concepts designed to divide the Soviet Union by forcing the regionalization of its population and economy and potentially destroying the ability of its ruling Russian majority to survive as a governing and social elite. It led to new priorities for both limited and large-scale military strike options against both residual Soviet strike forces and Soviet OMT – some of which were specifically designed to defend NATO and to counter the Soviet long-range theatre nuclear threat. It led to the development of carefully constrained population strike option concepts which could be used in limited wars or in combinations which would have a far more serious impact on Soviet recovery capabilities than striking at cities or fixed economic facilities. It led also to new targeting concepts for strikes at the Soviet economy which focused on the critical links that the country would need during the initial months of a post-nuclear exchange if it was to recover. It was found that, by concentrating strikes on these links, rather than trying to hit the entire base of major Soviet economic facilities, the US could vastly increase the lethality of her strategic attacks.

All of this work had an obvious impact in increasing the flexibility with which the US could use her strategic nuclear forces to execute limited strikes and support extended deterrence, and it had important effects in several related areas. The combined re-examination of US targeting strategy and ICBM modernization resulted indirectly in the first serious debate over the future of the triad that had taken place since the early 1960s. By mid-1979, the US had run through virtually every feasible basing and force improvement option for the 1980s. By the time the President reached his MX 'decision' in the Summer of 1979, the US had even seriously examined the option of shifting to a 'dyad' emphasizing SSBN. This debate was reopened, as the Reagan Administration reviewed the Carter basing decision, but during the Carter Administration it was resolved in favour of the triad for many reasons. These ranged from the need to gain political support for SALT II to a gradual shift in the Administration's views which led the President to doubt whether the USSR would ever provide reciprocal restraint, and to believe that the US had to match the rate of Soviet force build-up to achieve either substantial arms control or security. Accordingly, the main effect of this aspect of the PD-18 debate was to impose a delay in the deployment of MX, to delay the decision to develop the *Trident* II (D-5) SLBM with counterforce accuracies, to limit the upgrading of SLBM C³ links, and to increase relatively the emphasis on the cruise missile.

It was also accompanied by a growing debate over the implications of Soviet civil defence and the level of assured destruction that each side could inflict on the other. This led the Administration into the somewhat contradictory position of supporting major increases in the future number and yield of US strategic warheads while actively seeking limits on the numbers of delivery systems. It also led to a public debate (which still continues) over a possible 'recovery gap' with the USSR which is taken to mean that the USSR might be able to regenerate herself after a war faster than the US. However, this civil defence recovery gap debate has so far had only peripheral impact on extended deterrence. Soviet capabilities in this respect simply do not seem to be great enough to produce an asymmetry in population damage capability significant enough to confront the US with the risk that LSO would involve levels of US casualties unacceptably higher than those produced in the USSR, or that the Soviet Union could somehow prevent her population and economic facilities from being the assured destruction hostage that limits Soviet willingness to escalate any limited strategic conflict.

Finally, during the PD-18 exercise, separate initiatives by the Administration led to an initially rather subdued effort to re-examine NATO theatre nuclear forces. This aspect of the NATO Long-Term Defence Programme (LTDP) gradually began to take on real meaning in 1978, at the urging of some NATO nations (like Germany and Britain) and SACEUR, then General Alexander Haig. The Europeans pressed heavily for improvement of NATO's long-range missile capabilities as a counter to the *Backfire* and SALT II, and the Administration's original reluctance to take such an effort seriously gradually shifted to support as it became clear the Europeans wanted this as tacit *quid pro quo* for support of SALT, as the true scale of the Soviet SS-20 and ICBM build-up became clear, and as experience with the USSR indicated that SALT III was likely to have far better results if the US actively supported such TNF improvements. This ensured a closer relationship between US strategic planning and theatre nuclear planning than might otherwise have been the case. The whole issue of the targeting became enmeshed in the debate over the MX and, after the President's decision to deploy the MX in May 1979, the draft targeting directive was quietly shelved.

In June 1980, under the shadow of the election campaign, it seemed to senior White House and Pentagon officials that declaring the changes taking place in US planning would provide a clear signal to the USSR that the US was taking a stronger tone, had not rejected the concepts declared by Secretary Schlesinger, had plans to deal with ICBM vulnerability, and was improving – rather than reducing – the linkage between US strategic force and NATO.

The President actually signed the document, Presidential Directive (PD) 59, on 25 July, but the White House arranged to have the document leaked to the press almost immediately to counter the attacks being made on the Administration's defence policy by the challenger for the Presidency, Ronald Reagan. This timing meant that the strategy was published two weeks before Secretary Brown was ready to deliver a speech explaining it, and it caused a flood of misunderstanding, ranging from Soviet claims that the US was seeking a first-strike capability and supremacy to press reports claiming that the US had just rejected Mutual Assured Destruction (MAD) as a strategy (she had actually rejected MAD in 1974). It also inevitably forced a public debate over the fact that Secretary of State Muskie had not been consulted.

In any case, issuing PD-59 did not mean changes in the basic strategy that Schlesinger had declared, in the continuing development of LSO in the SIOP, or in force improvements that were designed to give the US a full range of LSO capabilities. If anything, the entire PD-18 effort, the continuing work on SIOP 5 and Administration policy after 1978, accelerated the implementation of NSDM-242, although it did delay or cancel some developments in strategic warheads and delivery systems. Secretary Brown's speech of 20 August 1980 was explicit on all these points:

> At the outset, let me emphasize that PD-59 is *not* a new strategic doctrine; it is *not* a radical departure from US strategic policy over the past decade or so. It *is*, in fact, a refinement, a codification of previous statements of our strategic policy. PD-59 takes the same essential strategic doctrine, and restates it more clearly, more cogently, in the light of current conditions and current capabilities.

This is particularly important in the light of Ronald Reagan's election, because the continuity of this aspect of US strategy since 1974 has been a powerful factor in ensuring that it would not change with a given Administration. In fact, the Reagan Administration is – if anything – even more committed to the rapid implementation of NSDM-242 and PD-59 than the Administration of President Carter.

Improvements in US Capabilities

While the debate over SALT II and US strategy received more attention than the Carter Administration's efforts to improve US strategic capabilities, the actions of the Carter Administration and the Reagan Administration, coupled to the programmes begun under Presidents Nixon and Ford, produced a wide range of force improvement programmes which affect both US capabilities to execute limited strikes and enhance extended deterrence.

C^3I Systems

In 1974, the Department of Defense estimated that it would cost between $300 million and $800 million to provide the minimum upgrading of its C^3 and warning systems necessary to support a suitable range of LSO strikes. Since that time, the US has spent several billion dollars in making relevant improvements. The strategic force improvement programme which President Reagan announced on 2 October 1981 will add billions more.

These improvements include the development of Command Data Buffer System (CDBS) for the 550 *Minuteman* III ICBM. This system, which started to become operational in 1977 and was completed in 1980, allows instantaneous selection from a number of pre-stored targets and the introduction of new targets in 25–36 minutes per missile, as against the previous 16–24 hours required to change tapes. This means that at least the *Minuteman* III force now has much of the targeting flexibility needed to provide a suitable range of LSO options. The associated electronics in the silos are also being hardened, provided with independent power supplies for sustained stand-alone operation, made resistant to electro-magnetic pulse (EMP) and given new suspension systems.

Major improvements are planned in the Airborne Command Post (ABCP) Programme to harden the system against EMP and to improve its ability to deal with complex attacks and provide LSO retargeting. Six advanced E-4B aircraft will be deployed by 1983, and the first entered service in early 1980. Several of those aircraft will include the Phase III airborne launch control system (ALCS). This will provide a jam-resistant secure data link to allow Strategic Air Command (SAC) crews to determine the status of each *Minuteman* III missile and the extent to which it has survived an attack, and it will allow encrypted rapid retargeting of *Minuteman* III missiles under attack conditions.

The Phase III system will be ready for 200 *Minuteman* III in 1982, and the USAF is now seeking to upgrade the remaining 350 *Minuteman* III, and possibly 450 *Minuteman* II, during 1983–4. Combined with the CDBS and improved B-52G/H capabilities, it will allow reprogramming and launch during a Soviet attack, and give the US a major launch under attack (LUA) capability.

The E-4B will also have a mix of UHF, SHF, satellite, LF and VLF communications which will improve the flexibility, reliability, and survivability of the US National Command Authority (NCA) in executing ICBM, bomber, ALCM and SLBM LSO even under trans-attack conditions, and it will have far longer airborne endurance. Coupled to the improvements in *Minuteman*, the B-52 force, and C³I links to SSBN, this will give the US an improved Secure Reserve Force (SRF) capability that will survive any forseeable Soviet counterforce strike on US C³I facilities.

The deployment of the USAF satellite communications system (AFSATCOM) netted *Minuteman* launch sites, B-52G/H and FB-111 bombers, KC-10 tanker aircraft, SAC Wing Command Posts, ICBM launch control centres, the E-4B, and the existing airborne command centres on EC-135 and EC-130 TACAMO aircraft by the end of 1980. As part of the strategic programme that President Reagan announced on 2 October 1981, the EC-135 airborne command posts serving military commanders will be hardened against nuclear effects, and will be equipped with upgraded satellite and VLF/LF communications.

This will also improve airborne warfighting capability, and greatly reduce the need to withhold a given number of US strategic systems from strike missions in support of NATO. Further, the US will acquire five mobile survivable ground terminals for AFSATCOM by

1985, and these will have considerable flexibility to conduct sophisticated LSO strikes and manage joint US and NATO strike plans even under worst case conditions. These measures will sharply reduce Soviet estimates of the probability that an all-out strike could somehow decouple NATO theatre and US strategic forces.

Other advances will take place in LF communication systems by December 1983, and high-speed encrypted digital land lines (SACDIN) will be established as a back-up between selected bomber and missile facilities during 1984–5. This will not only improve LSO flexibility and survivability, but again reduce any need to hold back warheads and launch vehicles from the support of NATO under attack conditions to avoid losing SIOP options because of the inability to retarget rapidly. Phase II of the AFSATCOM programme will also net the strategic satellite communication system into the Defense Satellite Communications System (DSCS) used for the theatre and tactical forces, and provide immediate worldwide communication and status coverage for planning, executing, and assessing extended deterrence and LSO.

Related improvements include the integrated operational nuclear detection system (IONDS) which will provide worldwide reporting on the location and yield of nuclear detonations, and provide far more rapid and accurate damage assessment information for LSO planning in the mid-1980s, plus deployment of satellite communications to theatre nuclear units in Europe. This will greatly improve US capabilities for launching through attack and will reduce the present vulnerability of the European Command and Control Console System (ECCCS). This system's nuclear C³ links are currently dependent on the survival of five fixed HF broadcast control stations, and help to integrate globally US strategic and theatre nuclear forces in much the same way that US strategic forces are being netted by AFSATCOM. The Carter Administration also completed a long term C³I plan for TNF forces in late 1980, which is going forward in a reinforced form under the Reagan Administration.

Although the revised 56-mile-long extremely low frequency (ELF) *Seafarer* System which President Regan decided to deploy on 8 October 1981 has a communication rate which is far too slow to allow flexible strike commands to be sent to US SSBN, this will be compensated for by other improvements in the quality and number of Navy EC-130 TACAMO aircraft, worldwide LF systems, fleet communications satellites, SSBN antennae and on-board communications. Taken together, these improvements will greatly improve LSO-capable communications with US SSBN by the mid-1980s and will allow a substantial increase in the ability to use *Poseidon* and *Trident* I SLBM in LSO against those fixed area targets which are in use by the Warsaw Pact. Combined with the Reagan Administration's tentative decision to deploy the *Trident* II (D-5) SLBM in the late 1980s, these systems will also eventually allow the US to employ SLBM in LSO strikes even at the lower levels of escalation where pre-planned targeting is often inappropriate.

Other new features of the US C³I system announced on 2 October 1981, include:

- Deploying mobile ground terminals for processing data from US warning satellites, and upgrading the satellites to improve their survivability. This will increase the speed and survivability of the command structure that would carry out a retaliatory strike and provide a better basis for linking US strategic and NATO LRTNF forces.
- The attack characterization capabilities of warning satellites and ground-based radars will be improved as well as their reliability. This will improve the ability to characterize the limits and intended target of Soviet strikes and to fight LSO conflicts. It will also provide a steadily improving launch-through-attack (LTA) capability.
- Additional *Pave Paws* surveillance radars will be deployed to improve coverage of Soviet submarines operating to the south-east and south-west of the US. This will improve bomber survivability, attack characterization and warning.
- VLF/LF communications receivers will be deployed and installed on strategic bombers to ensure the receipt of orders and retargeting capability under attack and trans-attack conditions.
- A new satellite communications system will be developed providing EHF communications channels to ensure two-way communication between commanders and forces. This will further improve LSO capabilities, and the ability to link US strategic and NATO theatre nuclear forces in the future.
- An extensive R&D programme will be initiated to provide a survivable C³I system that can fight an extended war, and force the USSR to face a situation where no Soviet strike could eliminate US or NATO capability to tailor long-range strikes to the nature of the Soviet strike or to desired tactical objectives. In effect, the USSR could not limit the US to the alternatives of mass strikes or nothing by attacking US C³I facilities.

This does not mean all the C³I problems affecting extended deterrence will be solved during the 1980s. Continuing delays in the Space Shuttle may cause some of these plans to slip, and there will continue to be severe gaps and problems in this mix of battle management systems, particularly in the ability to characterize and assess attacks on Western Europe and to assess damage to both Western and Eastern European targets. However, the US now has, or will soon acquire, many of the elements needed in terms of rapid communication and data management between US theatre forces, strategic forces and the National Command Authorities, to manage all but the smallest- or largest-scale strike options that might be used in defence of Europe. While their reliability and the netting of US C³I systems is still somewhat weak, the situation is much better than it was in 1974, and it will improve sharply over the next five years.

ICBM Forces

There has also been a considerable increase in the capabilities of the ICBM force. The somewhat unreliable NS-17 inertial guidance system in *Minuteman* III has already been replaced with the NS-20. This has vastly improved US ability to use specific ICBM in selective strikes with predictable results, and has increased the predicted lethality of each warhead against its target (single-shot kill probability, or SSKP) from 0.19 to 0.55 for hard targets. The US silo-hardening programme has raised the resistance of *Minuteman* silos to blast overpressure from 300 to 2,000 psi. While this is no defence against mass strikes from Soviet ICBM, and compares somewhat unfavourably with 3,500–4,500 psi for Soviet ICBM silos, it makes it difficult for the USSR to predict the results of attacks with only small numbers of warheads.

The deployment of the improved NS-20 guidance system on *Minuteman* III is further reducing its Circular Error Probable (CEP) from 400 to 200 meters and will improve its reliability. The effect will be a six-fold increase in lethality against semi-hard targets over the NS-17, and a further rise in SSKP against Soviet missile silos or other similarly hard targets from 0.55 to 0.70. Adding the Mark 12A warhead to 300 of the 550 *Minuteman* III missiles will double their yield from 170 to 335 KT, and raise their hard target SSKP even more – to 0.83.

Although, as we discussed earlier, the actual operational SSKP would be significantly lower, it would still be high enough to make a 'two-on-one' attack on most Soviet hard targets credible (also called 'cross-targeting', this involves aiming two RV – normally from different missiles – at one silo to give a high assurance of destruction). It will also allow the expansion of soft area target coverage for each RV from 50 to 88 square miles. Coupled with the fact that much of the force will retain warheads of lower yield, this provides a better mix of escalation capabilities with far less risk of a major miss. The Mark 12A improvement has, in fact, been so successful that SAC is pressing for all 550 *Minuteman* III to be upgraded, and consideration is being given to deploying this warhead in the *Trident* II (D-5) SLBM.

Similar improvements may take place in the 450 *Minuteman* II during the early 1980s, although the Reagan Administration has not yet chosen to fund this option. The NS-17 guidance system in these systems has already aged to the point where it is prone to failure, and SAC will also have to replace it with some variant of the NS-20. The boost motors in the *Minuteman* II missiles have already been replaced for the most part, and the missiles have been reconditioned to cure many of the problems of propellant and liner ageing. Further, 300 of the 450 *Minuteman* II missiles have had the same silo hardening, improved suspension and improved launch control upgrades as *Minuteman* III.

Serious study is also under way to improve the ballistic performance of the *Minuteman* RV to reduce the vulnerability of the warhead to various electronic effects. Finally there are plans to improve the ability to launch through heavy dust and residual radioactivity that might be expected over the silo after an attack. These improvements, if accomplished, will greatly improve the survivability and effectiveness of the US ICBM force against large area targets and very hard targets and in counter-value missions.

The deployment of at least 100 MX missiles will provide a major increase in LSO strike capability over *Minuteman*. The MX will be ready for deployment in 1986 and will have four times the throw-weight of *Minuteman* III, although it weighs only 2½ times as much. It will carry 10 RV and will have the potential for carrying 12. The warhead package has space to allow the incorporation of precision guidance or homing features and the ability to arm or disarm after launch.

The MX will also have approximately ten times the EMP hardness of *Minuteman*, and far greater reliability. Its computer will offer substantially greater capability to store target data and much greater speed and reliability in retargeting, particularly under attack conditions. The new inertial guidance system, AIRS, coupled with improved RV and platform design, will offer far better operational accuracy.

President Reagan's deployment decision of 2 October 1981 called for an interim deployment of 100 MX in a mix of *Titan* II and *Minuteman* silos, subsequently amended to *Minuteman* silos only. This is only half the size of the force the US had previously planned to deploy by 1989, although a 200-missile force would still be possible. It will also mean the phasing out of the obsolete and unreliable *Titan* II missile and temporary reliance on reconstructed silos with perhaps improved hardening through the mid-1980s.

The President has also announced, however, that by 1984 the US will select one or more improved MX basing options from among Continuous Airborne Patrol Aircraft (survivable long-endurance heavy-lift aircraft that could launch the missile), Ballistic Missile Defense (active defence of land-based MX), and Deep Underground Basing (deployment in survivable locations deep underground). While all of these concepts have their problems, they have gradually emerged as more cost-effective than the variants of the Multiple Protective Shelter (MPS) scheme, all of which would need some kind of ballistic missile defence by the late 1980s, and most of which would have proved prohibitively expensive. Equally important, the improvements being made to US C³I systems offer a high potential for reliable launch under attack by the mid-1980s, with any large-scale attack being characterized about 10-14 minutes after the launch and target options being selected according to its nature. While the Reagan Administration did not announce this option, it is steadily improving in technical feasibility, and a number of experts in the Department of Defense now believe that it will emerge as the preferred solution to ICBM vulnerability.

SLBM Forces
Improvements in the SLBM force will also improve US capabilities for extended deterrence. Although the total number of on-line warheads will drop slightly in the mid-1980s, the three last *Polaris* submarines are now being phased out of the force. This will create an SSBN force of 31 *Poseidon*-carrying submarines, of which 12 will be converted to carry the *Trident* I C-4 missile.

The C-4 missile increases SLBM range from 2,500 to 4,230 nm and thus increases ten-fold the area Soviet anti-submarine forces must cover in order to attack the SSBN. It will also have a nominal CEP of about 1,000 feet, or about 17% better than *Poseidon*, and will eventually have stellar mid-course correction. This increased accuracy, together with an increase in yield from 40 KT to 100 KT, will greatly increase the ability to use the system in LSO strikes against semi-hard OMT or industrial targets.

At the same time, the US plans to deploy up to 15 *Trident* SSBN. Although the programme has experienced considerable slippage and cost escalation, President Reagan announced in October 1981 that the US would continue to lay down *Trident* ballistic missile submarines at a steady rate of one per year, including one in 1981, one in 1982, and one per year in 1983–7. The contract for the 1981 submarine is underway, and the 1982 submarine has been partially funded. *Trident* SSBN will have 24 missile tubes, against 16 for the *Poseidon* boats, and will be able to carry the *Trident* II (D-5) missile.

The Reagan Administration announced at the same time that it would also accelerate deployment of the D-5 missile and begin deployment in 1989. This weapon will be able to carry a nominal 14 RV per missile, against 8 for the C-4, and will provide a further increase in SLBM range to 5,000 nm at full payload. The most important features of the D-5 missile, however, result from its being 10ft longer and 50,000 lbs heavier than the C-4 and having a throw-weight of about 6,000 lb. This increase in throw-weight allows the increase in warhead numbers to be accompanied by the development of a precision-guided RV.

The D-5 can thus for the first time enable the US to use SLBM against the full range of LSO and Soviet hard targets, eliminating the present need to rely on ICBM, bombers or cruise missiles. This, in turn, would mean the US would have no need to withhold ICBM from LSO missions because of their superior accuracy, or to rely on aircraft, ALCM and SLCM which lack a swift strike capability. Since the *Trident* D-5 warhead package is highly flexible and can hold even larger numbers of small RV, the US can also reduce yield to limit collateral damage while increasing the number of SLBM warheads available to react to any Soviet breakout in RV numbers.

Although the US has not announced it publicly, the *Trident* will also allow her to retaliate for a strike on her land-based ICBM force by using her SLBM. It will eliminate any possibility that the USSR could destroy so many of her ICBM that the US could only retaliate with slow-flying bombers or cruise missiles or by launching relatively inaccurate SLBM at area targets with large populations. Further, she could deploy the D-5 missile in a mobile land-based mode or on surface ships if forced into such an arms race by the USSR. This offers an important option in addition to the MX, and creates an added Soviet incentive to agree to arms control in the late 1980s.

Surface and Attack Submarine Forces
The Reagan Administration has further plans to improve the LSO capabilities of the US Navy, announced on 2 October 1981. It had already

announced in the Spring of 1981 that it was planning to deploy substantial numbers of sub-marine-launched cruise missiles (SLCM) in modular launchers on major surface vessels. These would equip each such ship with 32-60 SLCM, and 75% of these missiles would be designed for strikes against land targets, having the same precision and LSO strike capability as the air-launched cruise missile (ALCM). They would have an initial range of 1,500 nm and a potential range of 2,000 nm.

The first such SLCM missiles were to have con-ventional warheads and were to be deployed as early as mid-1983 on DD-963 destroyers. Others were to be added to the CG-47 *Aegis* fleet air defence cruisers in 1987. The initial deployments on the DD-963 would be limited in number, but armoured 32-missile canisters would be deployed from 1985. In addition, the Reagan Administration announced that it would reactivate two battleships and refit them with 60 SLCM each, and these could be deployed as early as 1983–4. The two ships would have the growth potential to carry 320 missiles each, and two more battleships might be activated by the mid-1980s.

While the Administration did not say whether such ships would also acquire SLCM with nuclear warheads, this was under study in the Pentagon and created a major new option for expanding US LSO strike capability. As a result, when it became clear that it would not be possible to solve the MX vulnerability prob-lem in the near term, and that the *Trident* sub-marine building programme would have to be limited to one per year, the Administration decided to put nuclear-armed SLCM on existing attack submarines. This decision means that US attack submarines will carry up to 12 SLCM each, and will act as LSO strike platforms with-out degrading their anti-submarine capabili-ties. Given these plans, the US opened five new land attack mission planning centres by the end of 1981. These are located at US com-mands in the Pacific, the Atlantic, Europe, Britain and at SAC. They have a capability for terrain contour matching (TERCOM) planning and are be able to launch a wide range of LSO.

The Strategic Bomber Force
While much has recently been made of the age of the B-52 force, the B-52 is undergoing a

comprehensive upgrading that should keep it functioning through the 1980s and will im-prove its survivability, accuracy and weapons delivery capability. The improvements in-clude a comprehensive upgrading of all aspects of the B-52G/H offensive avionics systems (OAS) and the conversion of the B-52G to an AGM-86B ALCM carrier.

The first B-52G with ALCM is now available for standing alert with external cruise missiles, and the first squadron should become oper-ational late in 1982. The 196-bomber force will then steadily convert to the ALCM, with the B-52G initially carrying twelve missiles exter-nally before being converted to carry eight more internally. The conversion programme is now scheduled to be complete by FY 1990.

The B-52G will also be greatly hardened against EMP to prevent 'barrage' type nuclear defence by the USSR, and will have the option of carrying short-range attack missiles (SRAM) for penetration missions. Although the ALCM aircraft will have very long mission flight times (12–16 hours), they can accommodate changes in the political and military situation while en-suring high survivability. They will also be able to achieve very high accuracy in LSO missions. (Under ideal circumstances, the ALCM will have accuracies of 300–600 ft. with a 180-KT warhead, and should normally have a CEP better than 3,000 ft.)

The Reagan Administration announced on 2 October 1981 that it would convert an un-specified number of the remaining 96 B-52H to ALCM. In the interim, both the B-52G and B-52H are being provided with modern com-puters to improve accuracy. Terrain map-ping/avoidance radar, necessary to correct the aircraft's current problems in low-altitude penetration missions, are also being improved. The aircraft will also have new data cartridge systems. These will allow data preparation centres on each base to programme new strike options rapidly and, in conjunction with cen-tral data centres at SAC, cut the time necessary to prepare a bomber for new LSO missions by hours. The OAS package will also increase the accuracy of the B-52H in dropping nuclear bombs by up to three times. The remaining B-52D will be retired in 1982 and 1983.

These capabilities of the B-52 force will be supplemented by those of the FB-111 forces

98

based in the US. The FB-111 can fly low-altitude penetration missions at half the height of the B-52H, and can use the SRAM in LSO missions, firing up to six missiles within a short period of time. Its terrain-following radar and navigational packages already provide much of the accuracy that is to be added to the B-52, and the communications links to the FB-111 are being improved to enhance control in flight.

In October 1981, the Reagan Administration also announced a decision to produce 100 improved B-1 bombers, with deployment of the first squadron in 1986, and 'vigorously' to pursue development for the early 1990s of a more advanced 'stealth' bomber which would be relatively invisible to Soviet radar. The 'simplified' B-1 that will be deployed as a result of this decision will have a limited-sweep wing and will be ideal for LSO and other extended deterrence missions. It will be tanker-independent and will have much more advanced defensive avionics and high multi-role payload capabilities. Even without an aft bomb bay, it could carry 22 ALCM – 8 externally and 14 internally. With an aft bomb bay it could carry 30 ALCM, 38 SRAM, 28–30 nuclear bombs, 142 500-pound conventional bombs, or 38 2,000-pound bombs. In combination with the B-52 force, the B-1 force will allow the United States to deploy over 3,000 cruise missiles.

These conventional and theatre nuclear mission capabilities are particularly relevant because, if the 'stealth' technology on the B-1, combined with low-power ECM, can keep its radar detectability low after prolonged service, the US could use it in NATO support missions with minimum risk of attrition and would have little need to withhold it so as to preserve it for strategic missions. (The B-1, while not a 'stealth' bomber, does have greatly reduced detectability and will be produced with several advanced features.) The B-1 variant is the Reagan Administration's choice for this role, and it is likely to enter service in 1987.

Finally, satellite navigation systems will improve the accuracy and reliability of all US bombers in LSO attacks during the mid-1980s, and advanced multi-spectral and enhanced imaging techniques, communications and data processing will also improve targeting and damage assessment.

Strategic Defence

While strategic defence has only a marginal impact on extended deterrence, it seems worth noting that the Reagan programme, announced on 2 October 1981, also included:

(a) Replacing five obsolescent F-106 squadrons with F-15s;

(b) Expanding the ballistic missile defence R&D programme;

(c) Bringing space-based missile defence to the development stage;

(d) Buying at least six additional AWACS airborne surveillance aircraft to augment ground-based radars in peacetime and to provide surveillance and control interceptors in wartime;

(e) Expanding the US civil defence and continuity of government programmes;

(f) Improving the US–Canadian air surveillance network by buying some combination of *Over-The-Horizon Back-scatter* (OTH-B) and other improved ground radars.

War Fighting Capabilities and Extended Deterrence

The rationale behind these force improvements is summarized in Table 5, which shows the estimate of the balance that former Secretary of Defense Harold Brown used in his SALT II testimony to the Senate Foreign Relations Committee in July 1979. Although both US force plans and the estimated capabilities of Soviet forces have changed somewhat since then, these estimates are important because they reveal the Carter Administration's thinking when it shaped the basic structure of the US ALCM, *Trident*, MX and bomber programmes, and the 'balance' the Reagan Administration considered in making its October 1981 decisions.

The US increased her force loading from 3,950 warheads in 1969 to 9,200 in 1980, while the USSR increased hers from 1,659 to about 5,100. Under the Carter programme, the US would have further increased her on-line warheads to about 15,000 by 1990, while the USSR would have a maximum of 10,000–12,400, if she continued to modernize within the limits set by SALT II. It was also shown at the time that deployment of the ALCM, *Trident* I, and MX were estimated to maintain rough parity in hard-target capability, and gradually to give the US significant superiority in soft-target kill capability, provided that the USSR did not respond with radical new force improvement initiatives.

It was also demonstrated that, if the US carried out all the force improvements programmed under the Carter Administration, and, if the Soviet Union did not change her force mix radically from that predicted by US intelligence, the US would never suffer significant inferiority in the number of targets she could hit. This estimate is particularly important for extended deterrence because it means that the Carter Administration had concluded that no set of worst-case Soviet strike options could pre-empt the American ability to conduct limited-strike options in the 1980s. Even after an all-out Soviet attack on US ICBM and a US response in kind, she could carry out extended deterrence options involving several thousand weapons while still preserving at least three times the number of warheads required for the civil-economic recovery targets in the SIOP assured destruction option.

The Reagan Administration's decisions of 2 October 1981 change the force mix underlying the US data in Table 5, but they do not change the essence of the balance. They emphasize bombers and ALCM over ICBM, and they slightly slow the rate of MX and *Trident* submarine deployment. At the same time, they could lead to an even faster MX deployment in the late 1980s, and they add SLCM and two additional bomber types to US strategic forces, and confirm deployment of the *Trident* D-5 missile. The net result should be to strengthen the US by comparison with the estimates shown in Table 5.

As has been discussed earlier, a pure counterforce retaliation against Soviet ICBM of the type shown in Table 5 would also be an unrealistic worst-case response to an attack on US ICBM. As the supporting analyses for PRM-10, PD-18 and PD-59 revealed, a much better response to a Soviet counterforce first strike would involve some mix of the several thousand key Soviet economic and military facilities which are critical to both Soviet sustained warfighting and recovery capabilities but involve no significant increase in the population damage than would result from a Soviet strike on *Minuteman*. The US thus has almost no incentive to retaliate by striking Soviet ICBM

where the exchange ratio is relatively unfavourable.

Secretary of Defense Harold Brown hinted at this in his long discussion of countervailing strategy in his FY 1980 *Annual Report*. He also made several points about counterforce targeting (pp. 75–9) which need careful attention. He stressed that such retaliatory targeting would require at most one warhead per remaining Soviet silo, command bunker, nuclear weapons storage site and soft strategic facility. In practical terms, this would mean that the US would need at most 2,000 warheads even if she could not determine whether or which silos were empty and yet felt that she could risk an all-out launch on all residual Soviet strategic capabilities.

Over 7,000 of the approximately 9,000 US warheads are on relatively survivable SLBM and bombers. Although these systems have the wrong mix of yields, cannot react quickly and lack the desirable degree of accuracy, surviving US forces could still carry out extensive extended deterrence strikes without jeopardizing either the option of OMT retaliation or assured destruction strikes. Further, as US attack characterization capabilities improve, it will become extraordinarily difficult for the USSR to launch large-scale counterforce attacks without the US locating many of the empty Soviet ICBM silos. This means that the US will need to reserve steadily fewer residual warheads for retaliatory counter-silo strikes each year, while simultaneously increasing the total number of survivable warheads she has available.

The 'Counterforce Gap'

It also cannot be overstressed, given the attention that the 'counterforce gap' has received, that this scenario was never intended to be a basis for sizing US forces, but rather to be the worst-case test for measuring Soviet capabilities. The gap applies only to US ICBM, non-alert bombers, and SSBN in port, and only if all the Soviet ICBM used launch at the proper time and perform according to the theoretical predictions, with no significant cumulative degradation for any of the anticipated readiness and C³ problems caused by the 'law of large numbers'. It requires the US to accept a minimum of 5–10 million casualties, and to reject 'launch through attack' despite her steadily improving C³I capabilities.

The gap also occurs only because of the asymmetries in the US and Soviet triads, which have the effect of making it easier for the USSR to attack US ICBM because they are a much smaller portion portion of the triad. Further the gap only becomes serious if it is measured in aggregates like effective megatonnage; these are poor measures of each side's ability to destroy targets, given the lethality of even a 100 KT weapon against 90% or more of the unhardened targets on each side.

There have been many different unclassified assessments of the consequences of a Soviet counterforce first strike on US ICBM but none are entirely satisfactory. Obviously the alert status of US forces is critical but it is now generally assumed that the US could cope with even a major increase in the rate of Soviet expansion in on-line warheads by either deploying more MX or accelerating *Trident* II, and could do so

even under conditions where SALT I and SALT II constraints no longer apply.

The MX or *Trident* II programmes are clearly important if the US is to avoid inferiority in the middle and late 1980s. However, the US can also offset much of her inferiority in a preemptive Soviet counterforce strike by either increasing her alert rate or converting to a launch-under-attack posture. While such a shift to LUA retaliation would be far more risky than deploying new delivery systems and continuing to plan to ride out any Soviet attack, the new C³I systems described earlier will massively reduce the risk of a 'false alarm' or overreaction by the mid-1980s. This will again help to ensure that the US can maintain a suitable margin of retaliatory capability to execute LSO even under worst-case conditions. In short, the 'counterforce' gap does not seriously threaten US capability to employ strategic forces in extended deterrence missions during the 1980s.

VI. EXTENDED DETERRENCE AND THE UNCERTAINTIES OF THE 1980s

Existing and planned US strengths and capabilities do not mean, however, that the US and NATO do not face major challenges from the USSR. Specifically, there are a number of problems which the US and NATO must deal with if extended deterrence is to be secured in the 1980s.

The USSR is clearly outspending the US on strategic forces and now has equal overall technical capability and a vastly superior production base. The details of this Soviet lead are shown in Table 6 (although some of the data on Soviet spending in the Table is the subject of an intense debate within the strategic studies community, the broad trends seem certain to be correct). While it is difficult to translate a superiority in expenditures into military superiority, it is clear that the USSR has the potential ability to improve her nuclear forces faster than the US.

The US must be ready to deal with a far greater range of Soviet force improvements than those projected in Table 5. While US plans seem adequate to cope with the known trends in Soviet forces, the USSR has the initiative in many areas, and the US must be pre-

pared to respond. Moreover, US strategic forces still lack a number of highly desirable capabilities which, though not essential to meet the minimum criteria for extended deterrence, provide insurance against miscalculation or uncertainty.

The gap between NATO's present theatre nuclear capabilities and those of US strategic forces has taken on a different character since the mid-1970s. It now presents serious problems of both range and capability in ensuring a proper spectrum of deterrent options, and NATO long-range theatre forces must be improved, as must the mid-range capabilities against fixed targets (and their associated air defence weapons) and against mobile or imprecisely located targets in the various echelons of Warsaw Pact forces. Nor has the US developed adequate forces suited for limited nuclear strike options in other areas of the world such as Korea and the Persian Gulf. The actual need for such forces may be arguable, but the inadequacies of current and programmed US capabilities are not.

Finally, the US has failed adequately to explain her strategy and capabilities to her European allies and to declare her intentions in a way that would help to restore the belief that a US President would implement extended deterrence in a crisis.

Uncertainties in the Soviet Threat

It is clear that even conservative estimates about the improvements taking place in the Soviet threat will mean that the USSR will lead the US in some major measures of total force strength during the 1980s, although she will have only parity or inferiority in others. Estimates could shift substantially further in favour of the USSR if additional Soviet and Warsaw Pact force improvements take place.

Soviet Strategic Forces

Even if the SALT II limits were implemented in some form, the USSR could greatly improve her bomber forces, the warhead loading and overall reliability of her ICBM and the number of warheads in her SLBM forces. There have been strong indications recently that the USSR may be moving in this direction. She has increased the tempo of her R&D effort to develop five new ICBM and may be developing improved variants of the SS-18 and SS-19. She can certainly deploy 8–10 RV per missile, and her ICBM accuracy has now reached 0.15 nm for SS-19, with Soviet ICBM in general now being expected to reach 0.08 nm by 1985. This would reduce or eliminate the Soviet need to allocate two RV per US ICBM in counterforce strikes. While the initial SLBM launches for the new SS-NX-20 missile to be used on the *Typhoon* SSBN were failures, the SS-N-18 missile in *Delta* 3 submarines has demonstrated the Soviet ability to give her SLBM 7 MIRV and a range of 6,500 nm with high accuracy; and the USSR has since deployed the *Typhoon* SSBN and seems to be making enough progress with the SS-NX-20 to deploy an SLBM with 12 RV, an 8,300-nm range and accuracies substantially higher than 0.3 nm by the mid-1980s. Work is also proceeding now on two new Soviet strategic bombers – a large supersonic bomber and a low altitude penetrating aircraft – and ALCM tests have shown that the weapon load of a heavy bomber (plus *Backfire*) could be raised to 8–10 systems per aircraft by 1985.

Under worst-case conditions, such developments would allow the USSR nearly to double

the number of warheads she could deploy by 1990 to a total of over 20,000. This is important because the estimates in Tables 4 and 5, and in current US strategic analysis, depend upon the assumptions that the Soviet Union:

(*a*) Will not quickly load her ICBM to the 10 RV permitted in SALT II;

(*b*) Cannot quickly improve the fractionation of her SLBM or bring them up to the 14 RV permitted by SALT II in the near future;

(*c*) Cannot greatly improve the bomber loadings with larger cruise missile numbers;

(*d*) Will not introduce a less vulnerable ICBM basing mode;

(*e*) Will not have any kind of SLBM with depressed trajectory and precision-guided RV capability before 1990.

Unfortunately, there is no firm intelligence evidence that the USSR will not do any of these things, and strong recent indicators show that she may. The real exchange curves of the 1980s could thus be very different from those shown in the previous Tables. In fact, the balance could shift in favour of the USSR as early as 1983.

However, as Part 2 of Table 6 has shown, the US does have a number of rapid countermeasures she can take to such Soviet actions. She could deploy more MX missiles into the presently planned basing structure and increase *Trident* SSBN production to one to two submarines per year. She could speed deployment of the *Tomahawk* SLCM in the 8 *Polaris* submarines being replaced by *Trident*, produce FB-111 variants to increase her bomber strength, increase B-1 bomber production and ALCM loading, and add ALCM capability to the 96 B-52H as well as the 169 B-52G.

It seems unlikely, therefore, that Soviet actions could greatly affect US strategic capabilities for extended deterrence before the United States could react with longer-term and more intensive force improvements, or that unanticipated increases in Soviet capability could threaten a substantially greater portion of the US ICBM force or civil population than the Soviet force improvements currently planned. Nevertheless, unless the United States acts decisively the perceived balance – in terms of static measures of force strength – might be much worse, and this could have significant political effects.

Soviet Theatre Nuclear Forces
The USSR is in the process of deploying large numbers of *Backfire* bombers and SS-20 missiles. Over 70 *Backfire* were deployed with her Long Range Aviation in mid-1981, with a matching number in her Naval Aviation. Most were the improved *Backfire* with a payload of more than 5,500 kg, an unrefuelled range of over 8,900 km and the ability to fit a probe for in-flight refuelling. By July 1981 the USSR had deployed over 250 SS-20 launcher/missile combinations, with one reload missile per launcher, which put more than 1,500 SS-20 warheads on line. About 175 of the launchers were deployed where they could be used against NATO. The resulting force had more than 350 missiles or 1,050 warheads.

The *Backfire* is being produced at a rate of 30 per year, and the rate of SS-20 production is accelerating. Since January 1981 the pace of SS-20 base construction opposite NATO has increased sharply, and bases now under construction will add 65 launch positions and 390 warheads to the force. As many as 100–150 additional launchers, or 600–900 warheads including re-loads, may be deployed before the end of the programme. An improved version of the SS-20 may also be in the process of deployment, and a follow-on version may now be reaching advanced development.

The USSR is also starting to deploy the shorter-range SS-21 and SS-22 and is completing final testing of the SS-23a – all of which have superior range and performance capabilities to *FROG*, *Scud* and *Scaleboard* that are presumed to be obsolescent. She is also greatly improving the capability of the fighters that can be used for nuclear strike missions. Accordingly, the balance of Soviet theatre systems in the 1980s could be very different from that currently projected by US intelligence in Table 1.

This could affect extended deterrence quite profoundly in two ways. First, there are indications that the Soviet Union may have targeted SS-11 ICBM on Europe in the past, and may now employ SS-19s extensively when Warsaw Pact exercises simulate 'counterattacks' against NATO. As the overall mix of Soviet theatre systems improves, she could either shift these SS-19 warheads to targets in the US or combine them with a vastly greater theatre first-strike and escalatory capability against NATO. All SS-20 in the USSR can also be fired against NATO (and not simply those normally counted as targeted against Europe), and the relatively short-range SS-22 and SS-23a have sufficient range to cover 70 to 90% of NATO's European military target base. Major improvements may also occur in the Soviet submarine-launched cruise-missile (SLCM) and naval bombers forces. All currently deployed Soviet submarine-launched missiles and naval aircraft with a nuclear capability, except the SS-N-6 and SS-N-8, have been used in exercises in simulated strikes against European land targets as well as in naval roles.

Such improvements in her theatre systems also allow the USSR to deploy her mix of systems with far greater flexibility than can the US in potential limited nuclear options against NATO's flanks, the Middle East, the Persian Gulf and Asia. Recently published maps of SS-20 deployments show that the Soviet Union is already taking such options seriously by orienting her SS-20 forces to maximize coverage in areas beyond China and the NATO Central Region.

Soviet C³I and Warning Systems
The Soviet C³I and warning systems have always been oriented towards fighting a nuclear war, rather than triggering retaliation. Unlike the US, the USSR had a system that could put limited strategic options into effect in the early 1970s, and she has been steadily improving that system ever since. The US currently estimates that she has a greater ability to conduct limited strikes in the 1980s because of her superior computer, satellite and communications technology. However, such superiority is extremely difficult to predict or to prove. There is no real way at this point to determine which side will lead in the targeting, damage-assessment and battle-management capabilities which could be more important in a limited strategic exchange than the size and capability of the nuclear forces on each side.

Soviet Strategic Defences
A Soviet breakout in either passive or active strategic defence cannot be ruled out, though it does not now seem likely. However, anti-ballistic missile (ABM) and anti-submarine warfare (ASW) technologies and other aspects

103

of strategic defence are evolving rapidly and the USSR has active programmes in all these areas. 'Breakthroughs' are by definition not predictable, and there is growing uncertainty about the progress the USSR is making in ABM and ASW technologies. It is clear from Table 7 that she already has a major lead over the US in strategic defences, and this is certain to continue, given the fact that the US has gradually reduced her constant dollar spending on strategic defences from nearly a third of total expenditure on strategic forces in FY 1971 to token amounts from FY 1976 onwards.

The importance of this Soviet strategic defence effort is illustrated by the fact that recent data on the Soviet surface-to-air missile (SAM) threat has evidently led Strategic Air Command to reconsider using the B-52H as a penetrating bomber for the 1980s. It is also clear that the USSR is carrying out extensive R&D efforts in SAM, ABM and anti-satellite (ASAT) weapons. Many of the advanced Soviet C³I and warning systems – such as *Cat House* and *Dog House* defence radars – could be used rapidly to expand the Soviet ABM force, although they do not now seem to offer much potential for a 'breakout' or a massive rapid deployment of ABM defence.

Successors or modifications to virtually all the air defence radars, interceptors, and SAM launchers shown in Table 7 are now being deployed. These may significantly degrade the penetration capability of all NATO fighters and medium and heavy bombers and may offer a significant defence capability against NATO's older LRTNF missiles. US experts expect about 1,700 new early-warning radars to be added to the totals in Table 7 by 1989, including *Over-The-Horizon* and phased-array systems with ABM capabilities, plus major improvements in C³ systems to integrate radar, missile and fighter forces and provide the command centre and integrated defence management capabilities that Soviet forces now lack.

The obsolete Tu-126 *Moss* airborne warning aircraft is being replaced by a variant of the Il-76 *Candid* with a capability similar to the American AWACS. The SA-10 SAM will provide greatly improved low-altitude coverage; it accelerates beyond Mach 5, has greatly improved electronic counter-counter-measures (ECCM) compared to the SA-3, and will have a

significant theatre anti-ballistic (TABM) capability. The SA-11 and SA-12 SAM will probably replace the SA-2, and the resulting system promises to have far better range and ECCM capabilities against US bombers flying at high altitudes. Finally, modifications to the MiG-25 *Foxbat* will give it a deployed 'look down/-shoot down' capability by 1982, and advanced Sukhoi (Ram-L) and MiG (Ram-K) strategic defence fighters are expected to be deployed by 1985 with greatly improved ECM, radars, look down/shoot down capability and air-to-air missiles.

While the USSR now has only 32 obsolete *Galosh* ABM in the Moscow area, there are indications that she has recently begun to upgrade this force, and she can still deploy up to 100 launchers under the ABM Treaty. This would allow her to test several aspects of an ABM defence of her ICBM forces in the field, and permit much more rapid deployment of such defences if she chose to abrogate the ABM Treaty. The USSR is known to have a hypersonic exoatmospheric ABM and associated radars under development; she has also recently tested an anti-satellite weapon successfully after several failures, and there is firm evidence of an intensive effort to develop laser missile defence technology.

Soviet Planning and Doctrine

All of these uncertainties are compounded by the uncertainty over how the Soviet Union views extended deterrence, and how she would react to the limited use of strategic weapons by the US. It is clear from Soviet literature that the USSR does in fact practice limited strategic exchanges in her games and exercises, although she uses very different terminology. However, she has publicly taken a strong line against the feasibility of such options. She has shown a far greater tendency, in her discussions of nuclear warfare, to focus on the value of massive preemption or escalation than have US or NATO planners confronted with the same sort of military situation. There are also disturbing hints that some Soviet planners may believe that full-scale and rapid escalation is an inevitable result of any limited nuclear strike and act accordingly. Yet such a belief would cut two ways. It could make the USSR afraid of a US strategy of extended deterrence and its escalatory consequences.

It is true that there does seem to have been some shift in Soviet planning and doctrine over the last five to seven years. Particularly in recent years, the Soviet Union has analysed a wide range of conflicts against NATO involving some limited use of strategic weapons, and she has discussed the use of steadily lower yields. She now seems to be tailoring her strikes to minimize collateral damage and the risk of escalation, and to be deploying improved theatre forces at least partly so as to be able to fight a broad range of limited nuclear wars.

However, major uncertainties remain as to whether Soviet and Western perceptions are sufficiently alike to allow extended deterrence to operate in a crisis, and there are good indications that the USSR may seek to improve her combined strategic and tactical nuclear capabilities against NATO to the point where she could try to force some kind of decoupling between the US strategic deterrent and NATO forces.

Limitations in US Capabilities

Perhaps the most serious potential limitations in American and NATO capabilities for sustaining extended deterrence lie in the fact that so many of the key improvements in existing US strategic forces are still being implemented or are uncertain to receive full programming support and to reach deployment, notwithstanding the new impetus the Reagan Administration is giving to improving US strategic forces. There is also no way to assess the probable success of each system, or how they will interact. Many operate at the leading edge of technology, and such efforts have often fallen far short of their predicted performance in the past.

Doubts also exist about whether the US can bring in new systems like the cruise missile, MX, *Trident*, B-1 and 'stealth' bomber at anything like the rate now projected in her plans. Some slippage in operational date or performance is almost inevitable, and the problem of cost escalation and competition for funds is serious enough, even under the new Reagan defence budget, to threaten cut-backs in all the major efforts now underway. This compounds the risks of comparing US plans against observed Soviet trends.

The current emphasis on upgrading US ICBM and SLBM forces to increase their assured destruction capabilities and the counterforce retaliatory capabilities of US ICBM will significantly raise the yields of weapons in the US strategic forces. The deployment of cruise missiles will not ease this situation, since they also have comparatively high yields. This could tend to limit US targeting flexibility, although it is easy to exaggerate the impact of such changes because the number of targets where truly low yields are necessary to limit collateral damage is restricted. Moreover, the effect of a given strike can be reduced very sharply by raising the height of burst of the warhead, and the cumulative damage effect of doubling or tripling the yield of a weapon detonated on or over a soft or area target is much smaller than the increase in yield implies.

Any delay in developing precision-guided RV technology for strategic missiles could deprive the US of the ability to deploy a *Trident* II (D-5) force with low yields and extremely high accuracies in the mid-to-late 1980s, despite the recent Reagan decision to accelerate D-5 development. This force would be an important addition to US extended deterrence capabilities since it would provide a launch platform which was not on US soil and which was not vulnerable. A delay or problem in the D-5 programme might be critical if the vulnerability of US ICBM increased strikingly. Nor has the US yet matched the improvements being made in the ability of strategic C^3 systems to retarget and manage LSO strikes with suitable improvements in survivable intelligence and theatre systems. The US C^3I system will be unbalanced in the mid-1980s by an overemphasis on the ability to execute strikes and a relative inability to decide what to shoot at, or to measure the effect.

President Reagan's 2 October 1981 decision to deploy 100 MX in existing silos also leaves the issue of US ICBM vulnerability undecided. While he announced that the US would decide on some mix of ABM defence, deep silos and airborne MX launchers by 1984, it is unclear whether she will actually fund and deploy a survivable basing mode for her ICBM in the 1980s. This may well force the US to convert to a launch under attack mode if she detects a very large-scale Soviet attack on land targets in the US. This could reduce her ability to restrict herself to LSO under worst-case conditions.

The fact that most of the changes necessary to make extended deterrence effective are still in the process of completion has ensured that almost no real US planning and exercise testing of these capabilities has yet taken place. This has been compounded by the long-standing tendency of senior officials to delegate virtually all exercise participation to comparatively junior members of their staffs. It does little good to plan such force capabilities, and even to have effective plans at the level of SAC, if the US National Command Authority (NCA) is made up of people who would have to learn how to operate extended deterrence under wartime or crisis conditions. For similar reasons, only a few European officials have ever paid any really serious attention to their NATO crisis management or wartime responsibilities. The NATO battle staffs that would exercise oper-

ational control over theatre nuclear forces are not permanently established, nor do they have the capability to adapt or adjust plans using up-to-date intelligence. The success of extended deterrence, however, would greatly depend upon the quality of the link between US and European authorities and the depth of their understanding of US strategic and NATO theatre capabilities. Delegation of such European responsibilities to SACEUR might partly compensate for such a lack of national capability, but the spectacle of United States' and NATO officials trying to deal with the cabinets of European governments undergoing a crash course in nuclear war is a real possibility. Much needs to be done to make NATO staffs more capable and NATO's national leaderships more cognizant of the need for effective crisis management.

VII. COUPLING STRATEGIC AND THEATRE NUCLEAR FORCES

The problems in strategic capabilities cannot be separated from the trends in NATO theatre nuclear forces. The ability to sustain extended deterrence is determined both by US strategic capabilities and by those of NATO theatre forces – and particularly by the extent to which US strategic capabilities to execute LNO overlap, and are reinforced by, NATO theatre capabilities to execute long-range strikes. While extended deterrence is not absolutely dependent upon the existence of such NATO capabilities, it is obviously reinforced by them, and they can be of major value in insuring against the uncertainties or weaknesses in the relative capabilities of US strategic forces.

The Current Trend in Force Capabilities

The overall trends in the relevant LRTNF capabilities of each side, as projected by the US, are shown in Table 8. The first part of the Table shows the US estimates on 1 January 1981. The second shows the latest trends as projected in US intelligence estimates. Both show that the LRTNF balance has shifted sharply in favour of the Warsaw Pact, yet the Table understates the extent of this shift and the problems it creates for extended deterrence.

Table 8 does not count either the Soviet SS-19 warheads which may be targeted in sup-

port of the Warsaw Pact, or the roughly 400 *Poseidon* warheads assigned to SACEUR. However, the Soviet ICBM form a highly precise system with rapid retargeting capability which links well to a full range of Warsaw Pact theatre systems. In contrast, *Poseidon* has comparatively poor true system accuracy, and, while it has some retargeting capability, the *Poseidon* SSBN lack the C³ links to make effective use of this. This situation will not change materially if the *Poseidon* SLBM are replaced with the *Trident* I, since the near-term improvements in the *Trident* I's CEP and retargeting capabilities will still limit it to roughly the same strike options.

The USSR therefore has large strategic land forces in Europe to supplement her theatre forces which are better suited to creating a smooth spectrum of escalation between strategic and theatre forces. The US SLBM on the other hand act as a residual deterrent which is oriented towards comparatively rigid, pre-planned and large-scale strike options against fixed area targets like Warsaw Pact air bases.

Virtually every NATO theatre nuclear system is now outranged by its Warsaw Pact counterpart, and NATO systems are deployed in highly vulnerable and concentrated sites. There are only about 70 major NATO theatre nuclear targets in peacetime, and no more than 200–300 in war. The only long-range NATO theatre system which can truly disperse on alert is *Pershing* IA, and this system suffers from an array of targetability, reliability and flexibility problems which seriously limit its effectiveness. Moreover, NATO has still taken only limited steps to improve its C^{3}I capabilities for nuclear war. Its C^{3}I systems are even more vulnerable than its long-range nuclear forces – the loss of less than ten C^3 centres in Europe (many of which could be destroyed with conventional weapons) could virtually 'blind' all NATO nuclear war management. Limited improvements in C^3 capability, such as AWACS and at Boerfink (NATO's wartime HQ) will improve NATO's capabilities in some areas, but these will not be enough for dynamic nuclear planning in a crisis. The improvement of key targeting, damage assessment, intelligence and battle management capabilities are not even called for in current NATO force improvement plans. While there is no question that these weaknesses would not prevent NATO from fighting, they would sharply limit its ability to support extended deterrence with accurate and timely information, to draw up carefully measured response plans and to conduct accurate damage assessment. These difficulties are compounded by the fact that NATO cannot rely on survivable nuclear delivery systems.

Overall, NATO TNF have only a very inadequate first strike posture. Their vulnerability invites Warsaw Pact pre-emption in peacetime, and NATO has left a large gap between its largest or most capable systems and the smallest strategic system the US could employ in extended deterrence. This posture creates both an incentive for a Soviet first strike early in any conflict in the Central Region and the risk that such an attack could be so successful that the US use of strategic systems for extended deterrence would lose credibility or effectiveness.

Improvement of NATO Long-Range Systems
As has been described earlier, the Carter Administration did not initially believe that these problems would be serious enough to require significant improvements in NATO forces. In fact, President Carter showed as much initial opposition to improvements in

NATO's nuclear strength during 1977–8, as he did to many of the efforts to improve US strategic forces. Although a number of senior European leaders and politicians sought US support for providing cruise missiles to NATO in that Administration's early days, it still proposed the temporary protocol on cruise missile deployments in SALT II. When West German Chancellor Schmidt made his speech at the IISS calling for stronger NATO nuclear forces in the Autumn of 1977 (see *Survival*, January/February 1978, pp. 2–10), the Carter Administration continued to hold to the dogma of previous Administrations, taking the position that large-scale attacks on Western Europe by Soviet medium-range forces were deterred (or countered) by the US strategic deterrent, especially those *Poseidon* forces at sea that were committed to NATO.

During 1978, however, there was a significant shift in President Carter's views as he came to feel that such a US policy met neither Europe's political or military needs. The initial catalyst was political. Repetition of US strategic guarantees through 1977 and into 1978 had little effect on European expressions of concern about the unrestrained growth of Soviet long-range TNF and the extent to which the US might be limiting her long-range TNF options in SALT. Accordingly, despite US concern that the European Allies would lose their political enthusiasm when faced with the reality of missile deployments on their soil, the Carter Administration began to look seriously at the question of modernizing long-range TNF in mid-1978. It is also fair to say that the neutron warhead debacle had some influence on this decision.

In the process, US planners went beyond the politics of NATO TNF and began seriously to re-examine the military aspects of the theatre balance in Europe. After about five months of study in 1978, they produced estimates which concluded that there was indeed a military problem, although its dimensions were not universally agreed within the Government. Elements of the State Department viewed the problem as mainly political, and certain elements of the US military viewed the problem (and continue to view it) in terms of a perceived need to cover SACEUR's entire target list in a theatre equivalent of the SIOP.

In broad terms, however, the new US planning effort reached the following conclusions:

– Strategic parity had changed European and Soviet perceptions of the credibility of an American strategic nuclear response, even a limited one, to Soviet nuclear attacks on Europe. Although this was a perceptual problem, it was not one that could be rectified simply by resorting to rhetoric or structural solutions.
– In addition to achieving strategic parity, the USSR had developed capabilities for a variety of military responses at conventional and nuclear levels. The nuclear improvements were striking, not so much in their numbers as in their quality. These changes also suggested that the USSR was moving towards being able to dominate escalation at all levels, even if this were not the preferred Soviet strategy. Since it had been US strategy since NSDM-242 to dominate the process of escalation, this change suggested that the NATO strategy of flexible response, already vulnerable at conventional level, was now vulnerable throughout the nuclear spectrum. Thus the military/strategic problem was not simply the SS-20, but the range of nuclear modernization, of which the SS-20 was an important part.
– NATO's most serious deficiency in this connection was seen to be in LRTNF based in continental Europe and capable of striking Soviet territory. The Alliance had almost no LRTNF – only the 156 F-11s based in the UK, which were dual-capable and also had important conventional tasks, and the 50 British *Vulcan* bombers, which were practically at the end of their operational availability, were in the inventory. The vigorous Soviet modernization, represented not only by the SS-20 and *Backfire* but also by fighter aircraft such as the *Fencer* and shorter-range ballistic missiles (SS-21, -22 and -23a), suggested the possibility of Soviet efforts – in conflict or in peace – to decouple Europe from US strategic forces in the sense that the USSR could attack or threaten attacks with her LRTNF, and the Alliance would have no response other than to resort to US strategic forces.
– To these military/strategic conclusions was added the political assessment that some

new LRTNF capability was needed to reassure the Allies that the American nuclear commitment to Europe remained firm. The SS-20 had become a symbol of the potential weakness of NATO nuclear forces, and something was needed on the ground to 'counter' the SS-20. (Unfortunately, the 'countering the SS-20' argument became the predominant theme in the ensuing political debate, which, since 1979 has thus tended to overlook the overall requirements of NATO and US strategy, and Soviet across-the-board improvements in nuclear capability and ability to dominate theatre nuclear escalation.)
– There was an additional political dimension. The Europeans felt left out of the SALT process. They saw the US – whether justifiably or not – bargaining away theatre systems (i.e., the ground-launched cruise-missile) in SALT II, while the Soviet strategic threat to Western Europe remained unconstrained and was in fact being vigorously modernized. It was clear that any SALT negotiations beyond SALT II would have to grapple with the Soviet strategic threat to Western Europe. It was similarly clear that the politics of defence in Western Europe would make it impossible to obtain Alliance agreement to deploying US LRTNF in Europe, no matter how much they were needed, unless that deployment was accompanied by negotiations to reduce and limit LRTNF on both sides. This led to the ultimate decision by the US, with Alliance backing, to make an arms-control proposal to the Soviet Union in the context of SALT.

Most US analysts felt, however, that the Soviet build-up did not require the sort of 'force matching' solution recommended by some military authorities which involved deployment of 1,000 to 3,000 warheads to provide a 'theatre balance' and to be able to execute a theatre-level SIOP against SACEUR's targets without relying on US strategic forces for help. There was a conscious decision at the higher levels of the Carter Administration that NATO did not need to 'match' Soviet LRTNF warheads one-for-one, at least in its initial *Pershing* II and cruise missile deployments. The Administration also felt that the chances of achieving an Alliance consensus on deployment of

1,000–3,000 warheads were virtually nil, and that any US effort to seek it would ensure that no new LRTNF systems would be deployed at all.

The Carter Administration also rejected views within the Government calling for small deployments, such as simply replacing the *Pershing* I with *Pershing* II, mainly because such a force would be so small as to be viewed for what it was – a token – and because a small deployment of a single system would not hedge sufficiently against vulnerability problems. Many in the Administration also feared that such proposals would have adversely affected perceptions of the US nuclear commitment to Europe and would raise again the old fears that the US wanted to be able to fight a nuclear war in Europe without harm to US territory.

The end result was the development of a LRTNF improvement package designed to provide a strong 'bridge' between NATO's existing TNF and US strategic forces. While not replacing US strategic forces in any way, this package was felt to be large enough to counter the developing Soviet long-range threat and to force a level of Soviet escalation which would eliminate any doubt in the minds of Soviet planners (and perhaps of Western planners as well) as to whether the US would be willing to employ strategic forces in the improved mix of LSO capabilities being developed as a result of the PD-18 studies.

The Impact on Extended Deterrence
On the positive side of the ledger, NATO's decision of December 1979 could provide it with the LRTNF necessary to establish a far stronger link between its current theatre forces and US strategic forces, and with much improved military capabilities that would greatly reinforce extended deterrence. NATO plans to deploy a force of 464 ground-launched cruise missiles with 2,500-km range, and 108 long-range *Pershing* II medium-range ballistic missiles (MRBM), with initial procurement of the GLCM beginning in FY 1981 and its initial operating capability (IOC) in Europe being December 1983. About 160 systems would be deployed in Europe by the end of FY 1985, and all 464 GLCM would be deployed in hard shelters by the end of FY 1988. Virtually all of these missiles would be deployed on NATO airbases, with 160 in Britain, 112 in Italy, 96 in the Federal Republic, 48 in Belgium and 48 in the Netherlands. All of the 108 *Pershing* II missiles would be deployed in West Germany and would replace the present US *Pershing* IA systems by the end of FY 1985.

Also, as a result of the Carter Administration's reappraisal of the TNF balance, the US is already improving her F-111 training and deployment, and the F-111 force will soon have operational experience in Norway, Turkey, Italy and Greece in addition to the Central Region. Other improvements are being made in US C³ systems, and US forces in Europe will acquire AN/MSC-64 UHF satellite communications channels during FY 1981–4 to improve their links to the US National Command Authority. A comprehensive C³ improvement plan is now being developed to link US theatre and strategic forces as part of the preparation of the FY 1983 defence budget.

Britain has also committed herself to enhance these US-sponsored improvements by buying *Trident* missiles as a successor system to her existing *Polaris* weapons. This will increase the weapons loading on British SLBM from 3 multiple re-entry vehicles (MRV) per missile to 8 MIRV, and warheads carried will increase the total weapons of the British force of four submarines with 16 launch tubes each from 192 MRV to 512 MIRV. This is a much greater threat to the Soviet and Warsaw Pact target base, and the improvements in accuracy and retargeting capability would allow much more flexible use of the British force. The *Trident's* longer range will give British SSBN the same increase in patrol area and survivability that it provides for US forces, and British SSBN will be able to take full advantage of the improvements in US C³I systems without affecting their independent targeting in their dual role as a national deterrent.

British nuclear capabilities will be further improved by conversion of British strike aircraft forces to the *Tornado*, although there will be range penalties. The present strike aircraft, *Vulcan* and *Buccaneer*, are both comparatively obsolete in terms of reliability, delivery accuracy in long-range missions, attack mission computers and other offensive avionics, and low-level penetration capabilities. The *Tornado* should substantially increase the speed with which the RAF can change its targets, allow at least some reduction in yields or collateral damage, and increase the chances of any one bomber reaching a target by 50% or more.

These improvements are partially reflected in the estimates in Table 8. They indicate that NATO as a whole should have sufficient delivery and warhead capability to maintain a broad spectrum of extended deterrence in the 1980s.

Continuing Uncertainty

There is also a negative side of the ledger. For a variety of reasons, there has been little serious European attention paid to how LRTNF can be made effective by providing either a range of new strike options for NATO or firmer links between NATO and US strategic forces. The various West German, Belgian, Dutch and British debates over LRTNF modernization have so far tended to focus on its impact on arms control and detente, rather than on forging a sound mix of employment capabilities to strengthen its deterrent value. While NATO certainly discusses the need for such plans and concepts, it has made little real progress in developing them.

The GLCM has experienced serious recent development problems. There are difficulties in warhead design and reliability, and the guidance system is proving far more sensitive to mapping problems and other anomalies than had been hoped. The GLCM delivery date may have to slip 1–3 years, or it may have to be put in service with poor overall systems reliability. Furthermore, few US experts are happy about the present basing, deployment, C³I and targeting concepts for the cruise missiles. There is a fairly broad consensus that hard shelters on air bases leave the systems far too vulnerable to pre-emptive attack for effective survival and flexible employment at the levels of nuclear combat necesary to link theatre and strategic forces. Many planners feel that the current basing concept tends to invite a Soviet first strike and to act as an incentive to Soviet planners to develop dedicated forces to attack the GLCM bases and facilities.

Underlying this lack of attention to survivability is a continued attachment by the NATO military to SACEUR's existing target list and a history of reserving long-range systems for a general nuclear response in concert with the SIOP. Unfortunately, it has proved easier for the NATO military to demonstrate a need for more forces on the basis of a growing list of targets and SACEUR's inability to cover them all without assistance from strategic forces than to take limited nuclear option planning seriously and build the options and capabilities to support such a strategy.

Although French nuclear forces are improving in numbers and capabilities, and inevitably reinforce extended deterrence to some degree, they remain largely isolated from NATO. They also lack the kind of warning, C³I and targeting systems that would allow their effective employment in limited strikes in concert with NATO. Current and programmed French forces also lack survivability, and the French government has made it clear that it has little interest in joint planning for extended deterrence. The result is that French forces tend to retain a 'trigger force' character. They are potentially large enough to force NATO to join France if she should choose to escalate unilaterally or to force NATO into the position of attempting formally to decouple itself from any Soviet attack on France. At the same time, they increase the Soviet incentive to conduct large-scale theatre strikes against them by being significant and rather vulnerable.

As a result, even if NATO does implement its agreement to deploy the *Pershing* and GLCM systems, and France and Britain do upgrade their national nuclear forces, Table 8 shows that it is still not clear that this will close the gap between NATO and Warsaw Pact LRTNF quickly enough, and no convincing basing options have yet been advanced to ensure the survivability of NATO's theatre nuclear forces in conventional or nuclear war. To put this in perspective, the USSR now has 275 SS-20 launch positions, of which at least 175 are targeted on Europe. This will perhaps rise to a total of 350–500 launch positions in the future. These now have two missiles per launcher, but may well increase to 3–5. At three warheads per missile, the USSR now has 525 SS-20 warheads ready to launch against Europe at any given time, and 1,500 including reloads and missiles with dual targeting capability. These numbers could, on worst-case assumptions, rise to a staggering 3,150–7,500 SS-20 warheads targetable on Europe if all missiles, including those normally aimed at China and

Japan, are counted. And this does not include the SS-22 or SS-23. In contrast NATO is discussing the introduction of new systems with only 572 warheads, and then only in the mid-1980s.

Demonstrating US Intentions

The Carter Administration had obvious problems in trying to determine how it should express a declared US strategy for extended deterrence. There is no doubt that it strongly repeated its commitment to extended deterrence on every suitable occasion, nor that it backed the necessary improvement of NATO nuclear forces even at the cost of raising problems with the USSR and rejecting Brezhnev's recent arms-control initiatives. Nor is there any doubt that it set out to procure many of the necessary improvements in its strategic forces, and that the Reagan Administration is as firmly committed to this policy and will accelerate these force improvements.

At the same time, the issue of how the US would actually extend deterrence to Europe has tended to be left hanging in the air, and little public reference has been made to the changes that have been introduced in American LSO capabilities or to the impact of the other relevant changes taking place in the nuclear balance. Secretary Brown, for example, made reference to LSO in his FY 1980 *Annual Report* (pp. 84–5), but simply in order to discuss the problems affecting their implementation. He explicitly rejected US reliance on 'assured destruction' to implement extended deterrence: 'Our allies, particularly in Europe, have questioned for some time whether the threat of assured destruction would be credible as a response to nuclear threats against them . . . it is little wonder in the circumstances that for many years we have had alternatives to counter-city retaliation in our plans, and a posture substantial and responsive enough to permit the exercise of these options.'

Yet Secretary Brown went on to state that the American ability to protect Europe may be weakening, and devoted most of his twelve page discussion of strategic and theatre nuclear capabilities to the problems of deciding what to do about US strategy, rather than to what the US had decided to do (*Annual Report*, pp. 74–86). More American leadership is obviously required, and this may well be the Reagan Administration's greatest challenge in its dealings with NATO's European leaders over nuclear affairs. The United States cannot simply say to Europe that it is investigating the problems of implementing extended deterrence; she must declare the details of her capabilities, and her willingness to act. She must also state what her strategy is, and what concrete programmes are in hand for accomplishing this strategy, in far stronger and more precise terms than just using ritual reassurances. She must communicate to both Europe and the USSR just how great American capabilities are becoming, and she must show convincingly why these capabilities will not be threatened by improvements in Soviet strategic forces.

CONCLUSIONS

The United States and her European Allies face major challenges in making extended deterrence effective in the 1980s. If the West is to be successful, it must complete the transition begun in the early 1970s and end its reliance on US strategic superiority. It must develop an effective mix of strategic and theatre nuclear capabilities that can influence Soviet perceptions – and reinforce deterrence – in the face of the major improvements taking place in Soviet strategic and theatre nuclear forces.

The United States and NATO are already making major progress towards completing this transition. The United States has made many of the improvements that are required in her strategic forces, and the force improvement programme announced by the Reagan Administration in October 1981 will lead her to make most of the others. She is beginning to implement properly the strategy of limited strategic strike options which former Secretary of Defense James Schlesinger enunciated in 1974, and the Carter Administration added the missing focus by improving the link between US strategic forces and NATO's theatre nuclear delivery systems. Although NATO's collective progress is more halting, the deployment of GLCM and *Pershing* II forces can provide it with the long-range delivery systems needed to improve the coupling of theatre and strategic forces, and Britain is planning independent improvements in long-range strike capabilities that should tend to further reinforce extended deterrence.

Yet this level of progress provides no firm guarantee that the West will continue to meet all of the basic criteria necessary for the United States to extend deterrence to Europe, or that it will develop a sound mix of capabilities to reinforce its credibility and stability. While the US and NATO are now in a far better position actually to execute the nuclear strikes that extended deterrence implies than they were in 1972, the Soviet threat has also increased sharply, and the West faces a broad spectrum of problems that both the US and Europe are still not prepared to deal with.

Extended Deterrence in the 1980s
The extent to which the joint ability of US and NATO forces is adequate to sustain extended deterrence is best illustrated by the extent to which these forces do and do not meet the criteria set forth in Chapter II.

Meeting the Minimum Criteria
The West should have a relatively high capability to meet the minimum criteria for extended deterrence in the 1980s, if the US continues to improve her strategic forces at the pace necessary to match the changes taking place in the Soviet strategic threat. The central criterion must be that the risk of using US strategic forces in addition to NATO theatre forces ought, in terms of the resulting escalation, to be limited enough to avoid the US running an unacceptable risk of mutual civil and economic anihilation with the Soviet Union. US strategic forces and plans do now offer major alternatives to mutual assured destruction. The United States can plan to employ her strategic forces in many types of LSO where the risk of escalation to all-out war seems acceptable. If anything, the steady increase in the total strategic and long-range theatre forces on each side should reduce the incentive to escalate to all-out war if limited uses are made of strategic forces, and should reduce any tendency to

over-react to limited strikes without fully assessing their nature.

The second criterion is that the US must have sufficient survivable forces that even large-scale exchanges in defence of NATO will not lead to an unacceptable 'run down' of her strategic capabilities against the USSR. The present mix of strategic delivery systems in the US triad, and their current and planned warhead loading, offer the ability to launch far larger strikes in support of NATO – without degrading US strategic capabilities – than are ever likely to be required. The discussion of US counterforce vulnerability has shown that this capability is unlikely to be affected by the vulnerability of US ICBM even under worst-case assumptions, given the thousands of weapons on survivable US SLBM, bombers and attack submarines. Further, US capability to target OMT and civil facilities essential to the conduct of Soviet military operations has steadily improved since the early 1970s. By the mid 1980s the US should be able to draw on her satellite sensors and other intelligence capabilities to provide a significant amount of timely data for use in limited strategic strikes in direct support of NATO tactical forces. She can already use these capabilities to attack many Warsaw Pact targets which are in the US target base or for all-out strategic war. Such strikes in support of NATO do not by definition degrade US strategic retaliatory capabilities.

Third, the US must have flexibility in terms of rapid targeting and the control of collateral damage. The improvements in her intelligence systems have unquestionably given the US great flexibility in targeting, and she has steadily increased the sophistication of her target planning over the last two decades. The improvements to the *Minuteman* force will give very rapid retargeting capability, and the US SIOP contains literally thousands of Warsaw Pact targets of major military importance to the USSR where collateral damage to civil population is below the threshold that would be inevitable in any large-scale nuclear exchange. While the US may not yet have adequately planned to use this flexibility in a sufficiently wide range of LSO in her war plans, and does not now plan to provide her SLBM and bomber forces with enough rapid retargeting and C^3 capability to give them the highest possible retargeting and damage-limiting capability for use in theatre combat, she does have enough current capability to sustain extended deterrence, and her programmed C^3 improvements will substantially improve this capability by the mid-1980s.

Finally, US determination to use strategic forces in the defence of Europe must be credible. Soviet knowledge of US capabilities and war plans is sufficiently great for the USSR almost certainly to accept the fact that any large-scale theatre conflict might lead the US to use her strategic forces in limited nuclear strike options. If anything, the USSR may be frightened by the lack of flexibility in combined US and NATO plans and capabilities, and the possibility these would lead the US to escalate too quickly or to over-react. While there is a clear gap between US military plans and capabilities and the lack of any well-defined NATO declaratory strategy, the USSR is likely to shape her perceptions on the basis of those military capabilities and not on the conflicting and uncertain statements of US and European political leaders.

Accordingly, the problem does not seem to lie with the *credibility* of extended deterrence, which is likely to be continuously reinforced by Soviet intelligence as the US improves her capabilities, plans and exercising. It seems instead to lie in the lack of any clear Soviet belief that the West can manage such conflicts with skill and restraint, and in the Soviet perception that NATO currently has a mix of forces whose vulnerability and limited command-and-control capabilities have sufficient first-strike characteristics to create a strong Soviet incentive to launch large-scale disabling strikes in an initial attack, or to pre-empt at the first rough indicators that NATO may be bringing its forces to readiness.

Meeting Other Criteria
US and NATO forces seem equally likely to meet many of the non-essential, but desirable, criteria for extended deterrence in the 1980s, although both the US and NATO need to improve their capabilities. This is particularly true of NATO theatre forces, although a number of relatively low-cost improvements in the US forces could have major benefits. For example, there is no need for the US to be able to launch

counterforce strikes against Soviet strategic nuclear forces. However, while she will not be able to launch counterforce strikes in the sense of being able to degrade Soviet capabilities to strike at an unacceptably large number of US urban industrial complexes and OMT targets, she will, nevertheless, be able to strike selectively at those Soviet strategic forces which are employed in theatre conflicts, and to strike at Soviet strategic forces as an option in conducting LSO strikes.

Although it is semantically something of a contradiction in terms, the US does not need a 'war-fighting' capability. Yet, while there is no expectation that US strategic forces can develop a 'war-fighting' capability that can 'win' an all-out conflict with the USSR while acceptably limiting damage to the US, they can certainly 'fight' wars at many different levels of escalation. Moreover, the US can certainly extend deterrence by threatening to inflict high levels of damage, by seeking to terminate conflicts on terms favourable to NATO, and by demonstrating her willingness to increase the level of damage she inflicts until the Warsaw Pact accepts NATO's terms. There is little question that the US will have this capability during the 1980s. There are some major rigidities inherent in her present forces and force improvement plans, but these are not such as to leave large gaps between the levels of escalation (or intensity within those levels) that the USSR seems likely to be able to exploit. Most of these rigidities lie in US and NATO C^3 systems, and not in the force size or force structure now planned for the mid-1980s. They can, therefore, be largely eliminated at comparatively low cost.

Although there is no requirement for the US to have highly flexible and survivable C^3I, targeting, damage assessment and re-targeting capabilities (for the US can rely on pre-planned strikes, given her vast peacetime targeting capability and the dependence of the USSR on fixed facilities and the inherent value of the entire Warsaw Pact fixed target base), she does in fact possess such capabilities in some degree. The cost of substantially upgrading US, NATO and European national capabilities is in any case low enough to be feasible in the 1980s, and there are strong indications that such capabilities may be funded by the Reagan Admini-

113

stration. They could perhaps be on line by the mid-1980s.

It can also be argued that the US and NATO do not need a clear strategy for the use of US strategic systems in extending deterrence to Europe. While the US strategy may not be clear in the sense of reflecting a single approach to the problem – it has been declared in broad terms, and this declaration is supported by strike options and military capabilities which are known to the USSR. Nevertheless, the lack of any cohesive NATO doctrine, the confusing and shallow nature of the current debate over extended deterrence, and the problems in NATO theatre nuclear planning and force structures create difficulties for the convincing application of the doctrine of extended deterrence. While the links between US strategic forces and the defence of NATO are not now 'guaranteed' – indeed cannot be guaranteed – the US has clearly done more than utter empty reassurances to her European Allies. She has made those changes in her doctrine, plans and forces which are essential if she is to maintain extended deterrence in spite of the changes now taking place in the balance of strategic and theatre nuclear forces, and she continues actively to pursue the development of more effective links between strategic and theatre forces.

Further Desirable Steps
There are six relatively low-cost steps which the US and Europe could take which would greatly strengthen extended deterrence in the 1980s.

Rejecting Reliance on Strategic Superiority
US and European political and military leaders must fully accept the fact that extended deterrence can never again be tied to US strategic superiority. There is no possibility that the US can regain enough 'superiority' in fighting a general strategic war to allow any lowering of the threshold of nuclear deterrence. The steady increase in the number of strategic warheads available to both sides will make it less and less likely that the threat to escalate to general war can serve to protect interests. The USSR, for example, will probably at least double her deployed strategic warheads over the next decade even if she fully complies with SALT II. The US will probably increase her own warhead numbers

enough to retain her lead in total numbers of deliverable weapons, but this will not make the threat of all-out war more credible.

The US must continue to seek strategic parity with the USSR to preserve an ultimate deterrent to ultimate war, and to influence world perceptions of US military and political power. However, this search for parity cannot by itself provide the bridge the West needs between theatre and strategic forces. This can only be accomplished by a dedicated American effort to develop all the force capabilities necesary to employ strategic forces effectively in a suitable range of limited nuclear options and by ensuring that the US force improvement plans previously described are implemented. The new Administration seems firmly committed to this course of action.

Similarly, the NATO military authorities (SACEUR and SHAPE in particular) must reject the thesis that NATO nuclear war plans can consist primarily of a series of limited short-range theatre options linked to large-scale strike options in the SIOP. The Joint Strategic Target Planning Staff (JSTPS) and SHAPE must jointly develop war plans which fully implement the rethinking begun in NSDM-242, PRM-10, PD-18 and PD-59 and symbolized by US support of the GLCM/*Pershing* II force. NATO plans are now far too rigid, involve initial thresholds of nuclear conflict which are far too high, and owe too much to the threat to escalate to all-out war. It is unclear whether the Reagan Administration has yet recognized the extent of this problem.

At the same time, NATO and European military planners must accept that they will not get theatre nuclear forces large enough to 'match' Soviet long-range strike capabilities or to replace US strategic superiority. The issue for NATO military planning is not to justify more and more long-range theatre systems as a substitute for strategic parity, but rather to make the available and planned long-range theatre systems effective, and to establish a convincing bridge between NATO's shorter-range systems and US strategic forces. This may or may not require somewhat more theatre nuclear forces than are currently planned in US and British force improvements, but it definitely does not mean trying to establish a force of several thousand new long-range NATO systems simply because the Warsaw Pact has them.

In short, both US and European leaders must fully accept that what is needed is a mix of strategic and theatre war-fighting capabilities for limited nuclear conflict which will deter the USSR at all levels of theatre conflict and which will provide as seamless a continuum of nuclear options as possible so as to limit any conflict that does occur as much as possible. NATO must also seek to deprive the USSR of any incentive to sustain conflict at a given intensity or to escalate it to some higher level of violence.

Joint Strategic and Theatre Nuclear Planning
The steady increase in the complexity of strategic forces and in the ways in which they can be employed requires that both Europeans and Americans carry out joint and continuous nuclear planning and analysis that must be far more comprehensive than in the past. European defence authorities will have to become involved in the details of strategic forces and war-planning in the 1980s if Europe is to understand American capabilities and limitations well enough to place the proper degree of trust in the American ability to extend deterrence and pursue the required improvement in European-based nuclear forces.

Above all, European officials and military officers and the NATO Military Commands must be brought fully into the process of US LSO planning. There is no longer a place for 'tokenism' or largely symbolic NATO nuclear planning activities such as the NPG. The US must allow Europe to participate fully, and Europe must take that participation seriously. The current (largely *pro forma*) NATO institutions for nuclear planning must be made effective. Nor will it be enough just to develop the right plans at SHAPE. Nuclear war plans for the 1980s must be fully understood by national defence ministries and commands. Again, the intentions of the Reagan Administration remain unclear in this area.

Improving Command and Control
NATO should provide the range of improvements in C³ systems and in intelligence, targeting and damage assessment capabilities that would convince the USSR that NATQ could, if necessary, employ a mix of theatre and strategic forces proportionate to the theatre attacks which the West wants to deter. There are obviously many different levels at which such capabilities are needed if the US is to extend deterrence to NATO Europe. At present, European national authorities and NATO headquarters are so poorly provided with secure and durable communications and are so vulnerable that they are not adequate for any substantial theatre nuclear conflict. Only US theatre nuclear forces are now programmed to acquire some of the command-and-control links to US strategic forces that would improve their ability to operate in common.

These improvements do not seem likely to require massive increases in the funding of either European national command-and-control capabilities, or in the NATO infrastructure programme. They do require, however, that existing levels of investment in NATO C³I be adjusted and improved to support both conventional forces and NATO theatre and US strategic forces without reliance on large-scale or pre-planned attacks. The Reagan Administration is seeking some of these improvements, but there is as yet no adequate European plan for such improvements.

Improving US Support Capabilities
The US should fund all the improvements in her military satellites necessary to allow them to be used in conducting effective LSO and long-range theatre strikes, and she should share more of her national intelligence. Such a sharing of upgraded US strategic C³ systems may be the only method by which NATO can collectively conduct LSO planning and the management of joint strategic/theatre nuclear strikes. Sharing US intelligence systems also seems increasingly more feasible as much of the more sensitive classified data relating to US reconnaissance satellites and SIGINT sensors have become known to the USSR. There would also be substantial benefits for NATO's conduct of conventional operations.

It would be equally desirable to upgrade the retargeting capability of the US strategic forces, and to improve American ability to use all of the triad of strategic forces in limited strategic strikes. The US may, for example, be underfunding both the relevant C³ and retargeting capabilities of *Minuteman* and MX, and the link between her strategic command posts and NATO. She may also have failed to provide enough flexibility for employing her B-52G and ALCM in limited strikes, either in concert with the GLCM to be deployed in Europe or to compensate for Soviet theatre strikes against them.

At the same time, it would be desirable for the US to accelerate efforts to give the *Trident* II programme a capability to launch accurate strikes in support of NATO, tailored to specific theatre requirements. Similar capabilities might be given to US SLCM. This would fully decouple US capabilities for extending deterrence from the ICBM vulnerability issue and would reduce any need to use US strategic systems based on US soil.

While these improvements may not be essential for deterrence to be extended to Europe, they would greatly increase US capability to support NATO, greatly complicate Soviet planning and ensure that US LNO capability was not affected by changes in the vulnerability of any given part of the triad.

Improving Survivability
NATO also needs to make further reductions in the vulnerability of its theatre nuclear strike forces. It is true that reducing the number of dedicated nuclear strike aircraft will reduce the Soviet incentive to launch nuclear strikes at NATO air bases, and that GLCM and *Pershing* II should be substantially less vulnerable once dispersed. However, neither the *Pershing* II nor GLCM basing concepts reduce the incentive for the USSR to strike at their peacetime bases if she can do so before NATO's long-range systems are dispersed as the result of an alert.

The GLCM basing concept seems not entirely satisfactory. Current NATO plans envisage the basing of the 464 GLCM in hard shelters on a limited number of US airfields in Europe with the missiles truck-mounted and dispersable, given warning. However, the associated C³I links seem likely to be inadequate and such peacetime basing of the GLCM tends to reinforce the Soviet perception that NATO still focuses on a general release of long-range weapons and a first-strike posture, giving the USSR a continued incentive to escalate.

It is true that keeping the GLCM and *Pershing* II systems dispersed in peacetime and moving them often enough to disrupt Soviet targeting could double the operating costs of the force and the manpower required. This, however,

may be a comparatively small price to pay for assured survival of the force, and it would imply that NATO could use its theatre nuclear forces with restraint. Certainly, the Permissive Action Links (PAL) and C³I technology is available to allow such basing with safety. Such improvements in basing might also eliminate any subsequent need to increase system numbers to compensate for future increases in Soviet warheads and targeting capabilities, and that would improve the prospects of both European acceptance and TNF arms control.

Influencing Soviet Perceptions
Finally, both US and European policy-makers need to pay more attention to the fact that they should be attempting to deter the USSR by influencing Soviet perceptions, rather than winning arguments with each other. Much of the present debate over extended deterrence and theatre nuclear force modernization never mentions whether or not Soviet planners are likely to find the resulting capability convincing enough to be deterred by it. The West must begin to regard the USSR as a highly sophisticated opponent. The Soviet Union has never enjoyed the luxury of being able to keep her planning of strategic and theatre nuclear forces separate, and she has long focused on what kinds of long-range theatre forces and strikes are practical and credible. For all her declaratory rhetoric, she has always tended to look at capabilities rather than at the symbols of military strength, and she has enjoyed distressingly good and timely access to classified data on United States and NATO capabilities and war plans.

It follows that extended deterrence will be shaped in large part by capabilities and not simply by rhetoric. The USSR will also tend to judge the credibility of the United States to extend deterrence by highly demanding standards and to be more fully aware perhaps than most European NATO governments of any weaknesses or vulnerabilities that she can exploit. At the same time, the USSR is far less likely to be concerned with American will to use strategic forces or to risk escalation to general war if she sees tangible evidence that the US and NATO can jointly use strategic and theatre forces in a wide range of options and at several different levels of escalation.

In this regard, it is interesting to note that the USSR probably reacted more strongly to Schlesinger's initial announcement of an LSO strategy in 1974, to US plans to modernize NATO long-range theatre nuclear systems, and to the implications of PD-59 than to any other improvements in US strategic and NATO theatre forces over the last two decades. It is obvious that the USSR takes such developments with great seriousness when it looks as if the West will develop real capabilities.

If the US and Europe can take these six steps, this should provide a high assurance that the West can deal with any Soviet force improvements that seem possible through the mid-1980s. It would also demonstrate that the West has the unity to respond to Soviet actions and provide the basis for developing the coherent plans and doctrine to cope with unanticipated threats or new Soviet challenges in the 1980s. These changes in official plans and doctrine need to be supported by improvements in the efforts of the strategic studies community to analyse extended deterrence, and by changes in the character of the present debate over strategic and theatre nuclear forces.

In particular, the West needs to correct a tendency to polarize the debate about nuclear force improvements. On one side is the 'force size' or pro-nuclear camp. This camp structures many of its arguments for nuclear force modernization in such a way as to shift NATO from conventional options to greater reliance on nuclear forces and seeks to match every major aspect of Warsaw Pact nuclear forces, regardless of the need to do so. On the other side is the 'conventional' camp, which fears that any major improvement in theatre nuclear forces will come at the expense of improvements in conventional forces. It tends to oppose TNF improvements, not out of a conviction they are not necessary but rather from the unstated perspective that they are less necessary than conventional improvements. These two camps do little more than obscure the issue of what needs to be done, while pushing discussion of extended deterrence towards impractical extremes – over-reliance on conventional and strategic forces or seeking unachievable and unnecessary increases in theatre nuclear forces.

American capabilities to extend nuclear deterrence are only one essential link in the whole process of deterrence. They can certainly reinforce conventional capabilities at high levels of conflict, but it does not look likely that NATO conventional forces will ever reach the levels where feasible trade-offs can be made between conventional forces and nuclear forces. It would, of course, be cheaper to rely to a greater extent on nuclear systems, but that is no longer an option open to NATO.

A balanced combination of NATO theatre and US strategic capabilities can make both the US and Europe safer. The Warsaw Pact could come to see that any attack on Europe could result in unacceptable loss, and an appropriate mix of theatre capabilities would greatly increase the problems that the USSR would face in contemplating any attack on US strategic forces. There is no point, however, in increasing either US or NATO forces beyond what is planned. Such increases would not significantly enhance NATO capabilities, and the USSR is more likely to be influenced by capability than by size.

Finally, although political relations between the US and Europe are not the subject of this Paper, it is obvious that the NATO Allies need to do a far better job of communicating with each other and with their respective citizens. The recent split between the US and Europe over the 'twin track' approach to pursuing arms control and the LRTNF improvement programme could grow far more serious in the future. If the West is to develop a coherent approach to strengthening extended deterrence, that approach must be fully understood on both sides of the Atlantic and be understood by the public as well as the politicians. The current almost totally unrealistic debates about large-scale nuclear wars being fought over the heads of Europe or on European soil while excluding the US, grow out of a degree of ignorance that stems largely from a past failure even to try to communicate the reality of extended deterrence. If there is to be a 'strategic consensus' within NATO, this situation must change in the future. Europe must pay as much attention to US strategic developments as to those in theatre forces. Similarly, the US must recognize the linkage, and that it cannot unilaterally plan US strategic forces which are Europe's ultimate defence.

117

TABLES

Table 1: Delivery Systems Affecting Extended Deterrence

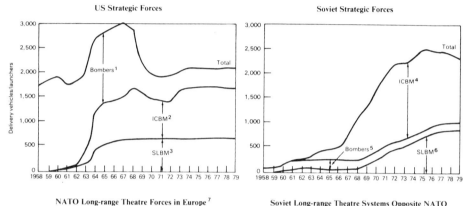

US Strategic Forces

Soviet Strategic Forces

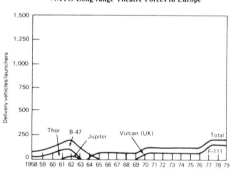

NATO Long-range Theatre Forces in Europe [7]

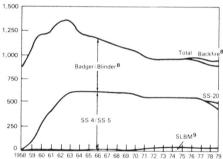

Soviet Long-range Theatre Systems Opposite NATO

[1] B-47 and B-52 bombers, excluding B-47 based in Europe.
[2] *Atlas*, *Titan* and *Minuteman*.
[3] Number of tubes on US *Polaris* and *Poseidon* SSBN. Includes SLBM dedicated to SACEUR.
[4] SS-7, -8, -9, -11, -13, -17, -18 and -19.
[5] *Bear* and *Bison*.
[6] SLBM tubes on active submarines.

[7] Does not include French Forces or 400 *Polaris/Poseidon* warheads assigned to SACEUR or British SLBM.
[8] Excluding naval versions.
[9] SLBM tubes directed against NATO.

SOURCE: Modified from DOD data of October 1979 by the author.

Table 2: US and Soviet MIRV Strength

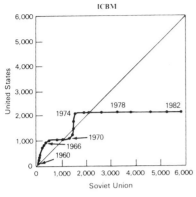

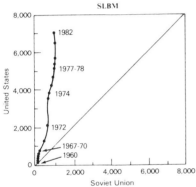

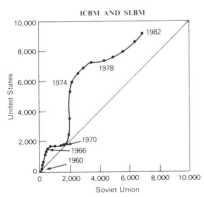

SOURCE: Santa Fe Corporation, 'Measures and Trends of US and USSR Strategic Force Effectiveness'. March 1978, pp. 34, 36 and 38.

Table 3: Changes in Strategic Capabilities, 1964–1982 (Rumsfeld Estimate)

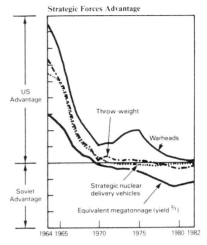

Table 4: Composition of Forces (1980)

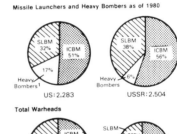

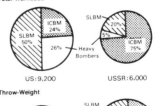

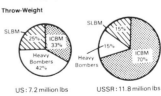

[1] Includes approximately 220 B-52 in deep storage.

SOURCE: Adapted from DOD FY 1981 Annual Report, Tables 5–3 and 5–6.

119

Table 5: Counter-force Exchange Capabilities (warheads)

On-line Forces

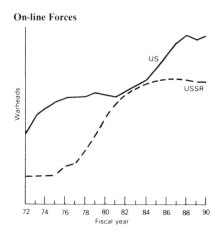

After Soviet First Strike

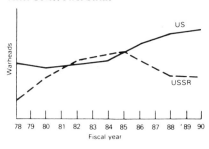

After Soviet First Strike and US Retaliation

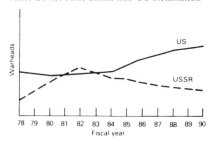

SOURCE: Secretary of Defense Harold Brown, Testimony to the Senate Committee on Foreign Relations, 9 and 11 July 1979.

120

Table 6: Comparative Investment in Strategic Forces

1. Cumulative: 1971–1980 (billion 1979 dollars)

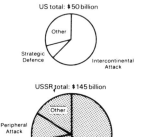

SOURCE: These comparisons use *US Defense Planning and Programming Categories* of November 1980 with minor adjustments to attain comparability. Investment includes all costs for the procurement of military hardware and the construction of facilities. 'Other' category includes nuclear weapons and strategic control and surveillance. Costs for pensions and RDT&E are excluded. Procurement excludes construction and nuclear weapons materials.

2. Trend: 1970–1979

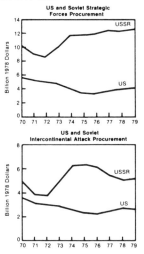

SOURCE: Adapted by the author from unclassified data provided by the Central Intelligence Agency.

Table 7: US and Soviet Strategic Force Strengths 1977–81

	1 January 1977		1 January 1978		1 January 1979		1 January 1980		1 January 1981	
	US	USSR	US	USSR	US	USSR	US	USSR	US	USSR
OFFENSIVE										
Operational ICBM										
Launchers[1]	1,054	1,550	1,054	1,400+	1,054	1,400	1,054	1,398	1,054	1,398
Operational SLBM										
Launchers[1,2]	656	800	656	900+	656	950	656	950	576	950
Long-range bombers (TAI*)[3]										
Operational[4]	419	190	349	140	348	150	348	156	347	156
Others[5]	184	170	225	0	221	0	225		223	
Variants[6]	–	–	0	120	0	120	–	–	–	–
Force Loadings[7]										
Weapons	8,400	3,300	9,000	4,000+	9,200	5,000	9,200	6,000	9,000	7,000
DEFENSIVE										
Air Defence Surveillance										
Radars[7]	59	6,000	59	6,500	59	7,000	88	7,000	91	7,000
Interceptors (TAI*)	416	2,590	324	2,600	309	2,500	327	2,500	312	2,500
SAM Launchers	–	10,000	–	10,000	0	10,000[9]	0	10,000	0	10,000
ABM Defence										
Launchers[9]	–	64	–	64	0	64	0	64	0	64

NOTES:

[1] Includes on-line launchers as well as those being built, overhauled, repaired, converted and modernized. Excludes test and training launchers and 18 launchers of fractional orbital missiles at Tyuratam test range.

[2] Includes launchers on all nuclear-powered submarines and operational launchers for modern SLBM on Soviet G-class diesel submarines. Excludes 48 SALT II-accountable launchers on 3 *Polaris* submarines now used as attack submarines.

[3] 1981 figures exclude 65 US FB-111 and over 100 Soviet *Backfires*, about 120 *Bison* tankers and *Bear* ASW and reconnaissance aircraft.

[4] Includes deployed, strike-configured aircraft only.

[5] Includes B-52s used for miscellaneous purposes or in reserve, mothballs or storage and 4 B-1 prototypes; includes *Bears* and *Bisons* used for test, training and R&D.

[6] Includes, for USSR, *Bison* tankers, *Bear* ASW and reconnaissance aircraft. US tankers (641 KC-135s) do not use B-52 airframes and are excluded.

[7] Total force loadings reflect independently-targetable weapons associated with the total operational ICBM, SLBM and long-range bombers.

[8] Excludes radars and launchers at test sites or outside North America.

[9] These accommodate about 12,000 SAM interceptors. Some launchers have multiple rails.

* TAI: Total Available Inventory.

SOURCE: Adapted from DOD Annual reports FY 78–FY 82.

Table 8: Estimated US/NATO and Soviet On-Line Land-Based Long-Range Theatre Nuclear Forces [1]

	Missile Range/ Aircraft Radius (km)	Weapons Per System	1 January 1981				Mid-1980s (Estimated)			
			Total Launchers/ Aircraft Worldwide	Total Launchers/ Aircraft Europe[2]	Total Warheads Worldwide	Total Warheads Europe[2]	Total Launchers/ Aircraft Worldwide	Total Launchers/ Aircraft Europe[2]	Total Warheads Worldwide	Total Warheads Europe[2]
Soviet										
SS-20 launchers	≥4,400	3	180	110	540	330	300+[3]	[4]	900[3]	[4]
Backfire bombers[5]	4,200	4[6]	65-70	40	260-280[8]	160	150	[4]	600	[4]
Older missiles	1,900-4,100	1	400	400	400	400	50-200[7]	50-200[7]	50-200[7]	50-200[7]
Older bombers[5]	2,800-3,100	2[6]	450	350	900	700	400	300	800	600
NATO										
UK *Vulcan* bomber	>2,000	_[8]	56	56	_[8]	_[8]	0	0	0	0
US F-111	1,800	2[6]	360	170	720	340	330	170	660	340
US GLCM	>2,000	1	0	0	0	0	464[9]	464[9]	464[9]	464[9]
US *Pershing* II	>2,000	1	0	0	0	0	108[9]	108[9]	108[9]	108[9]

NOTES:
[1] Soviet systems that can unambiguously hit targets in Western Europe from bases in the USSR, and NATO systems that can unambiguously hit the USSR from bases in Western Europe. Aircraft radii are illustrative for European missions.
[2] Inventory normally based in, or within striking range of, Europe.
[3] Because of the continuing construction programme, the SS-20 force may be larger than estimated here.
[4] Two-thirds of worldwide inventory could be deployed against NATO.
[5] Strike-configured bombers and ASM carriers only; excludes comparable numbers of *Backfire* and older bombers currently assigned to Soviet Naval Aviation.
[6] Illustrative weapons load. Actual load would vary according to mission and type of weapon (ASM or bombs).
[7] Numbers shown reflect uncertainties about the future status of the older missile launchers.
[8] Unclassified data not available.
[9] After completion of LRTNF modernization.

SOURCE: Adapted from *Department of Defense Annual Report Fiscal Year 1981*, p.66.

4 Nuclear Forces and Alliance Relations: Updating Deterrence in Europe — Inflexible Response?

FRANÇOIS DE ROSE

It is no longer possible to deny it. The European will to defend is in the throes of a serious crisis.

After a period of more than thirty years, during which the deterrent seemed to ensure the safety of Europe, there is today a loss of confidence in the ability of the Alliance, and in particular in its strategy based on the threat of use of nuclear weapons within the framework of 'flexible response', to forestall any conflict. The result is that the nuclear capability of NATO, which has long been considered to provide the most effective guarantee for maintaining peace, now seems itself to constitute a risk of war to many sections of public opinion in a number of countries.[1]

Fear, however, is always a bad adviser, and the reactions which it provokes run completely counter to that which could dissipate its cause. At a time when an objective analysis of the situation shows that the deterrent is not a thing of the past, it can be

seen that with an adapted doctrine and adapted means there is no reason for a hypothetical war to be less dangerous for the enemy than for ourselves.

It should not be understood from the following that a conventional or nuclear Soviet attack at a time chosen by the Kremlin is to be considered as the most probable prospect. The best strategy will always be the strategy which provides the fruits of victory without combat. However, whether during a crisis or in the daily running of affairs, international relations are governed by what each country knows of its own capabilities and vulnerabilities and of those of its adversaries. It is this balance, which is confusedly seen as unfavourable in Europe, which is grist to the mill of Soviet propaganda and which is prompting public opinion to take up the cause of neutralism. It is thus necessary to know the true strengths and the true weaknesses in order to steer oneself a bit less gropingly through this dangerous world.

NATO Doctrine and the Balance of Forces
In thirty-two years the Atlantic Alliance has had two doctrines of defence: the 'massive retaliation'

This article is a translation based on pieces by François de Rose which were published in *Le Mande* of 21 and 22–23 November 1981.

of 1949 to the beginning of the 1960s, and 'flexible response' from then onwards. The change from one to the other took place when the Soviet Union acquired her first intercontinental missiles. Today it is the balance of forces between the two European Alliances which has changed from what it was when the flexible response doctrine was adopted. It is possible therefore to ask whether the second concept is still valid and whether it will remain so in the future.

As long as the West had superiority in terms of theatre nuclear weapons, it was able to press home to the enemy the threat of their use when a conventional battle was not proceeding in its favour. The response would have been flexible, in the sense that instead of carrying out massive attacks on population or industrial targets, it would have been adapted to the need to prevent a victory on the part of the aggressor, whatever the level of violence he had chosen, whilst forcing him, on all levels, to raise the stakes to obtain resolution.

The situation could, to a certain extent, have been compared to that of two wrestlers, one heavyweight and the other flyweight. The former would have the power to adapt his pressure to the force of the latter, but not *vice versa*.

This situation has developed, as is well known. There is little doubt that the Red Army today could 'control escalation' in the same way as NATO. The Red Army will doubtlessly be able, at least in theory, to carry out a future strike which could eliminate a large portion of the conventional and nuclear elements of European defence systems.

Flexible response is therefore available to them as well, and the danger of escalation would be at least as great for the victim as for the aggressor. In other words, the justification or the internal logic of a doctrine based on a ratio of forces in which the superiority of one alliance was compensated by the advantages of the other elsewhere, may be questioned when this balance of inequalities no longer exists. We are now in the uncomfortable situation where this ratio of forces at different levels provides the enemy rather than us with the choice of weapons and, consequently, of the strategy to be used in the case of aggression.

During the period of American superiority in the field of tactical nuclear weapons, Soviet doctrine, as stated in the most authoritative texts, in particular by Marshal Sokolovsky, was that the destruction of the nuclear weapons of the enemy was 'indispensable to the victorious outcome of military operations'. Nowadays such statements put matters in a different light, such as those statements explaining that the Red Army would never be the first to resort to nuclear weapons. However, Marshal Ustinov is simultaneously warning countries which

accept Euromissiles on their territory that they are running the risk of being the target for nuclear attack.

Consequently, it is difficult to foresee the outcome. The fact is that the Soviet Union may choose between conventional and nuclear war. It is very possible that the views expressed by Marshal Sokolovsky are still valid. But it is equally plausible that the Red Army would exploit its conventional superiority to march on the West, leaving to the West the 'agonizing' decision of whether to use nuclear weapons, knowing that as soon as these weapons are used, even at a limited level in conformity with flexible response, the Soviet arsenal could completely destroy Europe, both with respect to its industrial and population targets and its military targets.

In other words, flexible response, based on the concept of providing the enemy with a problem which is more difficult for them to solve than it is for the West, no longer satisfies this requirement. It would be the West which would run the greatest risk if it took the nuclear initiative as called for by current doctrine: that of the destruction of Europe without the involvement of Soviet territory.

What has Really Changed
The European error is to take the threat provided by the SS-20 as the most important change in the balance of forces in their continent. This change has taken place on all levels, but the most important change has been the result of the increasing difficulty of NATO air forces to penetrate Soviet defences in full expansion. This has led to the need to introduce *Pershing* and cruise missiles, which is justified less from a desire to counter-balance or equal the SS-20 than from the desire to re-establish the possibility of attacking the main enemy, and the only enemy to possess nuclear weapons, on their own ground. Consequently, even if the Soviet Union had not modernized her arsenal, the West would have had to modernize theirs. The real changes have taken place in the area of vulnerabilities. The vulnerability of Europe has worsened whereas that of the Soviet Union has continuously decreased.

It is this imbalance which Moscow would like to freeze by negotiation. If Moscow managed to prevent the introduction of new American arms into Europe, this would be a major step towards 'de-coupling', i.e., the separation of the European theatre from the American strategic forces. Whereas if a strike was made against Soviet targets, even purely military targets, the Kremlin would be forced to choose between reprisals on American territory, which would be a considerable step forward on the scale leading to total war, or abstention, which would be to admit that the United States had the status of unilateral sanctuary. Neither of these options is particularly attractive. It is this dilemma which largely explains their bitter opposition to the modernization of NATO theatre forces. There should also be borne in mind the immense political consequences of a European acceptance of a precedent establishing that they could never have arms which were not tolerated by Moscow on their soil for their own defence!

This same error has led these European countries to accept, and even to demand, negotiations which would relate the SS-20 and *Backfire* to the *Pershing* II and cruise missiles. That this has become inevitable for political reasons merely shows that the governments involved have not been able to protect their people from the manipulations of Soviet propaganda. These negotiations would in practice involve all the American weapons in Europe capable of striking the Soviet Union and would leave out 90 per cent of the Soviet weapons which could destroy us.

It is also difficult to imagine that there is not something at fault in arguments which lead to the paradoxical situation in which public opinion in a number of countries is more concerned about the introduction of weaponry designed to defend these countries than by the existence and presence of thousands of missiles, aircraft and artillery in the USSR threatening these same countries and which only need to travel 1,500 km to attack them.

Key to Deterrence in Europe

If the arguments given above on the Euromissiles are correct, there is little doubt that the key to deterrence in Europe consists of the risk to the USSR that hostilities leading to the attack of military targets on Soviet territory by American forces would force her leaders to make the choice discussed above. Our problem is therefore to transform what is now the simple possibility of an extension of this type into a doctrinal concept different from the interpretation which could unfortunately be given to recent statements by President Reagan.

In plain language, this means that NATO, instead of basing its strategy on a response designed to stop the progress of the enemy offensive by a flexible response, should adopt the principle that, whatever the level of a nuclear attack on Europe, the response would immediately involve an attack on military targets in the Soviet Union whose destruction would be an important factor in countering the pursuit of Warsaw Pact operations – the idea being that, since the diplomatic and political aims of Moscow are to separate Europe from the United States, the military response of the Western powers would be to unite, in a way which would be inseparable from their defence operations, the Euro-pean territories with those of the USSR. The Soviet Union sees herself as a European power. Let us now draw the consequences for our security. Whereas the sea is an enormous gulf between the main Atlantic power and her allies, there is continuity between the Soviet land-mass and Europe. This is disadvantageous for us in all fields: communication lines, reinforcements, stationing of troops etc. to say nothing of the psychological consequences.

In all fields . . . except one – the likelihood that once military operations had been triggered towards the west of this continent, they could extend towards the East without interruption. The proposition that any nuclear attack in Europe would involve a response on USSR territory therefore appears to be the sole argument which could put geography on our side. As Bismarck said, geography is the only permanent element of international relations and, despite missiles and other modern weapons, it has not lost its importance in terms of strategy.

NATO Requirements for Conventional Defence

Assuming, consequently, that we could make a nuclear attack less probable, our problem is then to ensure that we are not in an inferior position in the conventional area, such that NATO would immediately be compelled to use its tactical nuclear weapons or to capitulate. The weaker the conventional forces, the sooner recourse would have to be made to nuclear forces.

The question of the level of the conventional forces which NATO must deploy and maintain is also inevitably raised by the evolution of the forces which we have identified. A reasonable compromise should be sought between the United States considering that it would be necessary to be able to contain the Warsaw Pact for some months, and the Europeans, who are not inclined to prepare for a resistance lasting more than a few days.

At this point it should again be said that hostilities in Europe would not this time be decided by the industrial potential of the belligerents, but by what they could put to use immediately. A strategy which consisted in giving ground in order to gain time would not provide, as far as Europe is concerned, a response to superiority in terms of land power.

In order to assess the time factor in relation to this discussion of our needs, it is necessary to take into account certain factors which are not all to our disadvantage. In the first instance, it is unlikely that the Soviet military hierarchy underestimates the forces of the West in a competition in which technology plays a considerable part . . . The second consideration relates to the availability of American reinforcements . . . As the speed of a presence counts for a great deal more than its volume in the first stages of a conflict, reinforcements, of whatever size and power, would be of no use if the forces on the spot were not capable of holding the ground until their arrival. However, the most important facts relating to this discussion are the events unfolding in Poland. Moscow's obvious hesitation to put an end to these events by military intervention is proof of the deep-seated political fragility of the Soviet system in her satellites. It is not difficult to imagine that, were these hostilities not victoriously concluded within a matter of days, gigantic subversive movements would arise in these countries, ruled by regimes maintained only under foreign domination. The lines of communication of the Red Army would be threatened, and not only in Poland. Each day which shows the inability of the Soviet Union to defeat her world enemies would increase the hopes and courage of her 'ally-enemies'.

How the Atlantic powers can deploy forces sufficient to resist for several weeks without abandoning most of Europe is thus the heart of our problem. However, it is too large a question to decide according to the percentage by which the defence budgets of this or that country should be raised. It would be less difficult to resolve in the framework of an overall strategic concept which restores deterrence and in which deterrence is the first and indispensable element.

The neutron bomb should be seen in terms of this concept . . . Unless we take seriously the notion that humanitarian considerations are inspiring the Soviet campaign against this 'cannibal' weapon, the campaign is no more than an indication of the complications which the introduction of this weapon would bring to the task of the Red Army if they were to attack us. Here, it is not a question of winning a possible war in Europe, but of making the concept of immediate victory more difficult for the enemy. In this respect, the Soviet threat to produce the enhanced radiation weapon should not take anyone in. It would not be to our disadvantage if the invasion forces used weapons which were ten or a hundred times less powerful than those which we know they possess.

The idea that the neutron bomb reflects a plan designed to ensure the non-escalation of hostilities to the territories of the super-powers, ignores the parallel decision to deploy Euromissiles whose function, as we have seen, is exactly to emphasize the threat of this escalation. In any case, President Reagan's decision on the enhanced radiation weapon is the reasonable consequence of the inferiority of the West in the conventional area. However, the West will never be able to fully compensate for this inferiority and nobody, whether in Europe or America, whether for or against this decision, should take advantage of this as a pretext for not developing their conventional forces.

What the West Should Do

In summary, it can be seen that the Western allies had worked out a concept which assumed superiority in certain sectors, and that they have retained this concept despite the deterioration in the parameters of this original superiority. However, as it is not possible to change the past, we must undertake an up-dating of this concept. For this we must take specifically into account the weak points of our enemy which he himself shows us by the efforts he makes to prevent us from taking advantage of them.

In order to put these factors to use in the European deterrent and to increase European confidence in this deterrent, the Western powers must:

1 Possess in the conventional area a force sufficient to prevent a surprise operation and to compel the aggressor to carry out a large-scale operation, whilst knowing himself that any conflict of some length carries great risk of domestic problems in the satellite countries.
2 Clearly state that the flexible response doctrine will be modified such that:
– recourse will be made to the neutron bomb as soon as necessary to counter the superiority of the enemy in tanks,
– nuclear strikes will be made against military targets in the USSR as soon as the Red Army has made strikes of this type against Western Europe.

As soon as it is established that vulnerability is not solely the lot of the West, that there are ways of exploiting the weak points of the enemy and that, if the structure of the forces and the concept of their use takes this into account, any nuclear or conventional attack would raise 'agonizing' choices for the aggressor, nations will again understand that the defence effort demanded of them is not to be seen in the context of a war which is 'lost in advance', but rather in the context of its prevention.

French Contribution to Deterrence and Defence

France would obviously have a part to play in this context. Giscard d'Estaing stated several times that the security of France was intimately linked to that of her neighbours. President Mitterand and his government have shown the fundamental importance which they attach to this security by taking a favourable position on the deployment of *Pershing* and cruise missiles. Raymond Barre had spoken of an 'enlarged deterrent'. His successor, Pierre Mauroy, in his first general policy statement on defence questions, did not merely reject in a categorical manner any idea of 'neutralism' or 'isolation'. He stated that 'an attack against France does not begin when an enemy enters her territory'.

To be more precise, it is necessary to examine the contribution of France in terms of overall nuclear, conventional and logistical defence.

The Ottawa declaration has recognized, since 1974, the contribution of the strategic forces of France and Britain to the overall deterrent position of the Alliance. There is little doubt that the sole existence in Europe of two independent decision-making areas capable of using nuclear weapons must seriously complicate the plans of a possible aggressor. If a strategic exchange were to take place between France or Britain and the USSR, these two Western nations could certainly disappear from the map. If this were the sole consequence, the deterrent would not be of great importance to the aggressor. However, the damage caused to the urban and economic infrastructure of the USSR would be considerable, and the Soviet Union is compelled to bear this in mind with respect to her position *vis-à-vis* America and China. In this perspective, the destruction of one or more medium powers in Western Europe could appear uselessly costly.

In the second place, the geographical position of France provides her with a vital role in the logistics of any conflict. It is not possible to defend the continent on the narrow strip of territory which separates the Oder–Neisse line from the Western frontiers of Germany and Belgium against an empire which has an unbounded depth from the centre of Europe to the Pacific Ocean. Only France can offer access to the Atlantic, airport facilities, communication lines, oil pipelines etc, without which it would be impossible to control a war even for a few days. A detailed preparation for this possibility is one of the main elements of her contribution to the strengthening of deterrence in Europe. Thirdly, if it were agreed to recognize that the Allies should be capable of sustaining combat for a certain period in conventional terms, it would be necessary for the First French Army, provided to act as a general reserve, to be subject to the same standards. If not, then France would not be in a position to play her part in the common defence of the continent. This would run counter

to her interests, her European policies and her undertakings.

The safety of France rests on one assurance: that provided by the Alliance to which she belongs, and on a counter-assurance: that with which her strategic armaments provide her. She cannot sacrifice one or the other, nor one to the other. However, she can strengthen the first without changing anything of her position with respect to the integrated system as defined in 1966 by General de Gaulle.

The President of the Republic and the qualified members of the government have repeated that France would be loyal and faithful to her allies. This means joining them if the Treaties of Washington and Brussels were called into play. Pierre Mauroy, in the speech mentioned above, made specific reference to the Treaties which established the Western European Union and which contain a much more precise promise of assistance than the Atlantic Alliance in the case of aggression against one of the signatories.

There are those who think that by asserting the independence of her defence policy, France is attempting to back out of her responsibilities to the free world in case of crisis or conflict. It would seem that the opposite is true. As a result of her political influence, her geographical position and the volume and variety of her forces, she holds the aces which may be decisive both for defence and for deterrence. Whether she decides to intervene or abstain would be to modify radically the basis of the confrontation for both camps.

It is well known that Paris has not approved the doctrine of flexible response. Is it possible to hope, if some of the ideas proposed here were considered to be useful, that this disagreement is a thing of the past and that there is greater unity between France and her allies with respect to the doctrine required to safeguard their common safety?

In these anxious times, a rapprochement of this type is perhaps the indispensable catalyst for a decrease in military vulnerability to attenuate the political vulnerability of public opinion.

[1]How many of our anti-nuclear supporters understand that, without these weapons, the assassination of President Sadat could well have become the Sarajevo of a third world war.

5 TNF Modernization and Countervailing Strategy

CRISOTPHER MAKINS

To a cynical observer, the subject of this paper would warrant succinct treatment. The present NATO theatre nuclear force (TNF) modernization programme, to such an observer, is a set of weapons without a corresponding strategy: the countervailing strategy is one without a corresponding set of weapons (and associated defence programmes). Like many simple formulations of complex issues, this cynical opinion is at once too skeletal to be useful and too nearly accurate to be comfortable. At the least, however, it has the merit of pointing towards the aspects of the subject which deserve further comment in this paper and, in political and strategic terms, further work in the coming months and years. Only in the light of such further efforts will it be possible to judge whether TNF modernization in Europe and the evolution of US strategy are not only compatible, but also susceptible to being combined in order to yield a more effective overall Western security posture.

Christopher Makins is with Science Applications Inc. in Washington.

Politics and the December 1979 Decision

It is by now widely recognized that the Alliance decisions of December 1979 on a long-range TNF modernization were motivated more by political than by military considerations.[1] Although the issue was discussed mostly in terms of counteracting the expanding Soviet threat to Western Europe, notably from the SS-20, this was in large measure a result of the fact that many of the deeper, intra-Alliance anxieties about the credibility of extended deterrence in Europe were too difficult and sensitive to raise openly between governments. As a result, some mutually acceptable, indirect language for discussing them had to be found. To say this is not to diminish the significance of the long-range TNF decisions or to suggest that they were militarily undesirable. That the decisions could help to stabilize the transatlantic relationship after a period of considerable strain was a powerful reason for taking them. That they helped resolve some bureaucratic political or programmatic problems (such as providing an application for the long-range cruise missile and compelling a decision about the *Pershing* II) was also significant, though still not directly relevant to strictly military purposes. But on the level of strategy and the Alliance military posture, the decisions settled very little. Nor, it is safe to assume, have the deeper internal tensions and anxieties within the Alliance been finally laid to rest. Rather, they have been put to sleep, with every prospect that they could quickly reawaken.

Two features of the long-range TNF decisions are important in this connection. First, they covered only one element of the allied nuclear posture and were deliberately insulated from consideration of shorter-range systems (both battlefield and mid-range). Although, as will be discussed later, this was done for apparently compelling reasons (notably domestic sensitivities in Western Europe), it made difficult, if not impossible, any thorough consideration of the relationship of the proposed new systems to the strategy underlying the allied TNF posture in Europe as a whole. Admittedly, the case can be made that the increasing vulnerability of aircraft on deep strike missions and the unsuitability in various ways of *Poseidon* submarine-launched ballistic missiles (SLBMs) for 'theatre' missions made it urgent to fill a 'gap' in the Alliance's spectrum of deterrence. Nevertheless, the fact remains that the allies did not pursue the difficult questions of strategy and employment doctrine affecting TNF generally during their discussions of the long-range system. Secondly, even in terms of the element that the allied decisions did treat, namely systems capable of striking targets in the USSR, the allies do not appear to have succeeded in developing a strategic concept which could provide a clear and easily understood basis for sizing the force. In fact there is little sign that they did much more than a simple and rather static analysis of target coverage, which is only one, albeit essential, step towards developing such a concept.

Both these features of the decision, incidentally, are likely to engender considerable problems if ever the US–Soviet negotiations on limiting TNF, which started in late 1980 in Geneva, become serious. The absence of an agreed and precise strategic concept will inevitably make it hard for the allies to derive generally accepted judgments about proposals which would involve changes either in the size of the current allied long-range TNF programme or in the scope of an eventual agreement (e.g., on the inclusion or exclusion of aircraft, sea-based cruise missiles, etc.).

The reason for recalling this line of critique of the Alliance decisions is not to suggest that they should not have been taken or that they should have been deferred pending resolution of the fundamental military and strategic questions which they implicitly set aside. Anyone familiar with the intricacies of Alliance politics is bound to sympathize with, and respect, the decision of the governments concerned to bite off only as much of the TNF problem as they thought they could digest politically at the time. Moreover, at one level, the decision to introduce the *Pershing* II and the ground-launched cruise missile (GLCM) in Western Europe was quite consistent with the recent drift of Alliance nuclear planning on the basis of the flexible response doctrine. While it was not strictly true, as was frequently argued, that the absence of long-range ground-based missiles from the allied inventory meant that a rung on the Alliance's escalation ladder was missing (given the existence of SLBM RVs dedicated to SACEUR and the F-111s in Britain), it was certainly reasonable to claim, as was suggested earlier, that the forces supporting that rung were insufficient to enable it to carry much weight in an escalatory process. Moreover, the relatively limited new capability which the allies agreed the US should procure was at the same time compatible with the general Alliance notion of selective employment and in some senses less threatening to the Soviet Union than a larger procurement would have been. Finally, by dealing with the element of TNF which most visibly embodied the cherished 'coupling' of a European theatre war to a strategic homeland-to-homeland nuclear exchange and setting aside any consideration of new short- or mid-range systems which might appear to facilitate the limitation of nuclear warfare to the theatre, the Western European governments could avoid raising a large number of delicate issues. In these and other ways long-range TNF modernization was the element of the overall TNF problem which was the easiest for the Alliance to tackle and resolve, even if the motives of the United States and Western Europe for supporting the chosen solution may have been divergent.

Even so, it is still by no means certain whether the results of the long-range TNF decisions will be such as to accelerate or to undermine the assimilation by European opinion, outside the narrow circles of government defence experts, of a clear and agreed role for nuclear weapons of all kinds in Alliance strategy. Even in the Federal Republic, it is not obvious that Helmut Schmidt's domestic political calculation will prove accurate and that the existence of some negotiating track will enable the Federal government to turn the long-range TNF deployments into incipient *faits accomplis.* There are still many hurdles to be jumped before the *Pershing* IIs and GLCMs are actually deployed in West Germany. Elsewhere the outcome is even more in doubt. In the Netherlands and Scandinavia, there has been little sign of increased assimilation of allied nuclear strategy since the long-range TNF issue broke into the open. In Britain, the latent disposition of a part of the society towards unilateral nuclear disarmament has again begun to rear its head in the wake of the government's decisions to purchase the *Trident* I and to accept the basing of US GLCMs, and the Labour Party opposition, while divided on this issue, is committed to an anti-nuclear platform. Perhaps only Italy has matched the Federal Republic in signs of progress towards broader assimilation of the nuclear dimension of allied strategy, though one should treat such indications as tentative and reversible. Yet in the medium and longer term, this process of assimilation is crucial if the Alliance's nuclear strategy as a whole is to have the base of public support necessary to make it credible for the purposes of deterrence.[2]

Striking the Soviet Homeland

Even such encouraging signs as there have been could easily be reversed in further allied efforts, such as are needed to deal with the modernization of shorter-range TNF, to come to grips with Alliance nuclear employment doctrine. Two major questions are likely to arise. Both can be discussed equally well in terms of deterrence or of war-fighting concepts. The first question is whether the West has any reason to suppose that it could strike targets in the Soviet Union with any kind of nuclear weapons without precipitating a massive Soviet strike against the United States (and other) targets. This question is central because the answer to it will show whether the Soviet Union can effectively place in

sanctuary an important fraction of her nuclear threat to Europe. The second question is whether the NATO concept of selective nuclear employment is self-defeating, given the apparently resolute Soviet attachment to the concept of large-scale, damage-limiting pre-emption of, or retaliation against, NATO's nuclear threat and other military capabilities once NATO first use appears to be imminent or has actually been initiated.

On the first question, there can be no certainty. At least two schools of thought on the subject can be found in the United States, and for once they do not seem to form entirely along the familiar hawk/dove polarization line. For example, Richard Pipes, writing in 1978, could say:

'The geographic criterion, that is losses of territory with the people and resources located on the homeland, has in their [the Soviets'] military thinking a secondary importance . . . the Russians . . . have learned over the centuries that the sacrifice of lives, territory and resources is not, in itself, fatal provided that the political authority and its military arm remain intact to mount a counteroffensive at the appropriate moment. The attitude also derives in part from intense thinking about the science of war, of which the Russians are today, now that the Germans have quit the field, the world's leading addicts'.[3]

This view, which is obviously historically correct, can be supported by suggestions from some Soviet observers that execution of the very limited strategic nuclear options which, among others, were implied by the 'Schlesinger' doctrine of the early 1970s would not necessarily have precipitated more than a limited Soviet response in kind (a perfectly logical response, after all, provided that the USSR could be confident of her ability to launch her major strategic strike options under attack, which by the early 1970s was probably a reasonable assumption for her). On the other hand, a strong case can be made that she would consider even relatively small attacks against Soviet homeland targets by US-controlled in-theatre nuclear systems as making a full-scale intercontinental nuclear exchange almost inevitable, and that she would therefore see an advantage in responding to such attacks with a large-scale, damage-limiting strike against the

US nuclear (and general military) threat worldwide. In any case, the question has to be raised as to how confident the Soviet Union could be in her assessment than an incoming attack against any significant number of Soviet homeland targets, whether by in-theatre or out-of-theatre weapons, was in fact limited, to the point that she would not have to consider an immediate large-scale response.

As a matter of fact, neither view is particularly comforting from the vantage point of the European allies. The second implies that there is no possible nuclear leverage on the Soviet Union above the level of attacks on the territory of her Eastern European allies without a full-scale homeland-to-homeland exchange, thus removing one or more rungs from the escalatory ladder at precisely the most critical point in terms of 'coupling'. The former view suggests that, while those rungs indeed exist in Soviet as well as Western eyes, they may serve relatively little purpose for the West because they would not necessarily (though they might conceivably) impose on the Soviet Union costs which she would see as great enough to justify a decision not to proceed with the pursuit of the aims with which she originally entered upon the war (e.g., the conquest of West Germany or expulsion of American forces from the European continent). This, of course, raises an even more uncertain issue, namely whether there are circumstances in which the Soviet Union, once involved in a nuclear war which had damaged her territory, might contemplate a negotiated termination short of realizing her stated goal of 'final victory'.

This is not the place in which to try to resolve these issues, which are indeterminate, given the uncertainties involved in forecasting human behaviour in nuclear war. For present purposes, there are two important points to note. First, that uncertainty on this general question inevitably leaves scope for transatlantic disagreement as long as the Soviet Union has a secure capability to retaliate massively against the US. It is by no means obvious that a measurable US advantage in long-range homeland-based nuclear forces would change the fundamental dilemma for America and Western Europe implied by these uncertainties. On this point, General de Gaulle's familiar view of Europe's position was almost certainly right. This does not mean, however, that the West can rest easy with the present state of the East–West strategic balance. Merely that even the acquisition by the US, were it feasible, of some quantitative advantage in strategic. forces would not be likely to change the West's basic dilemma given a secure Soviet retaliatory force. Secondly, and any contradiction with the previous point is only apparent, the West can influence Soviet calculations through the strengthening of its nuclear and conventional force posture. Both improvement of the pre-launch survivability of Western nuclear forces and Western capabilities to survive and dominate a general war would tend to affect Soviet judgments about the correlation of forces they would face in different contingencies. This is, of course, the point at which the Alliance's nuclear strategy dilemma leads directly into consideration of the 'countervailing strategy'.

NATO's Selective Option

The second major issue which the allies are likely to face in the future concerns the adequacy of NATO's concept of selective nuclear employment. It is not difficult to draw a plausible scenario in which NATO's attempt to use selective employment plans (SEPS) as a form of nuclear bargaining during a war would lead to a massive Soviet in-theatre counter-military response which would heavily degrade NATO's combat forces and in-theatre nuclear weapons and delivery systems, thus changing the theatre balance to NATO's disadvantage in terms of ground forces, while at the same time limiting its nuclear retaliatory capability short of a recourse to long-range 'strategic' forces. NATO's problem in targeting Warsaw Pact ground forces, other than those directly in contact, would be particularly limited in this scenario. Such a scenario could even include, using the first of the two views of Soviet behaviour described above, a limited NATO strike against targets in the Western Military Districts of the Soviet Union to which the USSR decided *not* to respond: the in-theatre consequences would be the same in all material respects. At this point, the aims of deterrence and abstract, pre-war concepts of escalation come into conflict with the need to fight the enemy as he declares himself to be.

The precise balance of risk and benefit in the concept of selective employment cannot easily be drawn. It could obviously prove to be a highly desirable concept if in the event both sides were of a mind to fight – and, more importantly, to terminate – a war in accordance with it. But the current NATO TNF posture would not appear to recognize clearly enough the need to hedge against the possibility that the attempt either to terminate a conflict or to achieve some military effect on the battlefield by the limited use of nuclear weapons will be substantially frustrated by a resolute adversary prepared to act on the belief that there is no logical barrier to escalation from limited or SEP-type use to all-out nuclear war in the theatre, if not necessarily to full-scale intercontinental nuclear war. Such a hedge could in theory be devised in several ways, from the denial to the enemy of lucrative targeting options, as will be discussed below, to the development of procedures which would enable SACEUR to launch a large-scale theatre-wide strike independently of the SIOP under a comparable Soviet attack, should that be the result of an initial selective employment.

This fatal risk in the concept of selective employment and flexible response would appear to be one which NATO cannot eliminate. While it is possible to imagine the conversion of the Soviet Union to some variant of a flexible response strategy, her possession of a secure capability to execute a large-scale damage-limiting strike in the theatre would always tend to raise doubts about the durability of that conversion. One obvious, and familiar, conclusion from such reasoning is that, in an age in which both sides possess a sufficient level of invulnerable nuclear forces, there is no wholly satisfactory means of using nuclear weapons to compensate for inadequate conventional forces. The real weakness of NATO in the scenario described above would be the absence of substantial ground force reserves in the face of the second and third strategic echelons of the Warsaw Pact, which would have remained effectively undamaged by NATO's SEPs while NATO's ground forces would have been heavily diminished by the Warsaw Pact response. This conclusion has, of course, historically been no more palatable to Western Europeans than the dilemmas of nuclear strategy. Again, however, the important point is that above a certain threshold of Soviet nuclear strength and sophistication, there is little that *additional* US nuclear forces can do to solve the problem, even though they may for a time serve as a balm to

jangled European nerves. Rather, to the extent that these dilemmas are soluble, the solutions lie in the direction of nuclear forces and associated command, control and targeting systems different from those now available and of different employment concepts and procedures. The relevance of the 'countervailing strategy' to these problems is close at hand. As might be expected, given that the idea of countervailing is an evolution from, rather than a rupture with, previous US strategy, there is little difficulty in fitting the general outlines of the flexible response approach in Europe to the broader countervailing approach to US nuclear strategy. Both, at the theoretical level at least, stress the need for a range of capabilities such that the enemy cannot reasonably hope to derive advantage from escalation to any level of violence and for the strong deterrent effect which the enemy's knowledge of the existence of such capabilities can and should have.

Much of the discussion of countervailing, as of flexible response, has been conducted in terms of US and allied targeting options and the different types of damage one can hope to inflict (or threaten to inflict) on the enemy. The relevance to European defence of this aspect of the problem has already become apparent in the earlier discussion of the likely Soviet response to allied nuclear strikes against targets in the USSR. It is also important in terms of NATO's requirement, in a variety of scenarios, to acquire and strike mobile Warsaw Pact targets deep in Eastern Europe – a requirement which NATO cannot adequately meet with its present mix of TNF and targeting capabilities and employment concepts. New systems, notably at the 'mid-range' of 150–500 km, and associated targeting and operational concepts are likely to prove essential for this purpose.

Denying Targeting Options

But it is also important to emphasize the reverse of the countervailing medal, namely the denial of effective targeting options to the enemy. This, too, has a direct bearing on the issue of TNF modernization in Europe. First, it reinforces the case for improved survivability of vital nuclear systems and casts some doubt on the wisdom of relying as heavily as the December 1979 Alliance TNF decisions did on ground-based systems. Although there can be no certainty that existing models of pre-launch survivability of TNF are highly reliable, it is by no means improbable that the effective mobility of systems such as the GLCM and *Pershing* II may turn out to be comparatively limited, not least because of their basing and training posture. And even at the best of times, such systems, being, theoretically at least, highly visible, merely create an incentive to the enemy to increase his efforts, conventional, unconventional and ultimately nuclear, to catch them. While the reasons which led to the *Pershing* II/GLCM compromise are well-known (German insistence on non-uniqueness, operational disadvantages of sea-launched cruise missiles (SLCM), the supposed psychological advantages of highly visible systems, etc.), the fact remains that that compromise is scarcely compatible with the strict logic of countervailing. Much more so would be either a dedicated SLCM force or, perhaps still better, an accurate, single (or low-multiple) RV SLBM which could avoid some of the weaknesses of the C-3 for theatre use, or even a penetrating bomber force sanctuarized in the US with the capabilities necessary to execute nuclear strikes in the theatre. Such alternative systems would match both the essential characteristics of the SS-20 and *Backfire* – their mobility and effective sanctuarization – and not just the first, as do the GLCM and *Pershing* II. The indispensable basis for judgment about which systems would be most effective in supporting a countervailing strategy is a realistic net assessment of the TNF relationship in the context of dynamic scenarios for combined arms conflict. Only in this way can the relevant attrition and other factors be properly accounted for. This point has more relevance in connection with that part of the countervailing strategy – and of PD 59 which seeks to implement it – which is concerned with the possibility of protracted war involving nuclear weapons after an initial large-scale exchange. While the discussion of this issue is hardly calculated to appeal to Western Europeans, it is none the less an important element of the conception of a countervailing strategy which adequately caters for theatre conflicts. If it is important at the level of intercontinental forces to demonstrate to the Soviet Union that she cannot hope to gain (and retain) advantage in a protracted general war, this must logically include advantage in the European theatre, which is likely to be one of the main issues in dispute. In effect, this would mean matching whatever may be the Soviet capability to prosecute the war in the theatre by either conventional or nuclear means after a large-scale nuclear attack. Although the most important element of such a capability might very likely be a substantial reserve of general purpose ground and air forces, the relevant concern for present purposes is the role of TNF in such a contingency. Again, the point is that even highly mobile ground-based systems would be unlikely to have the demonstrable survivability in a protracted general war needed to create a high level of deterrence in this way. Thus, the issue would appear to resolve around the ability of the allies (including the two European nuclear weapons states) to threaten to bring the necessary out-of-theatre (including sea-based) nuclear forces to bear on the theatre situation in a militarily effective way and quite possibly after a substantial loss of territory to a Warsaw Pact advance.

Civil Defence

A second way in which, consistent with the underlying concept of a countervailing strategy, effective targeting options can be denied to the enemy is through the use of both passive and active defences. Perhaps the most important issue in this connection at present is that of passive defences of all kinds, including civil defence. The issue of defences is important for two reasons: because of their intrinsic potential for limiting damage (and therefore reducing the attraction of certain options to the enemy) and because of their potential for creating a greater degree of public support and consensus for a given strategy. This latter point is one which has been emphasized in recent times with reference to civil defence in Europe by the British strategist Michael Howard.[4] Both the potential values of civil defence are important to the creation of a more comprehensive and broadly supported theatre nuclear posture in the Alliance.

At the level of the strategic forces, civil defence is probably the most glaringly absent of the various requirements for a convincing US countervailing strategy, though there are numerous other aspects of the US C^3 and intelligence posture, in particular, which are in need of improvement in order to meet those requirements fully. As to public support, while opinion in America has understandably been focused in recent years on the defence controversy in the Western European countries, it is important neither to overlook the parallel problem in the United States herself nor to assume its inevitable disappearance. Senator Sam Nunn's recent eloquent appeal on this subject highlighted the current existence and likely persistence of this problem for some time to come.[5] Dissension over the MX and concern among many defence experts at the spiralling cost of defence programmes only underline the point. A US–Soviet competition to proliferate and then defend (by anti-ballistic missiles (ABM), among other things) strategic targets in their respective territories, which could well develop in the wake of technological advances, would only accelerate the collision between political/economic constraints and the demands of defence. The importance of devising a defence programme that is politically supportable over the long haul has recently been emphasized by no less an authority than Melvin Laird.[6] To the extent that one of the most debilitating influences on the attitudes of the allies in Western Europe in recent years and has been the polarization of opinion in the United States on strategic and defence issues, the failure to develop a durable consensus around such a programme would only be likely to prolong this undesirable state of affairs and make substantially harder the evolution of broader support for a countervailing strategy for both the strategic and the theatre nuclear forces.

In sum, therefore, TNF modernization in the European theatre and the US countervailing strategy are two important pieces in a jig-saw puzzle which, if completed, could constitute a comprehensive and compelling combination of strategy, force posture and political resolve for the Western allies. But both these pieces still need to be attached to others in order to complete the puzzle. Unfortunately, those other pieces may prove to be extremely elusive. Neither the development of the necessary forces and associated programmes to back up the countervailing strategy – especially as it implies a need for a protracted general war capability, even if only as a deterrent to protracted war – nor progress towards the resolution of the long-standing dilemmas of Alliance nuclear strategy will be easy. Both are capable of arousing intense domestic political opposition which can delay progress.

134

The Role of Arms Control

Nor are there any obvious shortcuts to deal with the complex political, social and economic problems which underlie these issues. Certainly arms limitation agreements offer no such shortcut, as the SALT experience testifies. This is not to say that negotiated arms limitation is irrelevant to the problem. Looking back over the history of SALT, one is struck by the great significance of the American decision never to press seriously for the multiple independently-targetable re-entry vehicle (MIRV) test and deployment ban which it put foward as an option at SALT in April 1970. Many qualifications obviously need to be made about the negotiability and verifiability of anything like the original US MIRV-ban proposal, let alone the later Soviet counterproposal. Nevertheless, the failure of US policy[7] to foresee the strategic significance of unrestricted MIRV deployments by both sides in the following years sufficiently clearly to press harder, even though perhaps unsuccessfully, for some form of MIRV restraint as part of a SALT I deal involving ABM limitations appears in retrospect a serious one. On the threshold of major, but expensive, technological advances in the 1980s and 1990s, notably in the fields of space warfare and ABM development, there is an urgent need for a comprehensive net assessment of the advantages and disadvantages to the United States of various alternative regimes in some of these areas, covering in each case unrestrained development and deployment as well as a variety of negotiated limitations. This should be one element of the search for a more comprehensive countervailing strategy.

Another apparent shortcut to the achievement of both a more convincing strategic posture and a stronger position in the theatre is through a new burst of nuclear force procurement. But, while some procurement is no doubt necessary, it cannot in itself resolve the problems at hand. The implication of the earlier argument is that, in an age in which there is no foreseeable possibility of denying the Soviet Union survivable nuclear capabilities both in the theatre and at the intercontinental level, the attempt to use nuclear weapons, theatre or strategic, to close a gap in the conventional force balance is unlikely to prove successful. Once again, however, it is important to stress that this argument does not imply that no new nuclear forces are required.

What it does imply is that both nuclear and conventional force postures need to be devised more clearly in relation to one another so as to maximize both their deterrent and their operational effectiveness in the age of the 'integrated' battlefield.

Thus neither a hardware 'fix' for perceived US strategic force weaknesses (which are anyway less apparent to most European than to many American observers), nor an additional increment of modernized TNF would be likely in themselves to resolve the fundamental problems in Europe, which have to do more with an insufficiency of conventional forces and the unknown element in the desirability and the likelihood of America using nuclear weapons in Europe's defence. Even the European perception of US 'weakness' in the defence field might well be more readily countered by the reimposition of the draft and the improvement of the readiness of

US general purpose forces than by more visible actions affecting the strategic forces.[8] Possibly the most important contribution the 1980s could make to US defence policy is to end the compartmentalization of US strategy, as a result of which the term 'strategic' has been applied only to one part of the military posture and the world has been carved, for the sake of planning convenience, into half contingencies and half wars. Strategy needs to be made whole again and used with the entire force posture. Likewise certain quite plausible combinations of $1\frac{1}{2}$ or more contingencies need to be seen for what they would be – general wars affecting the whole globe, the conduct of which has to be thought about in a global fashion. It is against such a broad canvas that a countervailing strategy must be formulated and the role of theatre nuclear forces in Western Europe put in a strategic perspective.

NOTES

This paper was presented to the Institute of Foreign Policy Analysis' conference on the strategic problems of the 1980s in Washington, DC 4–5 December 1980.

[1] For a fuller exposition of this issue see Christopher J. Makins, 'Bringing in the Allies' in Foreign Policy No. 35, Summer 1979; and Michael Higgins and Christopher Makins, 'Theatre Nuclear Forces and Grey Area Arms Control' in Continuity and Change in the Eighties and Beyond, the proceedings of the Sixth National Security Affairs Conference, 1979, National Defense University. A compelling historical survey pointing to the same conclusion is contained in 'Intermediate-range Nuclear Weapons' by Kevin N. Lewis in Scientific American vol. 243, no. 6, December 1980.

[2] See on this subject Michael Howard's brilliant essay 'Forgotten Dimensions of Strategy', Foreign Affairs, vol. 57 (Summer 1979), pp. 975–86.

[3] See his article in the Wall Street Journal, 12 October 1978.

[4] See his 'Surviving a Protest' in Encounter: July 1980.

For a recent graphic account of actions under way in Britain to improve civil defence see 'Thinking the Unthinkable' by Polly Toynbee in the Manchester Guardian Weekly vol. 124, no. 3, week ending 18 January 1981.

[5] 'Defense with a Capital "D"' in the Washington Post, November 1980.

[6] See his 'Not a Binge, but a Buildup' in the Washington Post, 19 November 1980.

[7] Though not of all US policy-makers. See on this point Gerard Smith's Doubletalk: The Story of SALT I (New York: Doubleday, 1981). Appendices 2 and 3 contain Smith's eloquent pleas for serious consideration of limitations on MIRVs. He is, however, prudently equivocal on the question whether any workable MIRV limitations could have been negotiated.

[8] To quote Senator Nunn again: 'Among knowledgeable European defense experts, the weaknesses of the US volunteer force exceed the erosion of our nuclear deterrent in downgrading the credibility of America's treaty commitments' (op. cit. in n. 5).

Index

136

141